# PHOENIX

Jon Hilton

Copyright © 2022 by Jon Hilton

All rights reserved. No part of this publication may be reproduced, distributed, or transmitted in any form or by any means, including photocopying, recording, or other electronic or mechanical methods, without the prior written permission of the author, except in the case of brief quotations embodied in critical reviews and certain other noncommercial uses permitted by copyright law.

Published by WriterMotive
www.writermotive.com

# Contents

Prelude ..........................................................................5
Chapter 1. Crash .............................................................9
Chapter 2. Aftermath ....................................................25
Chapter 3. Paperwork & Decisions ...............................27
Chapter 4. Waiting for the Germans ..............................34
Chapter 5. Repairs .........................................................43
Chapter 6. German Excursion ........................................61
Chapter 7. The Why .......................................................86
Chapter 8. The Aircraft and the Details .........................94
Chapter 9. Take off. Day 1 ...........................................104
Chapter 10 - 7th June. France. Day 2 ..........................118
Chapter 11. 8th June. France. Day 3 ............................130
Chapter 12. 9th June. Italy. Day 4 ................................146
Chapter 13a. Crete. 10th May. Day 5 ...........................155
Chapter 13b. Mediterranean. 10th May. Day 5 ............163
Chapter 13c. Egypt. 10th May. Day 5 ..........................177
Chapter 14. 11th, 12th, 13th May. Egypt .....................186
Chapter 15. 14th May. Egypt. Day 9 ............................194
Chapter 16. 15th May. Day 10 .....................................209
Chapter 17. 16th May. Day 11 .....................................227
Chapter 18. 17th May. Egypt. Day 12 ..........................235
Chapter 19. 20th May. Day 15 .....................................242
Chapter 20. 24th May. Day 19 .....................................250

Epilogue ..................................................................256
Written Three Years Later ..............................259
Time Capsule ....................................................264

# **Prelude**

You should know that writing is not something that comes naturally to me, and I bloody well loathe commas. The buggers get everywhere and generally make me question my own sanity.

Now that that's off my chest, the reasoning behind the following 88,000 words is twofold. Firstly, that this narrative might make for interesting reading for my daughter, and other kin, to read at some unidentified point in the future.

And secondly, in a funny way, this is my concept of time travel, from writer to reader. The reader, you, have the benefit of being able to review what follows without the anxiety, stress, and fear that I put myself through.

Having said that, it's entirely possible I'll publish this, stash a copy in my wooden box of memories, then take it off sale. Alternatively, I may publish, but make it difficult to find unless a person goes looking. And in that case, few people, if any, will get to read this.

To summarise what follows, the text covers a 12 month period that I found a little challenging. The chapters stumble from the incident I'm about to outline, to the paperwork, and then life cocooned inside my airborne life raft.

Separately, and more of an indulgence than anything else, I've listed a handful of stories at the end of the book. These bring me to the point I find myself sitting on my settee typing away.

There are a few paragraphs covering my route towards aviation and life as a young tunnel engineer. There's also a couple of inappropriate tales about mature women chasing after a young estate agent. i.e. moi.

# Phoenix

Additionally, courtesy of my jumbled career path, I accidentally managed to mount searchlights to the Eiffel Tower. I also project managed the lighting on the Wobbly Millennium Bridge across the Thames. Both these stories are touched upon, and neither installation would have happened if I hadn't been a cog in the machinery.

There's also a general meandering around a couple of near-death experiences. And everything, rather embarrassingly, exposes my life for any and all to dissect.

And that's part of the awkwardness of writing a book based on actual events. In that it pretty much allows anyone to get a grip on a person's mindset and approach to life. I can't say what you'll think, but ultimately I don't want to know if you've read any part of what follows.

If we ever meet, and as a nod to our relationship as writer and reader, just buy me a bar of chocolate and that'll be our secret code.

There's no need to say anything at all. Just hand over the confectionary (I do like a Crunchie) and at that point I'll no doubt go a little coy, frown, and hurriedly walk off.

\*\*\*

Bringing matters back to Earth, and as a backdrop to what follows, I guess I should introduce my own personality traits.

Rightly or wrongly, I'd suggest I'm slightly mischievous, cheerful, and generally happy go lucky. I try to see the best in people, but sometimes that's easier said than done.

It also has to be noted that I can be both competitive, and stubborn. And those two adjectives have led to numerous confrontations over the years in which I've faced off against various assholes who've wanted to use their size, strength, or power of some sort to intimidate other folk.

Even though I'm what you might call middle-aged these days, if you put a bona fide bully in front of me my pig-headedness surfaces and my blood absolutely boils.

I'm not rich, but by the same token, I'm not poor. I live in a relatively nice cottage in Bolton and have no great ambitions to project any kind of impression to those around me.

I am who I am. At the same time, I've always had the somewhat misplaced feeling that no one is better than yours truly. Live and let live is my motto.

I'm round about 6ft tall, of medium build, and not what you'd call blessed in the follicle department these days.

With respect to India Zulu, my Microlight, she was given the nickname 'Samson' after one of my many ex-fiancées. The lady in question was a damned feisty bugger but someone I loved, and I guess those feelings were projected onto the aircraft.

So when 'we' crashed in June 2015, I was gutted. And I think that changed me a little.

Ironically the crash was two years, to the day, after returning from my somewhat idiotic Canada flight. I guess I'm a believer in fate, and certain coincidences seem nonsensical and interesting at the same time.

Maybe there is a god, or maybe the Universe has a quirky sense of humour.

***

And as a final comment, I should point out that I often use profanity as a way to express my situation. Outwardly I'm always very polite, but inside my mind there's a maelstrom of swear words jumbling around.

# Phoenix

For those of a gentle disposition I've tried to tone down such instances. In general, though, please replace the word 'fuck' with 'crikey.'

Hopefully that will help.

***

# Chapter 1. Crash

On the 10th of June 2015, the sun was shining. I kept wistfully staring through my office window at the small trees lining the car park across the road. Simultaneously my conscious mind was trying to think up an excuse to get to Barton that I could sell to my staff at Legal Brokers Ltd. My phone vibrated and I looked down to see a text from a lawyer friend of mine who was mincing about at Haydock Racecourse.

We'd talked about Haydock before because they allow aircraft to fly in and land between the horse races. The grass airstrip is in the middle of the oval racetrack directly in front of the grandstand. It's traditionally used to ferry jockeys in and out.

Flight time from Barton to Haydock is roughly six minutes. My mate started sending pictures of the fillies walking around, and that led to my absently staring out the window. Something inside me clicked and I decided I could use Dave as an excuse to aviate.

I then put my determined head on and spent 30 minutes on the phone trying to get permission from the Haydock management to fly in and land. The initial 20 minutes of the call included the phrase, 'please hold whilst I put you through to the right person.' That went on and on until the clearance, including a specific landing time, was given. I packed my work stuff away, left the office, and headed to the car.

The phone buzzed in my pocket and a text from my daughters mother popped up. We're not an item these days, we come at the world from different directions, and the relationship is somewhat strained. The message suggested Ava, aged 4, wasn't feeling well and I should head over.

A quick glance at the time said it was 4pm, and I tapped out a reply confirming that I'd do as requested.

9

# Phoenix

Surprisingly, very surprisingly, a follow-up text arrived saying it wasn't necessary and a later visit would suffice. And that was strangely odd because normally there's no leeway when an order's been issued.

Carrying on to Barton a few practical considerations started to tug at my conscious mind. How much time would be spent on the ground before getting airborne? How best to join the Haydock Circuit? What were the implications of the racecourse being in the middle of the Manchester 'low level' corridor? Would there be the potential to spook the horses and cause a mad stampede when landing?

In general terms, how the hell could yours truly fly in and out without causing anxiety to anyone?

Pulling in at the airfield car park my mind was racing, but also calm. No big deal. Just use a sprinkling of common sense and keep a good look out for aircraft heading North and South in the corridor. Then hope Manchester Approach had warned other traffic that I'd be pottering about courtesy of my 7000 Squawk. Or should I use a 7366 Squawk and briefly listen to the jets? What to do? My inner pilot was pulling apart conflicting scenarios.

Glancing over at the nearest windsock it was weaving around a little, up and down, but nothing scary. The sun was still shining, the skies were clear of clouds, and everything about Barton looked beautiful.

I carried both my green Dave Clarke headset, and red rucksack, into the hangar and laid my kit on the old orange plastic chair sat by the hanger doors. Then strode over to Samson, took the covers off both the propeller blades and the pitot tube, and pulled her out into the sun.

I checked her over, dipped the oil, looked for water in the fuel drain, and stared at everything. Then unscrewed the fuel filler caps in the wings, stood on tiptoes, and dipped the tanks.

There was three times more fuel in one wing than the other. Eh? They're supposed to drain equally, and 48 litres in one tank and 16 litres in the other seemed odd. It'd happened before when she'd been sat on an uneven surface, but that shouldn't have been the case in the hangar.

I involuntarily scratched my head, rubbed my hand across my chin, and took a moment to ponder. My infernal OCD bloody hates unusual things.

Even assuming the fuel system failed to work, 16 litres of fuel would be sufficient to get to Haydock and back with 30 minutes of juice remaining. And ultimately the gravity-fed system would, and should, make it impossible to run out of fuel.

Feeling the warmth of the sun on my face I stood there and stared skywards. Maybe she'd been sat slightly off-kilter and the fuel had just trickled from one wing to the other. That could be it.

I climbed aboard, wriggled into the harness, and pushed in the Master Fuses. Then shouted, 'clear prop' and fired her up.

With the propeller blurring away in front of my face, my left thumb pressed the red PTT button on the stick and asked the Tower for taxiing instructions. Then released the brakes and rolled forward a few feet before pulling the brake lever, and coming to a full stop.

With my brake check ticked off the list and everything else seemingly in order, India Zulu trundled across the bumpy grass towards the runway. Approaching the hold at Bravo 3 we turned into wind, stopped, and I carried out the power and preflight checks before radioing for departure clearance.

A well-spoken voice gave permission to fly, and we rolled onto the runway, took off, and climbed into Barton's wonderfully blue skies.

Thermals were popping up all over the place and Samson was getting bounced around by columns of rising air. The harnesses

# Phoenix

were pulling against my body every 20 seconds or so as we took hit after hit.

The Rotax engine sounded loud inside the cabin. Her wailing pleas made their way through my old headset and started assaulting my ears.

A couple of minutes later I keyed the microphone and called Barton to request a frequency change. My voice faltered as India Zulu took another whack from a sharp-edged thermal, and I stuttered over a string of words before completing the transmission.

Regaining a little dignity, my right hand reached out to switch radio frequencies. Simultaneously, I started to feel twitchy, nervous. Manchester Approach should have India Zulu on radar and be able to warn other aircraft, shouldn't they?

No one replied when I radioed Haydock.

Nothing to be done about it. My head was swiveling around looking for metal, wooden, or composite aircraft heading in our direction. A sense of unease surfaced, and an inner voice said, 'do not fuck this up Hilton.'

Thirty seconds later my left thumb keyed the mic' and called Haydock, again. A tired voice somewhere on the ground answered and asked that Samson orbit for a minute or two. I banked the aircraft over to the left, and watched the scenery move past the window.

My new mate confirmed clearance to land and Samson ghosted over the Grandstand. We turned left base and descended onto Final approach. No big deal.

Except thousands of people were milling around and the last couple of hundred feet took us past trees, other parked aircraft, and a 50ft high plasma screen. We slowly floated by all the obstacles, and India Zulu lightly settled to earth.

# Jon Hilton

A gentle landing. The kind that makes a chap feel reasonably pleased with himself. She rolled along the grass and casually came to a halt. We slowly turned and backtracked along the runway as a fella waved to a parking space between two elderly looking Piper Warriors. I shut down the aircraft, climbed out of the cabin, and put my flip flops on. Then raised my face towards the heavens and felt the sun's warmth on my skin.

Walking towards the guy who'd been pointing I said, 'hi' and shook his hand. He grinned, complimented the landing, and gestured on towards the Grandstand.

A thousand or so people seemed to be glancing in my direction and I quickly walked across the churned-up racetrack to the public enclosure. Hordes of dressed up ladies and smart-looking chaps were milling around, and I felt underdressed in jeans and flip flops.

Dave let me know by text that he was mincing about with the wealthy lawyers, and I headed over. We met up and started chatting as a succession of beautiful young women paraded past heading towards the grandstand area.

We followed the crowd and an unfamiliar need to gamble led to ten pounds being invested in three races. The thoroughbreds sprinted past, time and again, and the last race yielded a moment of excitement as I 'won' £3.00.

The winning ticket was slipped into my front pocket as a memento of the afternoon. 'Chancery.' An 11/2 bet in the 5.10pm race.

All in all, a lovely day out courtesy of the privileges of my Private Pilot's Licence. Twenty minutes later I said my goodbyes to Dave and made my way back to Samson.

I saddled up, waited for clearance to taxi from the security chap, and took off. We climbed skyward and I changed frequency from my friend on the ground to Manchester on 118.575. Then reset the Transponder to 7366.

# Phoenix

Twenty seconds later my right hand reached out again and flicked the radio back to Barton's frequency, and tweaked the transponder. Then keyed the mic' and called up the chaps in the Tower to ask for joining instructions. The clipped reply was, 'Runway Zero Nine right, circuit Left Hand and QFE of 1025.'

Joining overhead the airfield Samson slotted in behind a slow-moving PA28 on its downwind leg.

Inside the cabin I quickly ran through my downwind checks and glanced around looking for anything unusual. Then slowed India Zulu a little to build in enough clear air to safely follow behind the lead aircraft as we turned left on to base leg.

A quick glance at the Dynon showed 66 knots. My right hand reached out and selected thirty degrees of flaps.

We rolled onto final approach, and I squinted to pick out the Warrior about to touch down. A very quick scan of the instruments showed we were somewhere above 55 knots.

My eyes took a swift glance over towards the orange windsock, then took in the aircraft on the ground. My left thumb keyed the mic', 'Golf India Zulu, Final to land.'

Another outside scan and I picked out the windsock, and mentally compared it against the wind reported on the radio. Then felt the growing intensity that comes with the landing phase. There's no headspace to think about anything other than the 30 seconds ahead.

Time ticked forward.

My comfort blanket has always been to move my mobile phone from the tray beside my seat, and wedge it under my right leg. Between thigh and seat. Done it hundreds of times, and it makes me feel better for some illogical reason. Helps me concentrate.

Five feet above the ground we started to level out, ready to flare and gently touch down. The grass runway has bricks set into it marking out '09R', and Samson and I were ghosting above the numbers.

The left wing dropped. Fuck!

Not the gentle mush of a stall. It just fell away. I felt it through the seat of my pants but didn't understand what'd happened.

I can't explain it other than as a microburst of time. A fraction of a second. Everything stopped. For a moment we were purely 'dropping' to the left. Time sat on a pinhead and my right hand rammed the throttle forward without any conscious thought.

The engine roared at me, and the nose of the aircraft rose as the sheer grunt of the Rotax forced my body against the seat. Instinct said not to let her get nose high, and my left hand was pushing forward against the stick.

We were accelerating and slowly climbing away. My scalp was tingling. Two or three seconds passed. Tick, tick, tick.

The left wing was still low, and we were close to the ground. No great thought in mind, but my hand lightly moved the stick to the right by maybe an inch. And all hell broke loose.

Something was wrong, but I couldn't explain it.

A second later my brain and sense of balance caught up with the fact that we were in a steeply banked left turn. Samson was maybe 20ft above the grass, flying through hell's half-circle.

I wanted to move the stick to the right, but an inner voice said, 'we're in a tight left turn, but not losing height, so stay with it.' Gravity was pinning me to my seat, the engine was screaming away at me, and my whole body felt electrified.

We slowly started to level out as another second or so passed by.

# Phoenix

Samson was cornering her way through the turn, and we were heading in the opposite direction. Each second felt like it was being diced into individual splinters of time.

Fifteen feet above the ground, now.

I felt the wind behind us and even with full power we were being forced to earth. Another microburst of moments kicked in and Father Time stood on his tiptoes and watched.

The left wing was still slightly lower, but we were flying. And we were being pushed down. Every hair on my body tingled. The wings were nearly level, but the left was still slightly lower. Samson was still being fractionally pushed to earth.

Ten feet above the ground.

I daren't yank the stick back in case she stalled and piled in headfirst. My inner voice urged me to push the stick forward to gain airspeed and allow us to fly away. The luxury of height wasn't with us, and I knew we were in a pickle.

Just another second needed, and we could make it. One or two moments, fractions of time, and we could break free. The ground was getting closer, and we were still being forced down.

Time speeded up again, and I knew we'd lost.

My focus was fixed on the hard ground as we hurtled towards it. No conscious thought, but my right hand lashed out and whipped the throttle back to idle. Fuck. Then it lunged out again in a blind attempt at cutting off the fuel. Double fuck. My eyes were on stalks.

There was grass in front of us, a path to the side, and a collection of shrubs and small trees. The ground had an unevenness and there were tufts of long grass.

There was the briefest moment of optimism thinking, 'we can make this, we can actually fucking survive this.' If we're lucky we might just kiss the grass with the left wheel and fly away!

Time caught up with us. The tyre met the grass. I felt the undercarriage strut 'snap', and watched the dismembered wheel fly forwards beyond the propeller. Bugger. Not good. Whatever happens, happens. Then the body of the aircraft hit the unyielding grass surface.

Fifty or so miles an hour, to a dead stop. My body jerked against the harnesses. No great pain. Felt stunned, body tingling, but alive and uninjured. The waist and chest straps had held me firmly in place. My numb hands reached for the door handle, but we were on our left and the door was pinned against the grass. Then a thought shouted at me to make the aircraft safe and shut her down before doing anything else.

Numb fingers pulled the Master fuses out, took the key out of the ignition, fully closed the fuel valve, and I pulled my headset off. Time to get out, Johnny. Don't panic. Just get the fuck out of the aircraft.

I couldn't smell fuel, but there was hot metal in front of me and most likely a fractured fuel line would be venting Mogas somewhere.

A moment of sheer terror hit me knowing I'd need to climb slightly upwards to the passenger door and clamber out. Had I remembered to unlock the passenger door?

My OCD said I had, but had I? Please don't let there be a fire. Please don't let there be a fire. Please. I reached up and moved the door locking mechanism. Mercifully the catch unlocked, and the gull-wing door opened outwards. Feeling numb all over I started to climb out, then stopped dead.

# Phoenix

The Tower would be worried. We'd flown through a 180-degree arc in a handful of seconds and were facing away from the ATC guys. They'd be staring out their windows in a state of horror.

There was no conscious thought involved other than to stop people worrying. I can't explain why but my head swiveled round to face the console. A tingling hand reached out to switch on the Master. I pulled the headset on, flicked the radio on, pressed the red microphone button, and said, 'I'm fine.'

There was an acknowledgement from the Tower, but all I really heard was a massive sense of relief from the voice on the radio. Then realised how stupendously fucking stupid I'd been for making the aircraft live again, and potentially causing a spark that'd set us ablaze.

I quickly switched the power off, and reached upwards to pull myself out. With arms and legs like jelly I dragged myself into the sun.

Then stood beside the aircraft and stared at her. And felt both incredibly sad and damn relieved she was so strong. I turned towards the Tower, waved, handheld high, and then sat down on the grass. From normal approach to impact had taken, maybe, five seconds.

Round about 90 seconds later the Barton fire wagon came racing towards India Zulu. I dragged my arse off the deck and stood there with hands in pockets watching the flashing lights move closer. The first face that appeared was the new fire guy. The look of anxiety on his face was palpable.

The first thing I could think to say was, 'Are you ok?' Then realised how bloody silly that sounded considering what had just happened. I shut up and he replied with a flurry of questions. How did I feel? Am I injured? How's my neck?

'I'm fine thanks', I mumbled. And with every question kept replying with the same mantra, 'I'm fine thanks.'

All the while I was reliving what happened and second-guessing what could have happened. Maybe she was destined to crash no matter what I did. Maybe I was too high in the flare or flying too slow. She'd felt fine. Maybe the wind had veered round. Maybe the wind had just dropped off a cliff and we'd lost 10 to 15 knots in a heartbeat.

Maybe there was an element of thermal activity rising up from the bricks embedded in the grass. Once upon a time the runway was known for wind shear and maybe that had been a problem. Or maybe I'd just been a woeful pilot who'd fucked up.

I kept staring at the windsock, as it weaved around, thinking, 'no one else has had problems today.'

Another fire engine rolled across the grass and moments later I was asked again how I was feeling. In response I heard my voice say, 'Yep, I'm fine, thanks.' Then started to think about what could have happened, and I sat down on the green grass again.

At pretty much any moment the left wing could have hit the deck and sent us cartwheeling. Flying through hell's half-circle I'd wanted to yank the stick back and pull up, but my inner pilot knew she'd have stalled and gone tumbling face forward. That would have caused problems. Cuts, fractures, bleeding, burns, death.

We were being forced down, pushed down, but if I'd pulled back ever so slightly maybe she'd have made it. Wishful thinking started to kick in.

In the space of the last one or two seconds I guess I'd accepted the crash was inevitable and prepared for impact. That had to be one of the hardest things I've ever, ever, ever, had to do. Accepting defeat was so intense. So difficult. Maybe that'd saved me.

The **'fight on v's accept defeat'** thought process had been carried out in the time it takes to click my fingers. The last second of whipping back the throttle, and trying to cut off the fuel, made me feel better that my subconscious was working. But… still.

# Phoenix

Turning on the Master to speak to the Tower was incredibly stupid. Majorly fucking dumb. Nearly suicidal. My illogical need to stop people fretting was idiotic beyond belief. That moment of stupidity might have started a fire that could've had dire consequences.

And then the slow-motion image of the grass rising up towards the cabin started replaying through my mind. Over and over and over again.

With the fire guys milling around I ducked my head inside the aircraft and started to get my kit out. Numb fingers started undoing the securing bolts under the seats and began moving my bits and pieces out into the sun. Maps, blanket, spare headset. I then began removing the kit from the footwell storage. Fuel strainer, emergency beacon, basic toolkit, spare inner tubes, oil.

On the third trip one of the fire guys came over and asked how I was feeling. The reply was, 'fine, thanks.' My need was to do something, anything. Emptying India Zulu was soul-destroying, but she was a person and I needed to be near her.

My friend, the fire guy, asked me to sit down and I understood I was supposed to play the role of the injured person, but couldn't. I didn't want to upset anyone but needed something to occupy my mind.

A couple of fellas in fire retardant jackets helped me open the rear baggage doors and take out my emergency stores. A sleeping bag, emergency food supplies, spare clothes, and a foot pump all made their way outside.

I stood staring at the crumpled body of India Zulu as an estate car 'ambulance' moved across the grass towards us. A paramedic emerged from the Mondeo and he seemed both amiable and concerned at the same time. He gently suggested that it'd be best if I lay down on a stretcher and wore a neck collar.

I wasn't up for that, and said so. He very generously said it was optional. I raised an eyebrow and gave him a lopsided smile.

It made perfect sense to play the injured party, but that just wasn't going to happen. He made a show of not looking at me and got out a heart monitor. Then attached it to my finger and waited. Nothing happened. I frowned, and he looked confused. Then he looked sheepish and said, 'the battery must be flat.'

I stood there feeling stupid and he took hold of my wrist and started checking whether I was about to have a coronary. '90 bpm,' he said. Things were a little bit of a blur, as a succession of new faces came and went, but my inner health monitor said 90 seemed high and surely I should be fitter than that.

I found myself forlornly staring at the grass and could smell escaped fuel. It was draining from the left tank, running down the sloping wing, and being absorbed into the lush grass. A pang of guilt hit me that I'd be responsible for killing a patch of perfectly innocent field.

Blankly staring at the bent aircraft, it dawned on me that no one else was landing. The realisation crested my horizon that they'd had to close the airfield and I was now the focus of everyone's attention. Oh, for fucks sake.

Someone had a hand-held radio and I could hear various voices wanting to land. A decision was made by the high ups to move everyone off the runway, leave the carcass of India Zulu, and reopen the airfield. The ambulance fellah suggested riding with him, and we trundled across the grass to the Tower.

More people milling around. A dozen or so. Everyone was looking at me out of the corner of their eyes. I avoided all eye contact and became fixated with the windsock. I stood there, staring at it, feeling numb and hollow.

For some reason all the surrounding colours seemed more vivid than usual.

A police car pulled up by the hangar. And then a full-size ambulance. My first exchange was with the Police. What happened?

# Phoenix

Was I hurt? Was anyone else involved? Had I been drinking? Would I mind being breathalysed? Was I the only driver and had someone hit my vehicle from behind?

Eh? Pardon? I hadn't been listening and was still staring at the windsock. Driver? My conscious mind surfaced and corrected the chap that I'd been in an aircraft. Or something that used to be an aircraft.

He apologised and said, 'sorry, force of habit.' Making small talk I noticed he wore a heart monitor on his wrist. He saw me stare at it, as I was preparing to blow into the breathalyser, and commented that heart monitors can become an obsession. He volunteered that his girlfriend made him take it off at night.

I wasn't listening to anything he said after that and my mind wandered off in different directions. The police were in a rush to get gone, and I signed the chap's piece of paper and turned away. What should I do now? Who should I call? My girlfriend, Cindy? My Sister?

I pulled my phone out, raised my head to the blue skies, and shut my eyes.

Twenty seconds later I found myself texting Dave. Quite a simple message. 'Crashed at Barton.' His reply was instant and said he was on his way.

One of the paramedics tapped me on the shoulder and asked me to get aboard the ambulance. I obediently climbed in the back, and they slammed shut the doors. Three of them, and me.

Feeling awkward and out of my comfort zone, I found myself sitting on their metal stretcher making slow-witted small talk. I was checked over again and generally interviewed. My jaded eyes stared at the row of magnetic catflaps opposite me. My guess was that they were used to keep medical kit secured in-situ instead of drawers. For some inexplicable reason my headspace became properly fixated on them.

Were the NHS being charged too much for commercial solutions to keep stuff from breaking loose when an ambulance veered around a corner? Had some genius cat owner proposed the idea? Had the NHS made a sound financial decision or gone bonkers?

A blood test was taken. Another heart monitor attached. More questions. Hands were placed on my neck. My head was examined, and a light was shone in my eyes. One of the two lady paramedics, the pretty one, said, 'We really think we should take you to hospital for an X-Ray.'

I heard myself say, 'I'm fine, thanks, and I'd like to go.' A stupid mindset, but I felt caged in and wanted out.

There was a tap on the ambulance door and the larger paramedic lady opened it. There stood Dave, handsome chap, competent looking fellah. He had a smile on his face and cheerfully asked how the patient was. My reply said, 'fine thanks.' And I used his appearance as an excuse to climb outside into the sun.

We chatted and he randomly commented that from his perspective, as a whiplash lawyer, that I'd probably be fine. And if I went to hospital now completing the later AAIB (Air Accident) forms would be much more complicated.

He followed up with, 'course, you might have serious neck problems right now and end up paralysed if you don't go to hospital this very second.' What to do? I thanked him for his concerns, moved my head from side to side, frowned, and then lightly punched his arm.

Ten minutes later we shook hands and he left. The police had already departed and the two ambulances had moved off the apron and headed elsewhere. Everyone else went about their business, and I started wandering around. Lonely, and completely numb.

My brain was weighing up what happened and a long list of possible outcomes. I found a vantage point to watch the windsock.

# Phoenix

It flapped about and my gaze simultaneously took in the wind rustling through the distant trees.

In the distance sat the wreckage of a forlorn looking Samson as she sat angled on her side a couple of hundred yards away. I'd killed her.

I found my way to the Airfield Lodge and sank a cup of tea and a piece of chocolate cake. One of the duty guys from the Tower appeared and we had a brief chat. He suggested wind shear might have been involved and added, 'these things happen.'

And it dawned on me that sometimes a few words from someone you respect is just enough to make the world a slightly less daunting place. He absently mentioned that someone had damaged their aircraft by banging a wing against a hangar door earlier that day.

He went on to say that a couple of hours earlier a chap had landed on the same runway, and had had a 'prop' strike' on touch down.

During the landing phase, that aircraft had pitched forward and a propeller blade had hit the ground. It'd been ripped from its mounting and flown off into the distance.

The pilot would have been shaken up, but he'd walked away from the impact. The Barton fire crew had looked for the missing propeller but hadn't found it. It was out there, somewhere, with its own story to tell.

Two hours later I was back in Bolton reading Ava a bedtime story. My voice was telling her the Rapunzel fairytale for the dozenth time, whilst my head was reliving what had happened.

She fell asleep halfway through my narrative, bless her, and it was all I could do not to wake her and say how very much I loved her.

## Chapter 2. Aftermath

I've heard the phrase CFIT before but as many AAIB reports as I've read, I didn't think it would apply to me. 'Controlled Flight Into Terrain,' is that what happened?

Was she flying at the last second or so, but we'd just ran out of height? Was it wind shear? From the screenshots I'd taken of the Barton ATIS, on the day of the crash, the Wind Direction and Wind Speed graphs were showing the wind veering around and sometimes dropping off a cliff.

I subsequently called up the guys in the Tower and asked about the readings. The duty manager was in the middle of something, but I managed to snatch a couple of minutes. 'The readings can fluctuate,' he said.

And for good measure added, 'anyway, the anemometer is 500 meters away from where you crashed so our readings could be way off. And sometimes birds sit on the damn thing and that screws up the readings.'

Every scenario went through my mind, and I saw the grass coming towards my face and felt the impact. I offered my thanks for his time and hung up.

The following two nights were punctuated by cold sweats and constant replays of what had happened. The same video clip kept repeating itself, over and over, and I could hear the Rotax screaming at me.

A week went by and I felt incredibly grateful to be alive, but also acutely embarrassed by what had happened. I'm supposed to be a decent pilot, for god's sake. Or is it just that I've bluffed my way through so many things I've no concept of what being competent actually means?

# Phoenix

It's time to get on with your life, Johnny Boy, and stop second-guessing every bloody thing. None of us will live forever. The important thing is to squeeze what enjoyment and experiences we can from our lives before it's too late. Onwards and upwards, fellah.

I found myself at Barton 5 days later having booked a flight in a Eurostar. If I didn't fly soon there was no shagging way I'd ever get in an aircraft again. After generally saying hi to anyone who'd make eye contact, I made my way over to see the Fire Crew.

I sat in their office and spoke to Craig, the first guy I'd met after climbing out of India Zulu. I awkwardly passed over a box of Cadburys Hero's and generally chatted.

One of the younger chaps appeared. He's the spitting image of the singer George Ezra, and he asked how I felt. By return I heard myself mumble, 'Fine, thanks.'

He followed up by asking how my ear was. I frowned and said, 'sorry?' A smile crossed his face as he offered that before the incident he'd thought my right ear lobe had been red.

My mind returned to the day, I saw the grass coming towards me, felt the impact, and then it made sense. A smile travelled across my face as the penny dropped.

Middle age is a bugger. Hair starts growing out of your nose and embarrassingly out of your other protuberances. Rather than allow a conifer to grow from my ears I'd taken, occasionally, to shaving the blighters.

That morning I'd shaved various bits above my neck and nicked an earlobe. The morning had been spent with a succession of irregular sized pieces of A4 paper stuck to the side of my head.

Laugh all you want, but one day, if not already, your ears will sprout leafage and will need the occasional pruning, too.

# Chapter 3. Paperwork & Decisions

What to do? Simple, really. Pray that all the relevant paperwork is up to date and get the insurance money sorted out. Then do something different with your life, Jonathan.

I spoke to the dashing 'Silver Fox' at Barton and tried to get my head straight. He suggested, keep flying, get my mojo back, and buy a new aircraft. Then just move on and fly some more.

Separately, and more as a gesture than anything else, I spent a chunk of money on a voucher for Dave to fly a Spitfire. I'd appreciated his driving over to Barton when he'd got my text and that meant a whole hell of a lot. Can't explain it more than that. I'd needed someone there, and he'd not let me down. I owed him.

That weekend I took Ava shopping to the Trafford Centre. We were walking along the upper concourse, holding hands, surrounded by throngs of Manchester's finest citizens. She looked up and innocently asked, 'Daddy, do you know everything?'

I looked down and offered a mixture of a frown, and a smile, and gently said, 'No baby'. There was silence.

Then she chirped up with, 'I think you do'. There was a slightly longer pause, and she added, 'except you don't know anything about flying.' I was prepared to accept that but asked why. She replied with, 'because you crashed.'

I smiled, bent down, and picked her up. Then wrapped my arms around my 4-year-old angel and gave her a bloody big kiss.

That made me think, though. Maybe I need to prove to myself that I can still fly, and that I'm not scared of flying. Should I face that

# Phoenix

fear by pointing myself towards another challenge? Or maybe I should accept my good fortune to be alive, uninjured, and stay safe for Ava's benefit.

Ultimately, I felt a great wave of sadness that I'd let Samson down. And felt terrible, as laughable as this sounds, about the insurance company taking a loss.

The days ticked by and I started eating more. The pounds piled on.

A message came through from Barton that they'd moved Samson from the impact point, by tractor. Why? Because it's bad form having a dead aircraft by the side of an active runway. It could best be described as, off-putting.

Her crumpled remains had subsequently been lashed to a JCB and moved out of sight. That day I polished off five Mars Bars.

The following day I left work early and went to have a look. She'd been moved to one of the airfields Exit Gates. India Zulu was both an open grave and a tourist attraction for visiting pilots.

She was lying on her side, with her right wing pointing up at the sky and the left digging for truffles. The Fox had helpfully removed the radio and transponder from the cabin to stop any light-fingered heathens from forcing entry and removing the spoils.

He suggested getting her carcass removed immediately and destroyed. The less people saw her the better. I understood the sentiment, the good intentions behind it, but just couldn't.

I spoke to the airport duty manager and asked if I could leave her there for a while to think about my next course of action. Regardless, she'd need the insurance assessors to have a look before any final decisions were made. The Fox was adamant she was a write-off, though. And even if not, there was no way to have 100% faith in any repairs.

Sitting in his office the tall fella was good enough to chat about the accidents he'd seen and heard of. His opinion was simply that I'd been too slow. First stall, secondary stall, crash. Simple as.

Condensing a near-fatal accident into five words dug into me. It felt like a knife had been angled upwards into my chest. He didn't mean anything other than these things happen. But it hurt. Not just that, the words burrowed under my skin and I knew they'd fester there.

I said my goodbyes and left Barton feeling queasy. My need was to buy a tarpaulin and get her covered over, protect her, and give her a little privacy. Two hours later I was back with B&Q's biggest covers.

Like a zombie I found myself slowly walking towards Samson. A light rain was falling all around and an inquisitive wind was pulling at my jacket. Everywhere I looked seemed drab and miserable.

I spotted the fireman, the George Ezra look-alike, through the tired-looking windows in the fire crew's office. We nodded to each other, and I put my head down and walked on.

Thirty seconds later I found myself stood beside Samson, slowly unfurling the sheeting. George appeared by my side and volunteered to help. Between the two of us, in near silence, we began to cover her. The wind tried to stop proceedings, but she was covered and secured in 15 minutes.

If there's ever any basic wisdom I can give to anyone, it would be to be friendly whenever you can. Why? Because there'll be days when you're feeling absolutely demolished inside, and the offer of help, in the rain, from a person you don't really know means more than I can possibly explain. He didn't need to help me, but he did. Thank you, George.

Over the next week or two, I went backwards and forwards to Barton to see how she was doing and generally mourn. The sheeting kept coming loose as the winds tugged at her and I kept

# Phoenix

trying to re-secure them. It was like visiting a lonely unkempt grave, with her bones protruding from underneath the sheeting.

All the while the question was whether to get her repaired or not. Or let her be taken away and broken up for parts with her carbon fibre skin compacted and then destroyed. Repair or destroy?

I kept reminding myself to stop lapsing into moments of sentimental bollocks by referring to India Zulu as a, 'she'. It's just a bloody machine...

Simple scenario. Either get her written off and then buy another aircraft, or simply realise I'd used up all the luck I was ever entitled to and stop flying. I owed her nothing. She/it was just carbon fibre with a Rotax 912 engine bolted to the pointy end.

I went and spoke to the Fox, again. Sitting in his office I sprouted out more mournful drivel and sat feeling glum and stupid. The conversation changed again to accidents, incidents, and engine failures he'd experienced.

And the ground started coming towards my face as the crash replayed through my mind. I changed the subject and ventured a comment that I'd consider flying a Flexwing in the future.

By way of reply he said a chap had just written off the resident Flex by flying into an electricity pylon. Another guy walked into the Fox's office and I mentioned my taking up Paragliding, maybe. He came across all doom and gloom about parachutes failing.

Feeling stupid and confused I made my way home and tried to decide what to do. Take the romantic route and try to repair her? Or put my business brain to the fore and cash in my survival bonus?

Lying on the settee, on a wet Tuesday evening, I found myself Googling possible repairs. A website popped up from a firm in Germany that might be able to do the repairs, or there was the possibility that a UK company could get her airborne. I fired off a number of emails and started to think about a possible repair schedule.

Would any repairs be economical? Could she be fixed in a realistic timeframe? Would she ever fly 'well' again? Would the work add too much weight and knock her out of the Microlight weight category? Is the Fox right to say she can never be trusted again?

And then there are other considerations. Personal ones. If I keep the money and don't buy an aircraft would a chunk of cash going to Ava's Mum help maintain an ongoing spirit of goodwill? And will that allow me to keep the relationship with my daughter alive?

At one point I'd bought Ava's Mum a Mini Convertible, but that hefty investment hadn't made our relationship any easier. But when a four-year old slips her hand into yours, and calls you, 'Daddy,'…. it can be intoxicating. And you'll do almost anything for her.

I have an obligation to Ava to stay alive. Does that mean not flying anymore? Can I be that person?

Decision required. Repair or not repair. The decision-making process, and that of the insurance company, is getting to biting point. The Fox is adamant she's a write-off and that common sense says she can't be trusted in the future.

An aircraft engineer visited Barton the following day to look over India Zulu and assess her for the insurance company.

I arranged to meet him, drove over, parked up, then started trudging across to her open grave. An overcast covering of clouds frowned down from the skies.

I'd met the fellah previously over the course of life at Barton. Amiable, good looking, very experienced. He looked up as I approached and shook his head.

# Phoenix

We had a very brief conversation. She's not repairable. A write off. My empty stomach twisted inside out and I wandered off to the car to fill it with my misery. India Zulu was an open wound, lying there for all and sundry to see, with my shame on show to the public.

I woke up the next morning and bizarrely realised that I loved India Zulu. You may well be reading this thinking, 'what a damn fool.' India Zulu is just carbon fibre, nothing more than that, and it's pathetic to think she's anything else.

But I'd given her a name. She'd kept me alive when I'd needed her strength, and she meant something to me.

Is she really a write-off? Is there any way I can get her airborne again? Is it a waste of time to even explore the idea?

A week later I sent pictures to both the UK repairers and the Germans to get a price for the required repairs. Plus asking for a cast-iron guarantee she could be fixed without busting the Microlight weight limits.

Interestingly, the English repairers came back with a 6 to 12 month timeframe, but no promises on the total repair cost. The Germans said three months, gave an itemised quote, and promised no additional weight would be added. Both scenarios were interesting.

And both replies implied she would fly again.

I called the insurance agent and asked his opinion. He commented that she was being written off, and I had first refusal on buying the wreckage. The cheapskate in me asked how little she would go for, but he wouldn't say.

I rang round half a dozen people and came up with a plan. During my calls, emails, and texts to various people, it became known that the assessor's firm had made an offer to buy her. And that made me think.

The engine has a slipper clutch to protect it from impact damage, therefore it might be salvageable. Maybe that was worth £8k. I wasn't convinced the structural integrity of the aircraft was compromised. And the Germans didn't think so.

Feeling distinctly uneasy I took my balls in my hand and offered £4,000. I was asked if that was my best offer. I cringed and said yes. Fate could decide what happened next.

The insurance agent said he would put forward my offer to the insurance company. Twenty-four hours later I was informed by phone that I'd bought the beat-up remains of my former fiancé, Samina, nicknamed Samson.

She'd kept me safe flying at 10,000ft over the Alps. She'd looked after me whilst skimming the waves at 30ft above the frigid waters of the North Atlantic. More recently she'd kept the ground from crashing through the skin of the aircraft and breaking my bones... or worse, finishing me off. There was a misbegotten attachment that just wouldn't go away.

I subsequently signed the insurance documents and the offer to buy her remains were deducted from the overall settlement figure. I was told the money would be forthcoming shortly.

A sense of anxiety started to well up as it dawned on me that a bloody stupid leap of faith was required. Can she actually be repaired? Will she be as strong after the repairs?

Subsequent to that I exchanged voice mail messages with the English repairer. And made contact with the Germans. Who to use? I trust the English guy implicitly, but the Germans offered a defined price and suggested they'll be finished in a couple of months.

Aren't the Teutonic Germans supposed to be uber reliable?

I slept on the UK versus German decision. And on the basis the British firm wanted more money to move her to their location in

England than the Germans wanted to get her to Berlin, the decision was taken to embrace our European brethren.

## **Chapter 4. Waiting for the Germans**

Can't get my head round a serious feeling of anxiety. It's not the end of the world if financially things go tits up with the aircraft, but it's stopping me sleeping.

I've tried to put all doubts to one side and have organised a date for the Germans to collect her. Four weeks away.

Maybe I should take the opportunity to put extra fuel tanks in the wings and try to go round the World. Do I need to prove to myself that I'm not scared of flying?

I've not got Ava this week and Cindy's trying to fit hair extensions to someone's head, which is a bonkers thing for a Social Worker to want to do. I'm bored and doing the Telegraph quick crossword.

My mind starts to wander. Should I do another long trek? Will she be safe to fly? Can I trust the German repairs? Will the repairs come in on price? I've always said I'd go RTW and I should do that, shouldn't I?

What would Dad have said?

I've been grumpy this week. Mum hasn't replied to my texts. Ava's Mum has been mucking about and not allowing me to see Ava. I've been harsh at work and just text Matt, in the office, to apologise for being an arse earlier in the day. Cindy's been lovely, but I haven't been able to share my insecurities with her.

On the plus side, I seem to be getting slightly funnier as the, 'survivor of a plane crash.' I'm losing my filter and blurting out the first crap that comes to mind. My musings seem to make folk laugh, but I need to remember to be sensitive to people's feelings.

I'm still waiting for India Zulu to officially become mine, again. Hence I'm trying to juggle her transport to Germany and appease Barton's requirement to have her moved. Then tie that up with a date when she actually belongs to me again. It's getting stressful.

The suggestion has been that Barton might set the tractor on her again if I don't organise something very soon.

A couple of days later I went flying with Dave and we flew in his aircraft over the sea to Caernarvon. We landed, sat on one of the benches outside the Airport cafe, and just whiled away an hour in the sun. He mentioned the little matter of the AAIB report. 'Whatever it says, it'll be a stink that'll follow you around for the rest of your life,' he said.

The following morning I woke up at 4.30am and couldn't get back to sleep - too much to process. I started the Telegraph Crossword and then gave up when realisation dawned that I didn't know the answer to, 'Last drop in glass.'

Apparently, the answer is, 'Heel tap.'

Barton are threatening to move her again, I guess because she's an eyesore and not a pleasing sight. My anxiety is how much damage they'll do to her. And there I go again; she's not a bloody person. Get a grip, Hilton.

The Insurance agent mentioned, on more than one occasion, that crashed aircraft often sustain a lot more damage when they're moved. And that's been playing on my mind.

I couldn't help myself and sent an early morning email to Barton suggesting that if she's moved, and damaged, that I'll take legal action. Then immediately realised that was a bloody stupid move.

# Phoenix

Two more things happened over the next day or so. I weighed myself and seemed to have put on a stone in weight, and therein lies the problem with comfort eating. And I got my eyes tested. Everything seems fine, but my focus isn't quite as sharp very close up and it seems that middle age is kicking in.

The following morning's last remaining crossword question was; 'female ruff.' I've zero idea what the answer is, unless it's, 'a woman from Bolton.' The Telegraph crossword is full of language difficulties.

I was latterly Googling different things and watched a YouTube clip showing wake vortices from landing light aircraft. Very interesting. Maybe I flew through a tiny bit of that courtesy of the preceding PA28. Or maybe I'm just a shit pilot making excuses, again.

I subsequently phoned Barton and spoke to their Duty Manager, Mike Lobb. Quite possibly one of the nicest guys you'll ever meet. Friendly, likeable, genuine. And I'd sent him an email I'd no right whatsoever to send.

I organised to meet him later that day. Drove to Barton, parked up, and walked to the Tower. Climbed the concrete stairs leaning against the red brick structure, and found my way into his office. An aircraft propeller was idly leaning against one wall.

There was an element of small talk, and then we moved onto the open grave that was the rain-soaked skeleton of India Zulu. I apologised for my previous email and leaned forward waiting anxiously for him to say something positive.

The two options seemed to be, 'your wreckage is sat on our land, and we'll do whatever we want with it.' Or, 'we'll be a little bit more patient, but there are limits to our goodwill.'

I leaned forward in my seat and Mike said, 'Jon, we like you, Peel Holdings like you. We won't move your aircraft'.

There's no way to explain it, but I came over all emotional and felt a tear well up. A voice inside my head said, 'do not bloody cry in front of Mike.'

We chatted through the crash and my mind went backwards and forwards from sitting safely in his office to the impact, and how lucky I'd been. I mentioned my illogical need to refer to India Zulu as a 'she,' and Mike just smiled back at me.

I left his office and tottered down the stairs feeling light-headed. My headspace felt better about the world, but walking away from Mike felt like leaving the headmasters office after dodging a telling off.

\*\*\*

That weekend, 16th August, Dave and I flew to a place called Druridge in the Northeast. They were having a get-together for visiting pilots. We climbed out of his Jodel, I put my flip flops on, and both of us went to find a burger.

Sunshine was bouncing off the greenery and thirty or so people were milling around. A dozen or so different types of light aircraft sat neatly lined up on the grass.

The airfield is right by the beach, and I carefully worked my way through the barbed wire fencing, sluggishly climbed over the sand dunes, and found the shoreline. And stood with my feet in the sea staring at the horizon pondering life, the universe, and everything.

Twenty long minutes later I wandered back to find Dave and generally tried to be a bit more sociable. Shortly afterwards we climbed aboard Delta Lima with the intent to head back to Barton. A yellow Sherwood Ranger, microlight biplane, was taxiing ahead of us.

I was staring into space again, and only vaguely aware of Dave talking to me. My gaze was fixed on the tail wheel of the Ranger. It seemed to be digging into the soft grass as she taxied.

# Phoenix

The two-seat biplane lined up in front of us on the grassy runway and started her takeoff roll. She accelerated across the slightly uneven surface, and my disconnected gaze watched her wobble from left wheel to right wheel as she tried to get airborne.

Dave was looking inside the cabin as my eyes absently followed the departing aircraft. And then the Ranger flipped over and came to a dead stop. What? What the fuck?!

I told Dave to stop the prop', undid my harness, climbed out, and started sprinting over to the aircraft. Cars were driving over; other people were running. Please let the fellah be ok, please.

She was pretty much vertical, nose dug into the grass, with her tail wheel pointing up at the sky. The pilot, an older chap, had managed to release himself from the harnesses, dropped to the grass, and seemed dazed.

I tried to say everything would be ok, but his eyes weren't quite focusing on me. I knew exactly what was happening to him, and I wanted him to sit down and get his bearings.

And being told what to do was exactly what I'd rebelled against.

Looking over at him I could tell he was reliving the accident because I'd done the exact same thing a month or so earlier. A Police car arrived, the Air Ambulance flew over, everyone had concerned looks on their faces.

You watch something like that and it's impossible to understand the first time you replay it in your mind's eye. It was such an abrupt end to the takeoff roll.

Thirty minutes later, a decision was made by the high ups to roll over the biplane and allow other aircraft to depart. I added a little muscle to the strain of a few others and we pulled her from the runway.

Was the ground just a little too soft for the Ranger? Was he trying to haul her off the grass before she was ready to fly? Or was one wheel knackered and no matter what, she was going to crash that day?

As the Fox would say, 'she belongs to the insurance company now, and no one was hurt, so no big deal.' It could have been an awful lot worse.

Accidents are simply that, accidents. Mechanical failures are tough to battle against.

The following day found me at work as a call came through from the AAIB chap. He seemed pleasant enough, but my insides were twisting around my colon from the moment the phone was handed over.

His thought process was, 'initial stall, secondary stall, crash.' I didn't know what to say to that, other than, 'OK.' And then found the courage to ask about his flying experience.

He mentioned he'd got 10,000 flying hours. I asked about any scares he might have had and the reply was, 'Every 1,000 hours or so, I've done something stupid, and every 3,000 hours I've done something really stupid.'

That made me feel better, but I wasn't sure to what extent he was just being a thoroughly decent fellah offering a little cold comfort to a halfwit.

I weighed myself the next morning, and my chunk rating stands at 13 stone 10 lbs.

Have I been grumpy as a result of the crash? Or happier because I dodged a bullet? That Saturday morning Ava and I were walking along the busy main road on the way to her ballet class.

A warm day, beautiful, sun in the heavens. She started to run off and I screeched at her to stop, then felt a horrible moment of guilt.

# Phoenix

Ava had stopped dead and looked scared. I apologised for shouting and explained that roads were dangerous. And for some reason asked, 'are you afraid of me?'

She looked up at me, with her beautiful little face cocked to one side, and said, 'I'm not scared of my da da.' Without understanding why, I asked if she thought anyone was scared of me. She said, 'only monsters are scared of my Daddy.'

An hour later ballet finished, we got in the car, and I put the roof down. We took a detour on the way home and went for a drive amongst the narrow, winding, country lanes of Lancashire.

We raced past hedgerows, fields, up and over small hills, and generally felt the sun wash over us. The radio was on and 'Hooked on a Feeling' stormed the speakers (from the Guardians of the Galaxy film) and both of us tried to sing the chorus. And it felt glorious to be alive.

Later that afternoon the joy of life suffered a setback. Ava had a major tantrum after we'd been swimming. She didn't want to wash her hair and blurted out, 'you're just being nasty.' Then cried.

She got even more tetchy about the hair drying process and promptly tried to hide from the hairdryer. She climbed into one of the floor level wooden lockers and unsuccessfully tried to pull the door completely shut. I guess the logic being that if I couldn't find her, then her hair could stay wet, tangled, and untouched.

The following day the insurance money hit my bank account. To celebrate I bought a new set of bedding, purchased a Toaster & Kettle set for Cindy, and took Ava to buy a few goodies from Toys 'R' Us.

*Note to Jonathan from the future. Try to be more romantic when dealing with women. Whilst the language of love might suggest buying gifts for your girlfriend is generally a good thing.... purchasing, over time, bathroom tiles, a hairdryer, television, and a matching toaster and kettle set... are not the most romantic acquisitions.*

*And whilst the shiny black washing machine you bought Cin looks great, the fact that it wants to play a tune when it's finished a cycle gets really tedious after a while. You, I, need to understand how a bunch of Roses can say a lot more than a washing machine that wants to brag.*

The Germans are due to collect Samson on Tuesday. Where the hell that process will take me, I have no idea.

22nd August 2015.

An aerobatic aircraft crashed at an air display at Shoreham. What happened? Mechanical failure? Did the pilot blackout? The pilot survived, but ten or so spectators died.

25th August 2015.

The wreckage of India Zulu was collected today by two very nice German gentlemen.

A father and son team. Unfortunately their family name is Koch, which the child in me found very funny for some elusive reason. They arrived at Barton earlier than expected and very carefully started pulling Samson apart with a view to dragging her onto their trailer.

When I'd got the text saying they were in Manchester I'd raced to Barton without a portion of the paperwork they were expecting. So I stood there forlornly, on an overcast day, watching them work, feeling more stupid than normal.

Mark from the Tower was overseeing proceedings and we chatted idly as the Germans went about their work. Not for the first time I really appreciated how bloody supportive the Barton chaps are.

# Phoenix

The young German spoke very good English, but the father wouldn't communicate and, apart from nods and gestures, he didn't try to say anything.

I left Barton, drove back to the office, got the paperwork they wanted, then caught up with them as they were on the motorway driving her to the ferry at Hull.

After a few phone calls and texts, they turned onto a dual carriageway and I found them parked up in a lay-by. India Zulu was strapped to their trailer with her wings neatly folded alongside the fuselage. I clambered onto the trailer and had a quick look inside Samson. Cars were hurtling past, and drivers were looking confused at what they were seeing.

The pair had done a professional job of securing Samson, and they seemed very experienced at collecting crashed CT's. I looked forlornly at the first aircraft I'd ever bought, and Koch Jnr looked up at me and said, 'we've seen a lot worse.'

I sheepishly peered inside the cabin, almost embarrassed, and saw the broken undercarriage strut sitting on the fake leather seat. It was the thickness of my wrist and the skinny length of aluminium had been snapped in half by the impact.

It was no use to anyone, and I asked if I could have it, I guess as a morbid memento.

At that moment the older Koch interjected and used only the second English word I'd heard him say, other than OK. He presented me with the shiny strut and said, 'souvenir.'

The thought went through my mind that he'd probably used that word a few times whilst handing over redundant bits of aircraft to their former owners.

# Chapter 5. Repairs

I've discussed putting extra fuel tanks in the wings with the Germans. That'd help send Samson around the world but would take her to the limit of what she could structurally handle. And having seen the width of the Aluminium wheel struts and the way mine sheared in two, I figure that might not be wise.

Plus, the British Microlight Aircraft Association would most likely have issues with non-standard modifications.

My mindset has changed from, 'shall I go round the world?' to, 'I shall go round the world.' Something worthwhile has to come of this. But at the same time, I'm scared. And it's generating the kind of background anxiety that won't go away.

Maybe an extra fuel tank inside the cabin would work. But in the event of a crash, that could lead to huge amounts of fuel sloshing around and dousing me. It'd also make it difficult to get out the passenger side if an impact on landing was on my side.

I'm not 100% sure which decisions to make. Two commercial pilots went round the world in a pair of the bigger, modified, CTLS's. They had extra tanks in the wings, plus autopilots, and flew from South America to Africa in order to cross the Atlantic.

I really, really, don't want to fly via the Arctic again, so maybe…

But I can't really fit an Autopilot to a CTSW for weight reasons. And then there's the question, 'is that really flying?' Do I want to experience every second of the airborne experience? Isn't 'stick and rudder' what it's all about?

Having said that an Autopilot would make the flight a shit load easier. No fannying about trying to fly straight and level all the damn time. Simply let the electronics take the strain whilst I use the

# Phoenix

radio and put my feet up. Plus, it'd make navigation so much simpler and my headspace wouldn't be divided into too many compartments. Is that really flying, though?

The Germans have sent pictures of India Zulu being worked on, which makes me feel better. They're a whole lot easier on the eye than seeing her flatlined on the grass at Barton underneath blue sheeting.

I'm not sleeping at the moment, and my weight is ballooning again. I need to get away and do a long-distance trek but don't want to risk my life... Whichever way you add things up the bottom line is that I have a responsibility to Ava and Cindy. I can't afford to be reckless.

But then again, I'm getting restless and need something to focus on. Do I even want to fly anymore?

More speculation at Barton about the Shoreham crash. The suggestion is that the pilot blacked out for a second or two. That seems to be the consensus. Although someone thought he was carrying long-range fuel tanks and that might have screwed up the flight characteristics of the jet.

That weekend I agreed to go flying with Dave. Not flown in 2 months. Walking towards his Jodel made me feel sick. His aircraft, other aircraft, just looking at anything with wings makes me nauseous.

We climbed aboard Delta Lima and I could smell fuel. I said so, but Dave said he couldn't smell anything. He was preoccupied with his headset, it wasn't working properly, and he hit it a few times to fire it into life.

I was in my own little world, wondering about fire, flames, and sizzling skin. Maybe he'd sloshed fuel everywhere when fueling her. Maybe that was the smell.

# Jon Hilton

A warm day, sunny, no breeze, and Barton were using runway 27L. We took off and the fuel smell got to the point where we decided to make an about turn. To add insult to injury Dave's top of the range headset cut out, and yours truly took over the radio work as we turned back towards the airfield.

We joined the circuit and without any hint of anxiety or stress he very gently put her onto the grass runway. Textbook stuff.

For good measure I said it was a truly shit touchdown. A real whiplash-inducing shocker. I followed up with a suggestion that he should get the Fox to teach him how to fly before he properly broke his aircraft.

He glanced across at me, smiled, and said, 'shut up, fuckwit.'

We taxied back to the apron, got out, and started looking around the cockpit for the smell. There was a small amount of fuel dribbling around the footwell. The fuel line could be fractured, or maybe a seal was working its way loose. Dave made a phone call and the resident Barton engineer was booked to resolve the headache.

A few people waved at me and generally said hello as we pottered around the hangar. It's strangely odd when people you don't know say hi. A buried section of brain asks if you've been pointed out to them for a reason.

It's been a difficult week. Ava told me that her Mum doesn't like me, which is fine. Work has been stressful and heavy going. Ava asked if I was really her Daddy. I said yes, of course, but it made me feel very awkward.

I had a series of nightmares last night. I was being eaten by crocodiles, one mouthful at a time. Maybe I do need to get away and do a long flight. Maybe I need to disappear. Maybe Ava does need a new, permanent, father figure in her life, and not a weekend Dad.

# Phoenix

Ava pushed over a little girl at school this week. I found out from her Mum and had a chat with Ava about it. I explained that it was wrong to hurt other people, and in response she told me that she didn't like me. Then she followed up with, 'I don't want to stay at your house anymore.'

Her Mum is generally making life difficult for me. I'd put on a suit to go to Ava's school Assembly, wanting to look smart, and then got told not to go. From speaking to Ava the following day it seems that her Mum's new man went instead. I guess that's an inevitable part of folk moving on with their lives.

I headed to Barton the next day to meet Dave. Sunny, no wind, with a little lingering misty cloud. We jumped in his Jodel and I put on my pig-headed mindset and ignored all my airborne anxieties.

The plan was to head to Llanbedr in West Wales, and we took off. Yet again there was a fuel smell and we decided to turn around, head home, and check it out.

We landed back at Barton and there was fuel leaking into the cabin, again. We both took the pragmatic view that these things happen. What else is there to do if you want to fly?

Later that evening my friends Gary and Chris dragged me out for a beer and we called in to a few local pubs. For reasons I can't explain I tried to cheer myself up by using my mobile to buy three tickets to see Real Madrid against Barcelona. Cost price £1,100. It was a treat for both their birthdays, all courtesy of my unwanted windfall.

Life's been good over the last couple of days, but Cindy's been in floods of tears. Once a month she gets quite depressed and I don't know how to help.

The impression I'm getting from Ava's Mum is that I can have a relationship with Ava, if I don't have a relationship with Cindy. I'm outwardly smiling and being cheerful, but a heavy weight is settling on my shoulders. How do I keep everyone happy?

Maybe it's my subconscious fear of flying kicking about, but I've started paying much more attention to news reports of aircraft crashing.

### 3rd October

*Chigwell aircraft crash.*

*Two people have died in a light aircraft that crashed and caught fire in Essex. The Beechcraft King Air 200 came down in a field off Gravel Lane and Miller's Lane in Chigwell just before* <u>10:20 BST</u> *and burst into flames, police said.*

*A fire service spokesman said: "On arrival, crews reported that the aircraft was 100% alight." Essex Police said the plane was an eight-seater, but there were only two people on board.*

*Essex Police said it was working with the government's Air Accident Investigation Branch to find out what happened.*

*A statement released by the operators of the aircraft described both crew members, who have not been named, as "highly experienced professional pilots".*

*Ray Gibbs, who was at Woolston Manor Golf and Country Club when the crash happened, said: "We were playing golf and heard a loud bang and the ground rumbled a bit, but we couldn't see any smoke, so we were not sure how far away it was."*

### 4th October

A lovely day. Dave thought his fuel leak was a thing of the past, and we went flying. We landed at Wolverhampton and Dave spotted a great guy called James and his Citabria. My friend told him I wanted to get my tail dragger rating, which is most definitely not the case.

From what I can tell every tail dragger pilot thinks they're special. They're bonkers the lot of 'em.

# Phoenix

I ended up doing 0.7 hours with James in his aircraft. An example of a surreal experience is landing an aircraft you've never flown before, that doesn't have flaps, whilst juggling the demands of a 40-degree crosswind, in order to land on a 350 meter stretch of grass.

Plus, the instructor is sat behind you and it feels like only the Gods can help a chap touch down. So much concentration needed and I felt light-headed after the fan at the front had stopped.

Maybe that helped me overcome my general flying fears, but it wasn't an experience I wanted.

Dave, you're a dick.

### 22nd October

*Pilot killed as US fighter jet crashes into Suffolk farmland.*

*A US pilot was killed when his fighter jet crashed into farmland near a Suffolk airbase in the third crash near the airfield in the past two years.*

*The pilot died when his United States Marines F/A-18C Hornet crashed at around 10.30am yesterday, soon after taking off from RAF Lakenheath.*

*Witnesses described seeing a fireball erupt from the crash site in farmland near Redmere, just a few miles from the Suffolk base.*

*The plane from the Marine Attack Fighter Squadron 232 was one of six returning home to its base in California, via Britain, from operations in the Middle East.*

*Nearby residents said they had seen a parachute come down, but police said the pilot died in the crash and he was the sole occupant.*

*Patrick Turner, 72, who lives a few hundred yards from the scene, said: "There was a hell of a bang when it hit the ground".*

*'I have so much praise for the pilot ... he took the plane away from the houses. We are very grateful to him. It shook all of the houses. It was so loud you could*

not hear yourself speak. I went outside and saw the plane – it was a huge fireball'.

Karen Miles-Holdaway, 48, who lives nearby, said: 'I was in my garden when I saw the plane going over. It was much lower than they usually fly at.'

The crash comes just over a year after an American fighter based at Lakenheath crashed near a school in Lincolnshire.

The F-15 fighter jet from the US Air Force's (USAF) 48 Fighter Wing crashed in fields near Spalding on Oct 8, 2014.

The pilot ejected safely, sustaining only minor injuries, and no one on the ground was hurt.

\*\*\*

16th November

Nighttime and Ava's asleep in her room. White bed, pink wallpaper, white sideboard, and cream carpets. A large poster from the film Frozen on one wall and a dozen small foam purple butterflies stuck to another wall. A lovely room for a beautiful little girl.

She cried out in distress at 4am. I pulled myself from my duvet and tottered into her bedroom. It was dark in there with a faint glow from the landing light casting itself about. She reached out to me whilst half asleep. I lifted her up and rocked her in my arms until she settled.

Then whispered to her, 'I love you,' and she smiled with her eyes closed and replied with, 'I've got a new Daddy'… I stood there feeling devastated and alone.

The aircraft should be finished soon.

# Phoenix

## 14th November

*Four people from the same family were killed after a six-seater light aircraft crashed at Buttles Farm, near Churchinford, Somerset. Avon and Somerset police received an emergency call at 11:44. All four persons on board - a 56-year old man, a 55-year old woman, a 23-year old woman and a 20-year-old man - were pronounced dead at the crash site.*

*"The aircraft was approaching Dunkeswell Airfield, Devon after an uneventful flight from Fairoaks, Surrey. The weather at Dunkeswell was overcast, with rain. The pilot held an IMC1 rating, but there is no published instrument approach procedure at Dunkeswell. As the aircraft turned onto the final approach, it commenced a descent on what appeared to be a normal approach path but then climbed rapidly, probably entering cloud. The aircraft then seems to have stalled, turned left and descended to "just below the clouds", before it climbed steeply again and "disappeared into cloud". Shortly after, the aircraft was observed descending out of the cloud in a steep nose-down attitude, in what appears to have been a spin, before striking the ground. All four occupants were fatally injured.*

*The investigation was unable to determine why the aircraft made the initial rapid climb, but there was some evidence to suggest that the pilot may have manually overridden the autopilot, during the initial descent, without realising it was still engaged. This would have caused an out-of-trim condition that could have contributed to the aircraft pitching up rapidly. Evaluation flights showed that the pitch attitude achieved during this manoeuvre would have been disorientating for the pilot and may explain why control was not regained."*

(www.ogimet.com) *Exeter Metar SA14/11/2015 11:50->METAR EGTE 141150Z 21014KT 9999 -RA SCT020 BKN035 11/10 Q1022=SA14/11/2015 11:20->METAR EGTE 141120Z 20009KT 9999 -RA SCT020 BKN035 10/10 Q1023=*

## 3rd December

*A light aircraft went missing over the Irish Sea on 3/12/2015; aircraft is believed to have ditched into the sea whilst en route between the Isle of Man and*

Blackpool, Lancashire, after it failed to arrive as expected at Blackpool Airport at 9:15 am local time. The aircraft was last sighted on radar at 1,300 feet and approximately three miles off the Lancashire coast. According to the summary of the official AAIB report into the accident:

"The aircraft was on a VFR flight from Ronaldsway to Blackpool. A bank of low cloud was moving out to sea, and analysis of the radar track found that coincident with encountering this cloud, the aircraft descended, and its speed reduced until it disappeared from radar. Intensive SAR efforts did not locate the aircraft or pilot. The available evidence suggests that the aircraft may have stalled at a height from which recovery was not possible."

According to contemporary press reports:

"Fuel and debris have been found in the search for a plane that went missing off the coast of Blackpool this morning. The discovery was made by rescue crews scouring a 45 square mile area of the Irish Sea. The debris was collected by one of several RNLI boats and was taken back to shore for examination as the search came to an end for the evening.

Senior coastal operations officer for the UK Coastguard service, Adam Bradbury, said: "All I can say is there have been some objects recovered, but we don't know where they are from yet. It's too early."

The light aircraft was on its way to Blackpool Airport from the Isle of Man when it lost contact with air traffic controllers and vanished from radar shortly after 9am. The pilot was the only person on board. Duty controller Matthew Mace added: "We have used all the means and assets available to search an extensive area off the Blackpool coast. We have suspended today's search due to failing light, and we will review overnight what searches will be conducted tomorrow."

An earlier search along the coastline found no sign of the downed aircraft, sparking fears the plane had 'ditched' into the sea in poor weather conditions. The multi-agency response included volunteer RNLI crews from St Annes, Blackpool, Fleetwood, and Southport, two search and rescue helicopters, including one from Wales, and an onshore team of experts.

# Phoenix

*The Lancashire Fire and Rescue service and police were also involved in a search of sand dunes close to Blackpool Airport at Starr Gate.*

… More delivery delays with India Zulu. All getting very stressful.

<u>11th January</u>

Flying Medical required with Dr Donnan. A very nice, likeable, chap and his surgery is, bizarrely, only 100 yards away from Ava's first home.

I sat in his office and felt insignificant. Maybe everyone feels the same way in front of a doctor. I could see he was assessing everything about me as he passed over a questionnaire for completion.

He was still watching me from across his desk as I quickly scanned the paperwork. One question read, 'have you had a crash in the last six months.'

Whilst I was mid-scribble he asked if I'd had any excitement recently. For some reason, the question seemed like a loaded one. Rightly or wrongly, my guess was that he already knew my story. Maybe people lie on these forms and he was assessing my levels of honesty, so I told my tale.

The outcome of the medical is that my far vision is very good, better than the norm. My short vision is good, but I can tell it's deteriorating. Both would be sufficient for a Class 1 commercially valid medical, he said.

My heart rate is very good at 50 bpm, but I'm half a stone heavier than the last medical. My weight's been yo-yo'ing since the crash, but I reckon I'm getting it under control.

Leaving the Doctors surgery, I shook his hand and casually mentioned how it seemed harder to focus from close up to farther away… by way of a reply he shrugged and said, 'welcome to middle age.'

I smiled, he smiled, and then he stood there with an amused look on his face as I did a 6-point turn to get out of his small car park. You fool, Hilton.

* * *

A couple of days later I spoke to the Fox. He mentioned that the Barton Duty Manager, Mike Lobb, had been doing a runway inspection on New Year's Eve. Mike had been slowly walking up and down the grass runway, looking for AWOL bits of aircraft, and had had a heart attack.

He'd managed to get his radio out of his pocket and call the Tower. He asked for the Rescue truck to be dispatched and, when asked why, said, 'I'm having a heart attack.'

On the 15th of January he had a Triple Bypass operation at Wythenshawe Hospital. My Dad died there two and a half years earlier.

Cindy had been working the wards there as a contract Social Worker, so I sent a text asking her to call round and say hi. She's such a pretty, bubbly, likeable person, and just the sight of her would have cheered Mike up.

Like a twit I'd spelt his surname wrong and she couldn't figure out which ward he was on and Patient Services wouldn't help. And that made me feel like I needed to get more involved.

The fact that he was in Wythenshaw made me deeply sad, miserable even. Empty. I felt for Mike but was scared to go there. And there was no reason to visit him. I don't know him that well, but he'd been generous with his time and approach to me.

On the 22nd of January I picked Ava up from school and we drove round with a copy of my last book. The intent being to tell him I thought he was one of the good guys.

# Phoenix

We parked up and made our way onwards into the hospital. Clean walls and signs telling everyone to wash their hands welcomed us inside.

Ava was oblivious and was happily shouting out the kind of things young kids do. I was trying to keep her quiet by saying, 'We're in a hospital, you need to shush.'

We waited outside the ward and a couple of nurses rolled a patient past on a gurney. He looked like Dad. Similar age, pale skin, wearing a mask linked to a tired-looking oxygen bottle. The fellah looked scared, but smiled at Ava. She went quiet and I felt horrid for bringing her.

It was past visiting time, but the nurses seemed to like the look of us and let us through the security doors into the ward. I saw another nurse and asked where Mike was. She walked to a big wallboard listing patient names and bed numbers. She glared up at it and said, 'he's in bed 9.'

I looked up at the board and spotted another box on the right, it said, 'discharged'. He'd gone an hour earlier.

The inscription I'd already written in the book said, 'you are my hero, get well soon.' I've no idea what he's done with his life but he's a placid, easy-going, chap and someone I respect. The world needs more of his ilk.

Ava and I walked away. And then realisation dawned that if we kept the visit under 20 minutes the car parking would be free. With no reason to dawdle, and burn through cash, we pegged it back to the car.

* * *

More aircraft delivery delays and issues with her weight. Very frustrating. The Germans took three weeks off for Christmas and snow in Germany means she can't be taken outdoors to run the engine, apparently. Which sounds like complete bollocks to me. I'm frustrated and don't even know if she'll tick over.

I subsequently spoke to the BMAA about the aircraft's weight. Empty she was assessed at 268kg, and the repairs added half a kilo in weight which is absolutely minimal. An amazing job by the Germans, but she's still 20kg overweight.

I'd asked about this before the repairs started and was assured that she'd be fine, but she's heavy now. Either the Germans screwed up, or the sports seats, Dynon, transponder, bigger battery, and slipper clutch account for the extra weight. Which is bound to be the case.

There was a further chat with the Fox about India Zulu's weight, and he's been very helpful. She'd still be a viable aircraft if a ballistic rocket-powered parachute was added, he said.

So, ironically, by adding extra weight, that provides an additional margin to soak up the existing weight gain. And in that instance, she'd be considered legal under the definition of being a Microlight... But do I really want a rocket sat behind me?

I called the BMAA again and explained my circumstances and asked for further clarification on the weight rules. The chap said their attitude to weight limits had changed recently because aircraft were routinely having kit taken off before being weighed for their Permit Inspection. And then the 'extras' were being reattached after the paperwork had been signed off. With some aircraft this was affecting their Centre of Gravity.

He volunteered that a recent accident had happened where this was the case. I asked if the BMAA / CAA had thrown the book at the aircraft owner. He paused and said, 'No.'

Trying to be lighthearted I jokingly heard myself say, 'I bet the pilot's relieved the authorities have been so understanding.' The phone went silent for a couple of heartbeats, and then the chap said, 'Not really, the accident was a fatality.'

# Phoenix

A voice inside my head said, 'Shut the fuck up, Jonathan, and get off the phone before you say something really bloody stupid.'

* * *

Why the hell am I trying to get Samson back in the air? It would have made so much more sense to have given up on her and buy a new aircraft. New engine. Stronger landing gear. Completely weight legal. No issues.

A new CT would have ticked a lot of boxes. I'm so pissed off right now. Common sense says I should have just lodged my survival bonus with Flight Design and simply waited for a new aircraft to roll off the production line.

Separately, the pilot involved with the Shoreham crash has been interviewed by police. The suggestion is that he started his manoeuvre too low. And he's done it before, allegedly.

<u>7th February</u>

India Zulu is three months past the previously agreed delivery date, but she seems to be finished and needs assessing. The BMAA have said that as a result of recent rule changes there are three weeks to get the repairs inspected; otherwise the BMAA say it's unlikely she'll get approval to fly again.

The Fox mentioned a chap called Bob who's assessed crash-repaired aircraft on behalf of the BMAA. He also has a relationship with the Germans having previously signed off their work. It looks like everything could neatly fall into place. I spoke to this chap and swapped emails in which we agreed a price for him to fly out and inspect her.

Samson was check flown by Bob. He just went off of his own accord and did it. She passed.

Why have I refurbed India Zulu? Bloody stupid decision. She has a crash on her record and an old engine. It would have been so much smarter to have put down a deposit on a new CT, and then wait for it to roll off the production line. What a damned idiot.

18th February

Flight Design has gone bust! If I'd bought a new aircraft I'd have most likely lost all my money. This whole process feels like a slalom course. There's no right or wrong way to proceed, but there's a lot of anguish involved if I muck up.

19th February

I watched a TV documentary on the Discovery Channel about a midair collision in San Diego between a jet and a Cessna172.

The Captain of the Boeing 727 was described as a natural aviator, and the suggestion was they'd crashed because both the Captain and First Officer had their seats set too low. If their seating position had been slightly higher, they might have seen the light aircraft on a collision course.

By contrast, the Cessna 172 has a high wing configuration. Both aircraft were hidden from each other by their respective blind spots.

Everyone died. 144 people in the air and seven casualties on the ground. Maybe the whole world simply revolves around good or bad luck. Or fate.

27th February

The Germans are mucking about over the cost of the repairs, and I'm frustrated.

Additionally Bob has added £1,500 onto his bill because, apparently, his Company Chairman told him to renege on the existing agreement and charge more. Which is quite tedious as he

# Phoenix

says he won't forward the paperwork 'till the additional payment is made in full. And that strikes me as blackmail. Plus, there's no time to get anyone else over there, and he knows that.

I've sued half a dozen firms over the years, mostly law firms, and won each case. The only exception was a few years ago against the Law Society, but with the benefit of hindsight launching that action was a tad optimistic.

I felt completely in the right and, courtesy of an Early Day Motion in the House of Commons, eight Members of Parliament supported my case.

With all the disputes I've sat alone, across the table from lawyers and barristers, and argued. With respect to the Law Society, I was undone by my lack of Case Law knowledge. And if I'd won it would have had far-reaching consequences for the manner in which the Law Society of England and Wales operate. So you could say I was on a hiding to nothing.

And sometimes right and wrong doesn't come into legal disputes. It's either who best argues their case on the day, or whether a compromise can be reached before the door to the courtroom opens.

I take a certain comfort from the fact that the barrister acting for the Law Society proposed a deal fifteen minutes before the hearing started. I said yes, but by that point I'd upset too many people at the Law Society and the barrister's bosses rejected his proposal, and rolled the dice.

And twenty minutes after sitting down across the table from two solicitors, the barrister, and the judge, I got bitch slapped and was ejected from the courtroom with my tail between my legs.

I'm not a lawyer, and that was the risk I took. Any court case is a risk, but it's also a stressful battle of wills. Some things become a matter of principle and others just aren't worth the hassle.

With Bob it wasn't a huge amount of additional money. But changing the amount after we'd agreed the price and refusing to release the paperwork until the extra payment was made, was galling.

Two days later I'd agreed a compromise deal and the paperwork was sent to the relevant authorities.

\*\*\*

That weekend I drove Ava back to her Mum's. The streets were both dark and gloomy. Patches of yellow were splashed against the pavements courtesy of old sodium streetlights.

We climbed out of the car and my four-year old wouldn't leave my side. She looked up at her Mum and said she wanted to stay with me permanently. I told Ava not to say such things, but her Mum bristled and I knew I'd pay for Ava's comments in some way or other. It's heartbreaking dropping her off each week, gut-wrenching.

It's Ava's birthday party tomorrow, and I can't bring myself to go. Ava's Mum and her chap will be playing happy families, with Ava torn between us all.

Taking a step backwards, you could say that my initial romantic involvement with Ava's Mum was a whirlwind affair. There was the briefest flicker of love, but we'd been apart for a couple of weeks when she learnt she was pregnant. I tried to do the right thing by asking her to marry me, and she said yes.

Two months later she changed her mind stating that I still loved Samson. She also offered that as a strong independent woman she intended to raise the child on her own.

And there were threats of Police action if I ever got in touch again. Hence, I was cut from the picture during the last seven months of the pregnancy. Her family cut me off and wouldn't respond to text

# Phoenix

messages or calls. I was a pariah. An outcast. None of them wanted to know.

Why? Because Ava's Mum comes from a family of proud women where it seems men aren't necessary, apparently. And I was told that I'd served a purpose that didn't require any further involvement.

But just before Ava's birth she'd ran out of money and all of a sudden I was needed again. I don't want to socialise with any of them. And now poor Ava is stuck in the middle.

My insides are being twisted inside out and the pain of being an absent father sits with me every day. I'm hanging onto the relationship with my daughter by a thread… and unless I'm put in the position where I have nothing to lose, it's unlikely any of this will get published.

I have to go RTW to get away from all this. If I die, so be it. Then Ava will grow up with a new father figure. It'll simplify her life and she'll get a decent insurance payout. And if I come through it, then maybe I'm meant to be here. Cindy certainly seems to think the Universe has a purpose.

The following weekend Ava asked again, 'are you really my Daddy?'

With one thing or another my Fitbit monitor says I'm living on an average of 3 hours and 40 minutes of sleep each night.

Throughout all this Cindy has been a rock, but everything is taking a toll on our relationship. I need to give her more time and more affection. Possibly buying her a kettle and toaster combo (very nice though they are. Russell Hobbs. Black gloss, with dimples) from the insurance payout was not the way to go.

I subsequently went shopping and purchased blackout curtains and a memory foam mattress. I've also booked a course of relaxation therapy and bought a bouquet of flowers for my lovely girlfriend.

Two weeks later and my Fitbit suggests my sleep tally now averages 7.23 hours a night. I'm still stressed, but feel better. Life becomes a little clearer when you're well-rested.

# Chapter 6. German Excursion

The Germans have sent an email saying they want the final staged payment upfront before I head to Berlin, and that sets alarm bells ringing. But Bob has signed her off, and the UK importer has seen her and says she's in great shape. Or more accurately said, 'I saw yr a/c on Friday, it looks great.'

I need to have faith in Bob, and the Importer, and hope she can be brought back to Blighty. If there's any niggling problems they should be fixable in the UK. Surely there can't be major issues.

The cynic in me says, what can go wrong… will go wrong. Such a bloody pessimist. The fact the Germans want money upfront has got to be a bad sign. But I'm stuffed; there's no more time left.

Bob's flown her. He's signed off the paperwork. The importer has had a look over her. She has her Permit to Fly. There is no cause for concern Jonathan, stop being a pussy. Be positive, think positive thoughts.

Payment made.

Dave's offered to fly Delta Lima to Berlin to pick up India Zulu. The Jodel might sound like it has a tractor engine bolted to the front, but she should get us there.

I had booked a flight on EasyJet, but who wouldn't prefer a full day's flying in a draughty wooden aircraft when it was offered. Rhetorical question. No flying over water is 100% enjoyable, unless you're immortal.

<u>15th March</u>

We make it to Lelystad, Holland, and land for fuel. It's a chilly spring day. Time's getting tight and we're running behind schedule.

The immediate need is to sort out clearance into Europe and that means a visit to the onsite Police facility. There's a few sideways glances from the cops and we're welcomed onto the mainland. The clock's ticking and we purposely stride back to Delta Lima.

Dave makes all the radio calls, we taxi, line up, and take off. And at 400ft above the runway he says, 'you have control,' and gets out his mouse. What? What the fuck?

Instead of using an iPad or Garmin device for navigation purposes, he has a bulky 'device' bolted to the top of the binnacle. It's right in his sightline. It's a small Microsoft computer.

I sit there and just shake my head. My good friend, solicitor, very reliable and trustworthy mate, the fellah who saw me through the crash… and he's bloody well sitting next to me trying to get his 'desktop' mouse to work on his jeans.

I hear myself say, 'Dave, you are such a dick.' He pretends to ignore me as he continues plotting the route East.

We head into Germany and both of us feel odd flying at 3,000ft across the landscape. Maybe it's a World War 2 thing. An uncomfortable feeling starts to grip me, and I feel like we're intruding into a foreign land. There's no radio chatter from other aircraft, and we're disconnected from the countryside as myriad wind turbines disappear beneath the wings.

There's an awkward silence in the cabin that belies the industrial beat of the Jodel's Rolls Royce engine. I try to fill the void by talking about absolutely anything. In the confines of my mind I start with the letter A, and begin thinking about topics we can discuss beginning with A. Our Altitude?

A moment later Dave lowers the nose, and we dive at full power. Then crusade above the dark green fields, forests, and hedgerows following the Mosquito approach to Berlin.

# Phoenix

Darkness starts to take hold as we approach the remote, unlit, airfield. There's a brief moment of excitement as we can't distinguish between a muddy field and the runway. We guess right and touch down just as the night meets the day.

The German repair guy is waiting, and we walk into his smart-looking hangar to have a look round India Zulu. There are bright lights and parts of aircraft dotted around. And she's sat in the middle of the space, gleaming.

Courtesy of our late arrival there's only time for a quick glimpse. She's been cleaned, and polished, and looks fantastic. The memory of the crash clings to me and I feel nervous around her, like I've let her down and have come to apologise. And yet I'm buzzing as realisation dawns that my former fiancé is alive again.

I cautiously approach her, open one of the gull-wing doors, and poke my head in the cabin. Someone has sat a beat-up cardboard box on the right-hand seat. In it are bits they've found inside the aircraft after she'd been delivered by the Koch's. There's a couple of maps, wizzy wheel flight computer, and a thick towel is poking it's head out of the box.

The piece of carpet I'd had made specifically for the footwell is missing. I ask where it is, and the reply, in lightly accented English, is, 'it didn't look professional, so we threw it away.'

Oh, right. It was mine, it'd been purposely made to fit the space, but then again, maybe I shouldn't have left it there, I guess. But that piece of old, tired, thin, black carpet gave her a personality and without it she looks bare. As if a part of her has been stripped away.

The German tells Dave and me that he's booked us into a large B&B a couple of miles from the airfield. We pile our stuff into his people carrier and head off. In the darkness the town itself looks like a cold, sterile, place.

There's no one on the streets and it has all the hallmarks of a depressing East German town. The kind of place where the Child Catcher, from Chitty Chitty Bang Bang, would have rocked up, scratched his head, and figured one of his colleagues had already swept the place.

The Restaurant at the B&B has two other guys there. Burly Irish contractors working on some project or other. The four of us chat and, not for the first time, I feel that slight touch of, we're wary of the English.

Why? Some issue from long before I was born, no doubt. I play the role of cheerful chappy and all four of us swap stories across two tables.

The next morning our German appears and joins us for breakfast. He's a competent looking guy, all business. The money has been received, he says, and suggests that the plan is for me to test fly India Zulu and take her away. He looks down at his plate of ham and eggs, and say's he needs to be on his way within an hour to collect another bent aircraft.

Last night's sleep was sporadic. An uncomfortable bed, thin bedsheets, and a dose of anxiety kept me awake. Focus Jonathan, focus. Sitting there in my jeans and trainers, feeling tired, I get the vibe he's trying to play me. I feel his tension and my face reluctantly smiles at him as my inner cynic says, 'here we go.'

Twenty minutes later we're in his SUV driving through Germanic country lanes. Large unkempt houses are tucked away behind mature trees to our right, and there's open fields to the left. I make small talk and ask about the cost of German property as we head onwards.

His facility, and the airfield, appear in front of us and it looks like a smart looking operation hemmed in by Mother Nature. One grass runway, one tarmac runway, a small Tower, and this chap's extended hanger.

# Phoenix

It's Monday, and there's just us with maybe one or two others pottering around.

Our German is keen to get India Zulu out of the hangar so I can take her away. In return I hear myself say I'll get airborne and see how she feels. More importantly, I'll see how I feel.

I slowly pull her by the propeller out of the hangar and onto the tarmac. It's not that cold, but there's a chill in the air. It's a reasonable day in Germany, and if all goes well India Zulu can be back in the UK today.

Can I rely on her though? Will I feel comfortable in a CT again? They're known to be tricky to fly. What structural tests do they do after a crash? I ask a few questions and do my walk round the aircraft.

Standing on tiptoes I check the contents of the fuel tanks, then inspect the specific points where she bounced off terra-firma. My eyes are glancing all over her, and my fingers lightly move across her carbon fibre skin. My mood improves as it seems almost impossible to tell which sections have been repaired.

Looking at the screws that secure the engine cowling on the outside of the aircraft, the Germans have added tiny white washers. I've not seen that on UK CT's, and a feeling of satisfaction grabs at me. Someone's kept an eye on matters and attended to the little details.

The repairer chirps up, and volunteers that the pitch of the propeller has been reset to its BMAA setting because Bob had insisted.

The previous pitch setting had given her extra cruise speed and the change would degrade that strength, but if that's what's needed to tick the boxes, so be it. I'd bought her in that configuration so no point feeling narked. If she's been repaired to the letter of the law, that's perfectly fine by me.

I check the oil, then move to the cabin, and stare at everything inside the aircraft and compare it all against my memories of nearly ten months ago. A flashback of the crash replays through my conscious mind, and the grass comes straight towards my face.

I slowly walk round to the front of India Zulu, eyes scanning her sleek body, and bend down to drain the fuel. There's supposed to be a 50 mm diameter hole cut into her carbon fibre skin. The hole allows the pilot to push a little plastic tube into the underbelly of the Rotax and check for water in the fuel.

The Germans have provided the hole, but in the wrong place. Alarm bells start ringing. How has Bob check flown her? Had he forgotten to check the fuel for water? Had he flown with the cowling off?

I hunch down on the cold tarmac and look at the lower section of cowling. It's lopsided. One side is lower than the other. Oh, for fucks sake. It shouldn't affect the way she flies, but it doesn't look right.

The carbon fibre surrounding the nose wheel strut isn't right, either. It looks like a child has hacked at it with a saw… and done a crap job.

My left hand creates a facepalm moment, and I close my eyes. Then lean back and lie full length on the cold tarmac.

Think, Jonathan, think. None of these issues should affect her ability to fly. And she has a valid Permit. I'm still in credit between the value of the aircraft, the cost of the repairs, and her value in flying condition. The thought floats across my conscious mind that I can afford a certain degree of buggeration. But really, who needs this kind of bollocks?

I climb off the deck and speak to Dave. We speak to the German. He says the cowling could be made correctly, and the weight increase would be a matter of grams. So why wasn't it done

# Phoenix

properly in the first place, I ask? Why hope I wouldn't spot it? He just shrugs.

And the piece where they'd cut through the upper section of the nose wheel spat is absolutely shocking.

Looking into the fella's eyes I make my point without getting upset or annoyed. Just express my disappointment. Then walk round the aircraft again and look closer. The wingtips look good, the structural carbon fibre repairs look solid.

What to say? Do I shout? Call him incompetent? Generally rage? Deep down I knew something would be wrong, but had told myself that Bob's inspection would highlight any problems. And I'd had pictures forwarded at each stage of the repair process. Funnily enough the poorly repaired sections hadn't been visible in their pictures.

My gaze turns to the trees behind the hangar, and my focus extends into the distance. Don't lose your temper, just deal with the situation. Test fly her and see how she flies. The German wants to leave, and I can tell he's feeling uncomfortable, but fuck 'im.

He disappears and returns a minute or two later with a small battery-operated Dremel. Then hunches down and starts cutting away at the carbon fibre so I can check the fuel.

I want my aircraft back in the UK with people I know and trust. I finish my preflight and climb onboard. Everything seems normal inside the cabin. Sitting in the familiar bucket seat my gaze drifts across all the instruments, then focuses between my legs at the repaired section of carbon fibre. I can see the repaired areas because the Germans have destroyed my carpets.

The structural stuff looks good. Looking up at the wings, they look good.

Deep breath. Stay calm. I hear myself call, 'Clear Prop', and turn the key in the ignition. She fires into life first time. Is that good or bad? Good because it shows she's healthy, or bad because I might be 20 minutes away from a catastrophic failure of some sort.

The propeller's blurrily spinning away and the throb of the Rotax runs through my bones. My mind wanders off in different directions, again.

The engine repairs have been carried out by a firm I know and trust. The engine will be fine, it should be fine. With my headset half on and half off I listen for anything unusual, and she seems in good health.

What will happen to Ava without me?

With the brakes fully on and locked, my right hand tentatively moves the throttle lever forward. Full power surges from the beating heart of the Rotax. The cabin resonates to her power and the wings are rocking like a confused seesaw. She wants to leap forwards, but holds position.

First test completed; the brakes can be relied upon. Throttling back, I key the mic' and speak to the German on his handheld radio to let him know she feels good.

Then release the brakes, slowly move forward, and alternately push on each rudder pedal as we inch along. Feeding in a little more power we track through a tight figure of eight motion on the Apron. She feels better turning left than right. That's one thing to report back.

Deep breath. 'Golf India Zulu taxiing to the 24 hold.'

My bowels are not happy and my arse is twitching big time. The engine is fine. Structurally she looks in good shape. Someone's polished her and she seems like new. There's nothing else to do but fly.

Sitting at the runway hold my gaze stares through the spinning propeller. My focus extends to the trees on the East side of the

# Phoenix

airstrip. If the engine goes mid-flight we'll be in a pickle. Just remember to land straight on, Johnny, and if that means hitting the trees, so be it. I tell myself not to make any stupid attempts at turning back to the airfield if there's not enough height.

Any impact needs to be on my terms. I will not stall a wing and pile in face first. If the shit hits the fan, so be it. If I die, so be it.

The thought floats across my conscious mind that if I'm not comfortable with dying, that I'll perform poorly when the pressure mounts. An inner voice tells me to accept that shit happens. My eyes drift around the cabin and absently focus on the passenger door. What's Cindy doing right now? Is Ava in school?

The engine should be fine, shouldn't it?

My distracted gaze scans the skies for aircraft. There's no noise from the radio. My tired eyes can't see anyone on final approach, and Germany feels unfriendly.

'Golf India Zulu entering runway 24.' We slowly roll onto the active runway and stop at the threshold markings. There's a 30-degree crosswind running along at 10 knots.

Swiveling my head to the right I can see Dave and the German watching. I try to look competent and blasé and give them both a thumbs up. Drawing in a deep breath my left thumb key's the mic' and my voice announces, 'Golf India Zulu taking off.'

Nothing happens. I just sit there listening to my inner demons. After 5 seconds of forced relaxation my right hand moves the throttle forward, and we're rolling.

Wheels going faster. Full power. Engine roaring away. I'm trying to feel the runway through the tyres and allow for the crosswind. And then we're airborne and accelerating towards the heavens.

A feeling of joy washes over me. The skies are mine and I have wings again. A wondrous blue panorama is complemented with the occasional Simpsons-like cloud.

The cabin feels colder as we climb.

We bank right, leave the circuit, and clear a couple of thousand feet. Then in slow motion I push the stick forward, and she dives at maximum speed. I roll her to port and starboard.

Words can't explain. A corkscrew of a roller coaster ride. My insides churning. Feeling sick, yet thoroughly alive. Exhilarated, but also scared and anxious.

My brain is expecting something to break, but I need to know I can trust her. If I ever took anyone flying I need to be a million percent sure of her structural integrity. She needs to be tested. My left hand pulls the stick back, and she launches herself like a rocket.

Back at 3,000ft I push the stick fully to the right and put her into a spiral dive. The Rotax is screaming away, nausea starts to say hello, and the tall trees stare me in the face.

Then power back and level out. My wide-awake eyes are darting around the cabin looking for anything unusual. Every sense is keying into her sounds, responses, and vibrations.

My focus shifts upwards to look at the wing roots, whilst my right hand pushes the throttle wide open. The engine and wings battle gravity as we race skywards.

We level out and I pull the throttle back to cruise, let go of the stick, and fly hands free. She flies in a straight line and feels stable. My head space says, 'she might have aesthetic issues, but she's my baby, and she's flying well.'

One last test. The one I'd dreaded. At what speed will she stall? How will she react after the stall? How will my bowels react?

# Phoenix

There's a thick forest of trees underneath each wing.

Everything is in slow motion as my right hand incrementally pulls the throttle back. As we slip below 80 knots, I select fifteen degrees of flaps. The whining noise of the extending flaps sounds familiar as she slows. She slips below 66 knots, and it's time for 30 degrees, whilst easing the stick back to maintain height.

Our speed is bleeding away, and time slows. I take a long look around the cabin scanning for anything unusual. Eyes on alert. My left hand is hovering over the radio button ready to make an emergency call.

Fifty knots. Gently pulling back on the stick. Aircraft nose getting higher. My seating position changes as the skies fill more of my view. We're slowing, and pointing upwards. It feels even colder in the cabin.

My focus is the airspeed reading on the Dynon screen. 40 knots. More footwork needed on the rudders to keep her tracking east. Less noise in the cabin, clouds everywhere, and a lonely field in front.

36 knots. A gentle mugging sensation. Nothing intense. The wings have stalled, but she's still flying straight ahead. We're losing height but in a controlled fashion. A foot lightly presses against the rudder and gently nudges her onto a southerly heading. Nothing exciting happens, as perspiration inches across my forehead.

No big deal. A scratch of the head and a frown. And then another scratch of my jaw. I inch the stick forward, open up the throttle, watch the speed increase, and we fly away.

Landing configuration stalls, then standard recovery. The kind of stuff you practice.

There's no one else on the radio, there's silence. There's no expectation of other aircraft around as India Zulu and I rejoin the circuit. The throb of the Rotax is in my ears and the beat of the engine shimmies through the seat.

My cold thumb keys the mic' and my voice makes a Downwind call, then Base, and then Final. There's trees everywhere except the narrow stretch of tarmac getting closer.

A look to the distant windsock finds it both outstretched and pointing across the runway. Crabbing towards the wind we track the centreline. My hand blindly reaches for my phone and wedges the white iPhone under my right thigh, as usual.

The weather gods are making an effort to push us into the clutches of the trees on the side of the tarmac runway. And that's focussing my mind. Pay attention, Johnny Boy, and remember how to fly.

Ten feet above the ground we pass over the threshold markings, and my right hand smoothly pulls the throttle to idle. My left hand ever so slowly pulls back on the stick. She glides above the runway and a touch more left rudder is needed. A second or two passes. The nose is slightly raised, and the main wheels lightly touch down.

The nose wheel lightly makes contact with the tarmac and our speed gently bleeds away. Flaps up. Then walking pace. I key the mic' and say, 'Golf India Zulu backtracking the runway.'

It feels frigidly cold inside the cabin. The Germans have removed all my draft proofing, and with no chance of a crash my body starts to catch up with the fact it's bloody cold.

We track along the short taxiway and make it back to the hanger. She's slightly pulling left.

I shut down the engine then climb out the gull-wing door. Dave asks how it felt. I hear myself say, 'fine thanks.' My mind wanders to all the AAIB reports I've read where it states how many flying hours the pilot has had before that particular crash.

# Phoenix

Aside from a refresher flight in a Eurostar before leaving, my time in a CT would read zero hours in the previous three months. An underused section of brain tissue says, 'take nothing for granted flying her home. It was a nice landing, and you confronted your demons, but nothing more. Time to get on with living.'

Dave says he'd missed the touchdown, but the German says it was a great landing. I squint in his direction and know I'm being played, but then again he gets 10 out of 10 for looking competent. And the facility looks well organised. Surely if there's a long-term problem, it'll be fixable.

The German holds out a sheet of papers in his hand and a pen. The backdrop is the hanger and the trees, with clouds clinging to th' horizon.

'I think she's pulling a little to the left on taxiing, and the trim is out,' I say. He counters with, 'the brakes will just be a little stuck, and the trim wheel just wants a tweak,' then looks down at his feet.

Something is not right. But she's been signed off by the Assessor and a sticking brake should be fine courtesy of a little WD40. 'I need to go, please,' he says and holds out his pen and papers for signature.

Deep breath. I can be home for tea with Cindy this evening. India Zulu has a valid Permit to Fly. Any follow-up work can be carried out in the UK by people I trust. And I'm still in credit between the value of the aircraft and the cost of the repairs.

Fight or flight. Cause a scene? Argue? Or take the view she's airworthy and everything else is fixable. Worst case? Maybe £500 spent in the UK? And time's ran out to leave her in Germany. Just sign and get her home?

My right hand reaches out and a squiggle goes onto his documents. I reluctantly shake his hand and five minutes later he's driven away.

Dave and I find a wifi spot in one of the empty buildings and both of us lodge our flight plans home. We take off twenty minutes later and I inevitably lose visuals with Delta Lima as he climbs and picks up a tailwind. India Zulu and I stay lower and we take in the view heading West.

Germany looks cold and unattractive as greenery passes beneath the wings. I climb and descend irregularly. There's no rush. It's cold inside the cabin, but I'm happy to be flying.

We weave our way onwards at 100 knots. Sometimes at 3,000ft, occasionally at 5,000ft, but mostly at 1,000ft simply sightseeing and staying warm. There's no one on the radio and no ATC requirements.

Common sense says to fly higher and, if the engine fails, there'll be the luxury of time to find a field to land in. But if a wing comes off, I'll be screwed regardless.

My eyes lazily scan the countryside for emergency landing sites. My focus ranges from inside the cabin, and across the instruments, to the outside world. Just go with the flow, Johnny. Pay attention to everything, but don't stress or obsess.

Without my draught-proofing in place the heater can't cope and my skin begrudges the cold. The outside world is being vented into the cabin via a dozen entry points. I didn't bring gloves so my right hand awkwardly reaches across to the passenger seat and finds its way into my rucksack.

A couple of minutes later both hands are sleeved in a sock each. A white sock for my left hand on the stick, and a mismatched sock for the hand resting on the throttle. Ten minutes later and my OCD objects to wearing odd socks.

With eyes fixed on the horizon, my right hand blindly roots around in the bag for other sock shaped items. Taking a quick glance over I manage to grab the matching sock from the group I'd dragged out of the red rucksack.

# Phoenix

Then text Dave, 'Got socks on my hands & towel wrapped around my neck. Highest I can manage without my balls freezing is 2,000ft'... and then give him a position report and ask about his location. He's climbed to 5,000ft and picked up a tailwind

Germany looks bleak, dispiriting, and glum. There's miles of not a lot, interspersed with industrial complexes.

Leaving Germany and entering Dutch airspace I relax my grip on the stick and let go. The wings are level for a second, and then she starts rolling to the left. Ohhhh kay...

Why's that happening? Have I been flying her out of balance? Is something wrong? I tell myself to keep flying and stay calm. There's no need to stress. It might be a big issue, or nothing at all.

My focus takes aim at centering the balance ball on the Dynon to see if that makes a difference. Nope. No change. A sock covered hand absently scratches the side of my head as my anxiety levels start rising.

We navigate on towards Lelystad. It's a busy GA airfield accommodating a range of aircraft with a tarmac runway stretching 1,000 meters or so.

My eyes are continuously scanning the skies searching for conflicting traffic. Every time I relax my grip on the stick, she rolls left. Something's definitely wrong. A voice in my ear says the winds are picking up, and a 15 knot crosswind is now reportedly flowing across the tarmac.

I haven't flown a CT in nearly a year and mentally start searching for everything the Fox has ever said about flying. Then tell myself to forget his narrative that Samson could never be trusted again. Try to ignore that.

All I can do is sit still, watch the horizon, take in the landscape, and look for other aircraft. The throb of the engine is ever-present and it's cold in the cabin. I press the red PTT button, make my radio calls, and listen to the clipped Dutch accent replying.

Try to relax and stay calm, Johnny Boy. Inhale, exhale, inhale, exhale.

Worst case, just get close enough to the ground and crash at a survivable speed. And hope any impact doesn't render me unconscious or incapable of exiting the cabin.

My mind wanders away from me and asks if this is supposed to be enjoyable. And for some reason religion raises its hand. Maybe a better relationship with God is called for. Is there a God? Was I kept alive for a reason? Maybe I should convert to a religion, any religion, and express my amazement at being alive. Or yet again, maybe I should just shut the fuck up and concentrate on flying.

A foreign voice interrupts my train of thought. 'Golf India Zulu, you are number 2 to land.' Righty ho. Simply follow the distant twin-engined aircraft and set her up in the landing configuration.

The lead aircraft touches down.

India Zulu has her standard 30 degrees of flaps down. The reported wind is a direct fifteen knot crosswind, and my headspace knows that's technically beyond the limit of the CTSW. Should I pull up the flaps to 15 degrees and come in faster? My hand moves to the flap lever and hovers there.

What would the Fox say? Probably something like, 'don't adjust the flaps on Final approach. Leave them where they are. Maintain a steady approach speed. Control height with the throttle and speed with the stick. Aim for 55 knots. Trim for that.'

The trim mechanism isn't working right. Too much, 'down' and not enough, 'up'. Do your best and fly her down, Johnny. Don't let your mind wander again, and do what you can.

# Phoenix

If the wind drops off a cliff and we lose 15 knots we're still above the stall speed. The landing will be 5 knots faster than I'd like. And in a CT 5 knots feels like an extra 50 mph, but it's a tarmac runway and no grass 'bump' should launch us back into the air if we catch it wrong.

My eyes take a swift look around the cabin. All the readings on the Dynon look good. The temperatures and pressures seem OK. The black balance ball looks out of whack, though. Am I flying her out of balance? Is more rudder needed?

Sod it. Whatever happens, happens. My eyes are scanning outside the cabin and they take in a racetrack of sorts on the right. There's a couple of long taxiways, a grass runway, and a long tarmac runway. Another scan looks for the windsock and anything unusual.

A hand pulls on the harness straps to check they're tight. I wedge my phone under my right thigh. Then take a deep breath, and tell myself to exhale.

100 meters from touch down. Then 50 meters. We float over the threshold markings, and I pull the power to idle. The wind is pushing us off the centre line. More right rudder. She floats a foot or two above the runway, but won't land. The wind has hold of us and won't let go.

Don't do anything, let her settle, she will settle. The wind is holding her above the tarmac. I straighten the nose and we stop crabbing into the wind. She starts to lose height an inch at a time. The right wheel touches down, and half a second later the left wheel meets the deck.

And a gust. Both wheels are lifted off the ground. Fuck. Airborne. Stay calm. My numb hand moves the throttle forward half an inch and I tell myself not to let the nose rise, but not to force it down.

A second seems like a lifetime. One Mississippi, two Mississippi. Plenty of runway left and my right hand pulls the throttle to idle again. An inner voice says to let her settle back to earth and hold my nerve.

I'm starting to sweat, three Mississippi, four Mississippi, and touchdown.

Not a gentle landing. Hard, but down. I quickly pull the brake lever and lean forward to flick the flaps up. My forehead is creased with perspiration as a massive sense of relief washes over me like a wave.

We slowly taxi off the runway and I cock an ear to listen to the sound of the wheels. Then press the red microphone PTT button with my left thumb and ask the Tower where to park. And feel that light-headed sensation that comes with a flight coming to an end, for this leg.

India Zulu trundles to a stop two aircraft apart from Dave's Jodel. I shut the engine down and watch the prop' shudder to a halt. A cold hand switches off the avionics, takes the key out, and opens the door to the outside world.

My numb consciousness sits with me feeling abused. I awkwardly climb out and stand by the side of the wing as the whirlwind rushes around Samson. I stretch away a couple of hours of flying and face directly into the oncoming wind.

Then slowly walk round the aircraft whilst letting my left hand lightly touch every surface. Then walk around again, trying to see everything for the first time.

The onward flight should be doable without refueling. The fuel at Barton will be cheaper, but it might not be wise to miss a fuel stop. Bite the bullet Johnny Boy and pay the extra here?

I reach inside the cabin for my small kit bag and fish out the tool to unlock the fuel caps on the wings. Reaching up on tiptoes I undo both fuel caps and dip the fuel in each wing. One tank is full, and the other has 25 litres. The flight has taken 40 litres from one tank,

# Phoenix

which is not supposed to happen. They should drain equally. What the bejesus is going on?

The pitch trim is way off what it should be. I can't get her to fly in balance. The fuel isn't draining correctly. She's rolling left. And to add insult to injury I'm bloody cold because the sodding Germans ripped out all my bloody draft proofing.

A confused hand scratches my arse. I wrinkle my nose, point myself towards the wind again, and stare into space for a handful of seconds. Then cast my eyes over the well organised neat looking facilities. It's time to find Dave and tell him of my woes. Then wait for him to laugh and tell me how bloody stupid I've been for buying an insurance write-off.

He's been here for 30 minutes and is upstairs in an American style burger restaurant. There's a smart modern-looking bar overlooking both the two runways and a multitude of parked aircraft.

Dave and I make small talk and alternate between chatting about the flight and the pictures of aircraft on the walls. I tell him of India Zulu's issues, and he simultaneously smiles and chuckles.

My mind wanders back to the old Top Gear approach with Jeremy Clarkson reporting, 'it's with great sadness that I have to report that Jonathan Hilton died when his aircraft crashed. And in other news...' i.e. No great upset, just everyone else getting on with things.

The conversation turns to the onward leg and my life raft which is currently sat in Delta Lima. And I lightly suggest that I wouldn't mind having it back for the flight over the Channel. Dave smiles, finishes his Speciality Burger, and suggests it's time to go. He gets up and heads to the toilet.

I'm left sitting there, distractedly looking out the window at all the aircraft on the tarmac, and don't want to move. I'm tired, jaded, disillusioned, scared. And don't want to fly.

I fire up my iPad and email Barton with a copy of the GAR form for customs purposes. More minute's trickle by as I work through the flight plan, then close the cover on the iPad, and stand up, ready to go.

And then sit down and type a follow-up message to the same email address, 'Hi, just filed my flight plan. Leaving here in 30 mins with a 2.5hr flight time. I'm not expecting problems, but my right fuel tank doesn't seem to be draining properly (that was the case on the day of my bump). The trip is doable on one tank, and the gravity-fed system should mean I can't run out of fuel… But if my friends in the fire team could pay attention to my landing, I'd appreciate it. Cheers. Jon'

I finish my lemonade and push back the chair. Absently staring out the window my gaze takes in all the aircraft sat outside. I spot Dave clambering aboard Delta Lima, and that seems like a sign he wants to keep the life raft.

Ten minutes later I get back to Samson as Dave leaves the tarmac and climbs into the skies. Then reluctantly fill up the tanks with Avgas from the self-service pump and carry out my preflight, and feel lonely and uncertain.

Then find myself taking a slow walk round the crash-repaired, written off, aircraft and hate my pig-headed approach for ignoring the Fox's advice. My fingers run across the flight surfaces, and I look at all the securing screws on the control surfaces again.

A cold hand opens the gull-wing door and I force myself in and get my headspace ready to fly.

Engine checks, radio calls, taxiing, and take off. We gain height whilst I try to squeeze out positive thoughts to bully my anxieties. The throb of the Rotax shakes its way into my bones.

We clear the Lelystad airspace and I flick the radio to Amsterdam Schiphol's approach frequency. My eyes are slowly moving

# Phoenix

everywhere inside the cabin and beyond. It's time to think like a competent pilot and just bloody well get on with it.

Flying anything higher than 1,500ft and SkyDemon says the jets will be unhappy at our poking into their territory. I mentally rehearse my radio calls, key the mike, and tell the Controller of my intention to fly below their airspace and head back to Blighty.

Twenty minutes later we've skimmed over a reservoir and are coasting out. The North Sea beckons, and looks bleak.

One of the engine sensors starts to flash on the Dynon. The right Cylinder Head temperature sensor is issuing a warning. What does that mean? It means we're 5 miles out to sea at 1,200ft above the water.

And all I can see are wind turbines poking out from the miserably cold sea. Would I be able to land close to one and cling on if the engine folds?

Is it just a sensor issue, or an impending engine failure? And my mate with the raft has buggered off. Should I turn around and spend, at the very least, a day in Holland and get an engineer out to check the Rotax?

My fingers run their way across my forehead and I wrinkle my nose. Time to speak to Schiphol and ask for permission to climb into Class A airspace and get height on my side. A section of brain tissue tries to think through the request and it gets written down on my knee pad. I wait for the jets to stop talking and then key the mic'.

'Schiphol Approach, this is Golf Charlie Golf India Zulu'. They reply, 'Go ahead, Golf India Zulu'. I hear myself mumble through a position report and request a climb to 3,000ft.

Do I tell him I have anxieties about the engine? It could be just a sensor glitch, or she could be about to seize up. Time slows again.

Every jet pilot on frequency will be listening. Do I declare an emergency? Will they let me fly in their airspace as a VFR aircraft?

Stop thinking. Just let him know I'm here and see what he says.

The reply comes back as, 'Negative Golf India Zulu, you'd be climbing into Class A airspace. Please remain below 1,500ft until 15 miles out to sea.'

A thoroughly pleasant-sounding chap, light accent, probably not used to the faint-hearted. I hear my voice acknowledge his command. Then absently itch my balls, and wonder how long I'll have ownership of them.

We're flying at nearly two miles a minute and the throbbing of the engine offers a constant grumbling through the headset. How would another accident report read?

Tiredness begins pulling at my concentration levels. I reach over with my right hand, and open the vent in the window to scoop a cool jet of North Sea air into the cabin. This is a pickle of your own doing, Johnny Boy, deal with it.

My right hand pulls off the headset so I can listen to the beat of the engine. The high-pitched noise is the wrong side of comfortable. Not painful, but unpleasant. Twenty seconds tick by, and my ears can't pick out any change in tone. Is it just a dodgy sensor?

The phone is switched on, the Emergency Beacon is by my right hand, and the orange GPS tracker is flashing its light back at me. People will know where we are if I have to act quick.

How long will she float if we hit the water? How violent will a landing on the wet stuff be with a high wing aircraft? Will the wheels skim the surface and then flip India Zulu upside down? Should I crank open the door or keep it shut? Will I blackout?

# Phoenix

The flight plan says the short route across the Channel, but it's the longest way home. My headspace is overthinking things, and I want the flight over as quickly as possible.

A cold right hand pulls the headset back on as we pass over the international boundary, and I kick in the rudder and aim straight for Manchester. That means more time over water, but if Samson gently climbs to 5,000ft we might be able to glide to a beach in the event of a niggle.

Skimming past the East Anglian coast I relax my hand on the stick and let go for an instant. The left wing immediately starts to drop and continues dropping. A shake of the head and another scratch of the nose follows. I stay handsfree, and let the wing fall away to see how bad it'll become.

Twenty seconds later the left wing is pointing straight at the ground and the right is aiming vertically up at the heavens. A head rush of sound and dizziness starts to kick in.

My left hand gently pushes against the stick and slowly rolls the wings level. Try not to panic, Jon Boy. She has a problem, that's all. I tell myself it's nothing to get too upset about, and my subconscious shouts at me to be calm.

My right hand reaches for the Emergency Locator Beacon and clumsily extends the thin metal antenna. A glance over to the Dynon and the engine sensor is still flashing its warning.

A look down at the damned Turn Co-Ordinator, and it's all over the place. The ball keeps wandering around as I stare at it. Am I flying her out of balance? Is all the fuel being taken from one wing? I should have enough fuel to get to Barton on one tank, shouldn't I?

My T-shirt itches, I feel cold, and I'm bloody well missing my life raft. We're still over water and I'm micromanaging our progress on the iPad. The Sky Demon software extends a circle of sorts around the aircraft to replicate our glide range if the Rotax folds.

It's an overcast day outside the cabin and I find myself constantly scanning the horizon. Every handful of moments glancing down at the moving map. If the engine cracks open Samson can just about make a beach.

Time takes its course, and we coast in at Skegness. My achingly cold fingers let go of the stick, and she immediately rolls left and wants to enter a spiral dive. Every time I look down at my iPad, she wanders off course.

Worst of all my bladder tells me there's other considerations and that's starting to feel uncomfortable. I'm constantly frowning, feeling thoroughly pissed off, and it seems like every second is a minute.

Keeping a firm hold of the stick my right hand reaches up and takes the headset off again. My head is cocked to one side listening for anything unusual. My ears hurt and it's ice cold in the cabin.

I'm constantly scanning for emergency landing site after emergency landing site, and each moment is filled with its own awkward risk assessment.

We get within range of Barton and I broadcast, 'Barton Information, Golf Charlie Golf India Zulu 7 miles Southwest inbound Lelystad request joining information, please.' The reply comes back, 'Welcome home India Zulu...' I scribble down the rest of the landing details, Runway in use, Circuit pattern and QFE.

We join overhead the grass airfield and descend like normal, enter the circuit like normal, and line up on Final approach like normal. And see the fire truck, with its lights flashing, hoping for a normal landing.

Stay calm, Jon Boy. My right hand blindly wedges my phone under my leg, like normal, and I tell myself to forget adjusting the trim wheel because it's bloody useless. My eyes are outside the cabin, and a swift glance at the Dynon suggests an airspeed of 52 knots as we glide above the hedges in front of runway 27L.

# Phoenix

And I take a deep breath. A hand pulls the power to idle, whilst the other lightly pulls back on the stick. She flares and I lightly hold her off the green grass until we gently touch down. Then tell myself to exhale.

She slows, and I wave to my friends in the Firetruck. Thank fuck that's over. They wave back, and probably think the same.

Thirty minutes later I've secured India Zulu in the hanger, have relieved my bladder, and I'm sat in the Airfield Lodge with a pint in hand chatting to Dave.

I thank him for coming with me and tease him about leaving without me. 'I knew you'd be fine,' he says. And for good measure he adds, 'and there was no bloody way you were having that life raft back.'

We chat a while longer, and I say my goodbyes and head home for tea with Cindy.

# Chapter 7. The Why

More reading. More conversations with pilots. Different thoughts put forward. Was the crash the result of wind shear? Maybe a dynamic stall? What would have helped? Another second or two before tweaking the ailerons?

She seemed to be climbing away and accelerating like normal. Not drastically slow, but not supersonic. Maybe the wind dropped off a cliff? Maybe I should have used the rudder instead of the ailerons?

The Fox always warned of a wing drop on 40 degrees flaps, but on 30 she's supposed to be benign. Would it make sense if three-axis Microlights had stall warning horns installed?

Was the prop' ripped from the other aircraft a sign that something else was happening that afternoon? Was it a combination of things?

Whatever answers anyone gives, it'll be something I'll replay in my mind's eye for a long, long, time. And most likely something I'll try to replicate up at altitude. The motto has to be, 'live and learn.'

***

I'm getting grief from Ava's Mum, and it seems pretty obvious that if I accept anyone into my life that that will be deemed unacceptable. Ava genuinely likes, maybe loves, Cindy. But she seems to be putting up barriers, and I don't know how to pull them down and make everyone feel loved.

Do I have to rank each relationship in terms of how important it is to me and then revolve my world around the winner? Is Ava better without me so she can bond with the new man in her Mum's life? To what extent do I fight Ava's Mum? How can I create a loving environment for Ava? How can I offer Ava the love that her Mum, Samson, and Cindy all missed during their formative years?

# Phoenix

Which is the best way forward? Is the answer to just fuck off and use flying as an excuse? Is a person's strength measured by the manner in which they stand and fight for what they want? Or does a coward simply run away?

It seems Ava's Mum is trying to grind me down. It seems like I'm fair game. Is this how all estranged fathers feel from time to time? Like their heart is being slowly shredded.

The following Friday, I took Cind with me to collect Ava. We drove for an hour to get to her house and arrived at the agreed time. Cindy got out of the Audi, walked across the road, and knocked on the door of the terraced house. I was sat in the car watching via the rear-view mirror. I should have gone but didn't want an awkward exchange.

The old wooden door opened, and a wonderfully happy 4-year old literally leapt into Cindy's arms. Three seconds later, Ava was dragged away from her, pulled inside the house, and the door was slammed shut in her face. Nothing had been said.

Ava's Mum had met Cindy before. There was no need for that. I got out of the car and slowly walked to the house. My beautiful girlfriend was stood on the spot both visibly upset and completely nonplused. I lightly knocked on the door and a disembodied voice replied, 'you're not seeing her this weekend, go away.'

How is any of this healthy for anyone? And I know this is affecting Cind. She doesn't need this.

A week later, I picked Ava up, this time from school. We went to the Trafford Centre and played on the bumper cars and arcade games before heading home. We pulled up outside the house, and I was hurriedly dragging her school stuff and bags from the car whilst Ava stood supervising.

I'd previously bought her a Harry Potter 'wand,' and it'd been carried back and forth from her house and mine. It'd been accidentally left in the car a few weeks earlier.

Ava spotted the plastic wand and said, 'mummy was looking for this.' Before I could engage my filter, my response was, 'well, every witch needs a wand.'

Damn, damn, damn, I didn't mean to say that out loud.

Later that evening, after a hyper 4-year old finally flaked out, I sat on the settee and just stared at the wood-burning stove. The flames were lapping against the glass, and my inner voice told me to focus on anything other than what's happening in my personal life.

I sent an email to Eddie, from General Aviation Support Egypt in Cairo, about the ins and outs of flying around the world in a Microlight. He replied with the comment that there's a significant mental component to flying, and in return, I sent the following…

*More information than you need, but... I've ran marathons, finished the Iron Man, done a relay swIm across the English Channel, I'm a Blackbelt in JuJitzu, etc., and I can't see me giving up.*

*Seventeen years ago, I gave up on my ambition to be a commercial pilot when I had to pick between my girlfriend and aviation. Roundabout then, I also snagged a corneal ulcer which made matters easier to accept.*

*The RTW trip validates a few things (not least a feeling I've failed in my life). And wanting to make my Dad proud.*

*I'll hate being away from home and I'll miss my daughter and girlfriend. But it's something I need to do.*

*This year is my opportunity, and it'd be great if you'd help me, please.*

On the 10th March 2017, Eddie replied with…

*Hi,*

*Remember, I was an ardent follower of your flight to Canada and back, helped (I think) with your drafts for the first book, followed up on your ideas to go and do something spectacular - although the pogo stick thing seemed a bit pointless*

# Phoenix

*at the time... and dangerous;-)...* **Note from JH. I had a slightly bonkers idea to try and beat the Guinness World Record 'Mile Pogo Stick Record.'*

*I have on occasions also sent you ideas of what to do next, so yes, I have always been expecting a follow-up adventure from you at some time... dented only by the accident with 'GIZ last year.*

*So, I will never doubt your sincerity to accomplish something and to push yourself beyond what lesser people call normal, but I was making the point that you really need to have the mindset to fly around the world, which is a completely different mindset to say a normal long-range flight.*

*RTW's are never a normal journey. You are flying from your home airfield to your home airfield, the long way. From the second you take off from your home airfield, there are over 25,000 miles and probably 2-3 months before you touch down there again... the biggest circuit you will ever do.*

*The way to get through it is to forget you are flying around the world. Each day you have a new destination. So, the whole flight is made up of a lot of day trips. You let us do the worrying about what is ahead... our job is to make sure that all is in place, everything arranged and if possible, a friendly face to greet you. Your job is to fly your aircraft from A-B each day, take some photos, record your thoughts and enjoy the changing world below you.*

*We lost one aircraft two years ago. They had flown as I just suggested, enjoying the experiences. But as they got closer to home, they forgot the day by day thing and started to think three legs ahead and about home.*

*Pressure from their family and friends and some dangerous suggestions from 'expert pilots' led them to go against our suggestions, which was to spend a few days on the ground until the fuel had arrived in Kiribati and the weather had cleared, and they took off, way overweight with so much extra fuel on board, in complete darkness from an uncontrolled airfield with strong winds.*

*Next stop Hawaii, 2200 miles away... they got one mile from the end of the runway and crashed into the sea.*

*I mention this to make a point about the mindset...one day at a time... enjoy the experience... realise that delays can and probably will happen... the most dangerous legs are the ones closest to home...one day at a time.*

*OK, with that said, I will set up a file on your flight and start to send you the preliminary emails that we send out, which is to give us all the facts, documents and information we need to do our bit.*

*I will also inform the people who will be helping with the Russian legs and, along with them, get our Indian agents to start the process for your visa.*

*And it looks like I will be buying you a beer in Cairo at last :-)*

*Cheers*

*Eddie*

***

A couple of years earlier, I'd told my Dad about a future, 'Round the World' trip. I remember he smiled at me with a vaguely amused look on his face, as if to say, 'yeah, right.'

And then a neurological virus, picked up on a holiday to Portugal, led to a series of mini-strokes, also known as TIA's. He was subsequently rushed to hospital and lay, unconscious, in the stroke ward whilst various folk hooked him up to differing bits of medical kit.

Rightly or wrongly, I can only describe that particular ward as something akin to a 19th-century insane asylum. I will never forget hearing a group of nursing staff laughing in one of the side rooms, whilst patients on the main ward were alternately half shouting and half pleading for attention.

Possibly being around those whose minds are in bits makes a person immune to the noises they make.

# Phoenix

With respect to Dad, they put an adult nappy on him. That action in itself seemed to strip away the feeling of invincibility a son builds around his father. My Dad was the son of a coal merchant, but he'd made it to Grammar School, became a successful insolvency accountant, and retired early with a big chunk of money in the bank.

But there he lay, unconscious, without his dignity, whilst hell seemed to swirl around the hospital ward.

A drip stand stood to attention by the side of his bed, and it was intended to feed fluids into his body whilst he slept. For whatever reason, the saline solution meant for his arm didn't make it.

I can't say what the problem was, but he became badly dehydrated. And a day or two later, he had a series of heart attacks.

He survived, but as a consequence, his heart function dropped to 13% of its normal output. At that level, it becomes a struggle to talk, and walking becomes nearly impossible. Things were only heading in one direction after that.

'Frustration' is a difficult word. It means what it says, but some words are felt on a much more emotional level rather than simply letters on a page. I felt frustrated and a little heart broken, I guess.

Dad subsequently went through half a dozen hospital wards, including intensive care. Fortunately he never returned to the stroke ward.

As a family, we talked about his health, and I volunteered to spring the old sod from hospital and get him back to the family home. My plan was to move back in for a handful of weeks and do all the messy jobs involved with palliative care.

Ultimately, I wanted him to be able to sit on his favourite settee, watch a bit of telly, and have the family's Bernese Mountain Dog beside him. And be able to look out on the large garden through the patio doors. Dad desperately wanted that, but Mum didn't.

She was understandably struggling with everything, and I guess wanted her own respite and a place where matters seemed normal. So Dad remained in hospital.

Knowing a central figure in my life, such a strong man, physically and mentally, was moving towards death was difficult. Part of me wanted to start legal claims against the hospital and drag them into court; certainly, Mum wanted that.

It's horrible to say but, more than anything else, I just wanted his suffering to be over.

Over the next week or two, I got into the habit of visiting him after hospital visiting hours had officially ended. By that point, he was in a private room, and it was relatively easy to slip in and out without being noticed. The two of us just chatted about boring, mundane stuff.

On one occasion, the chitchat came to a head, and after taking a couple of extra breaths, the old boy said, 'I signed a do not resuscitate order today.' He paused and asked, 'how does that make you feel?'

I smiled, frowned, told him to 'shurrup,' and changed the subject. Twenty minutes later, I was back in the bloody car, bawling my bloody eyes out.

In a cowardly fashion, I needed a distraction and flew my Microlight to Canada as a way to occupy my mind. I landed in North America, slept for half a dozen hours, and raced home again.

The day after returning to the UK, I waited for the official hospital visiting hours to end and snook into the old fellah's private room. Between the two of us, we chatted about a few things, and I made a point of being lighthearted and generally cheerful.

He knew where I'd been, and I showed him a few pictures—glaciers, icebergs, and snow by the megaton. I had a photo of his

# Phoenix

name etched into a vertical snow face in Greenland. He seemed pleased but, struggling to breathe, murmured, 'you didn't make it round the world though, son.'

He died a day later.

***

Deep down, I don't want to go RTW but need to prove to myself that I'm not scared of flying. It will put matters into perspective with Ava. Maybe I just need to roll the dice and see what happens. And maybe this will help box away Dad's comments.

Anyway, it's time to shut up, stop whining, and focus on matters. And hope I don't run out of time to nail everything down.

One way or the other, I'm going to bugger off east.

# Chapter 8. The Aircraft and the Details

I asked Nigel to look at everything, and it turns out the binnacle hasn't been properly secured to the bulkhead. It's been attached by a screw at the bottom of the unit, but the German's haven't secured the top half. Hence the whole assembly is simply wobbling around like an upside-down pendulum.

This means the Balance Ball is useless, and whilst I've been trying to fly her 'in balance' to avoid stressing the airframe, well, that's just been a bloody useless effort on my part. Is she dangerous at the moment? Who bloody knows?

Nigel's drilled more holes and properly secured the binnacle in place. The current consensus amongst the 'clevers,' is that she's 'directionally unstable,' and we're not even sure if she's structurally sound. I've gone back to the Germans, but they're refusing to do any work on her.

The suggestion is, 'you signed the release documentation when you collected the aircraft, so you're screwed,' which is somewhat frustrating. I've threatened legal action, but practically that seems unlikely to force a German response.

I spoke to the Fox about the likelihood of getting the assessor to take some responsibility on the basis the guy must have realised she had problems, but that seems like a dead end. It's all getting irritating.

Annoyingly, I can't get insurance for a 'Round the World' trip, either. With the Canadian adventure I went without any cover, bluffed my way through, and got lucky.

# Phoenix

Seeking a different perspective, I emailed a chap at Sky Ferry and his reply was, 'third party liability is a legal requirement. You don't have to insure the plane's value however, that's a risk up to you, but it would reduce the premium significantly. Some countries want insurance papers before issuing permits, so it's a must realistically to have some form of cover.'

At the moment I can't even get third party cover, and I'm going nowhere. And there's health issues, will the inoculations from my Sahara trip be sufficient to protect yours truly, or do I need to go through that rigmarole again?

<u>18th March</u>

I sent a further email to the Germans outlining my frustrations. The intent being to use it as a mechanism to create a paper trail from which I can ask for additional repairs to be carried out, or request some form of credit. Extracts as follows...

1. *No allowance was made to gain access to the fuel drainer.*
2. *She enters an aggressive left hand turn when in level flight.*
3. *The rudder doesn't self-centre (the springs should have been checked).*
4. *The binnacle wasn't attached securely (50mm of movement), and it seems it was only attached against the bulkhead at its base.*
5. *The fluctuations of the right CHT are a cause for concern.*
6. *The vertical trim is out by about 30%.*

*I think you did a great job on the composite repairs, but the items above are cause for concern & will add additional costs.*

*Jon*

Unfortunately, I failed to mention the woeful lower cowling or the crap state of the nose wheel housing. I chased the assessor for his views, too.

# Jon Hilton

## 19th March

FREAK winds were blamed last night for causing a Dubai-based airliner to nosedive into the ground in Russia in a disaster that claimed 62 lives.

FlyDubai flight 981 from Dubai to Rostov-on-Don crashed and exploded while trying to land in strong winds at the southern Russian city early yesterday morning. All 55 passengers from Russia, Ukraine, Uzbekistan and India, were killed along with seven crew members in a blast that scattered fragments of the aircraft across the airport.

"Everyone at FlyDubai is in deep shock, and our hearts go out to the families and friends of those involved,' said Ghaith al-Ghaith, the carrier's chief executive, at a press conference in Dubai.

President Vladimir Putin offered condolences to the relations of the victims and ordered emergency officials and the regional governor to provide support for the bereaved.

Mr. al-Ghaith said there was no indication it was an act of terrorism. Airports in Russia have been on high alert since a suspected terrorist bomb destroyed a Russian airliner over Sinai in October, killing 224 people. Investigators are concentrating on 'pilot error caused by poor weather or technical failure' as the main lines of inquiry.

Weather data cited on Russian television indicate low cloud, rain, and wind speeds of nearly 70 miles per hour. Vasily Golybev, the governor of Rostov region, said a 'hurricane force' gust of wind seemed to have struck the aircraft, causing it to slam into the ground 250 yards from the runway.

The pilots had aborted an earlier landing attempt and circled for two hours before the second, fatal attempt to land. Fabrizio Poli, managing director of aircraft trading company Tyrus Wings and an experienced airline pilot, said that pilot fatigue could also have been a factor.

# Phoenix

<u>23rd March</u>

Reply from the assessor.

'*You accepted the aircraft and signed for it on collection.*

*The aircraft may have a turn when flown solo in the left hand seat, which could prove tedious on a long cross country. This can be tuned out by adjusting the aileron springs, but this is minor tuning, not a dangerous defect.*

*As far as I am concerned, that is the end of the matter.*'

He's not in any way interested in helping. Which, on the basis that I didn't kick off about his earlier blackmail effort, is frustrating. And my attempt at generating goodwill by agreeing to pay an increased sum seems to have been pointless. And the bollocks about, 'may have a turn to the left.' Really? That makes my bloody blood boil.

*\*\*\**

Assuming I'm still going to fly, I need to get a leaving date in my head for a Round The World trip.

When will the weather conditions be best? Typhoons? Heat? Clearances and Permits? Aircraft repairs? Inoculations?

If I can get the aircraft flying properly the provisional leaving date for the trip needs to be on or about the 24th of April. But can I get her to fly right?

The whole process is taking its toll on my relationship with Cindy, and I'm worried we may split up courtesy of this crazy obsession with flying. Will we split up? She seems to think I have someone else in my life.

More people at Barton have cast their eyes over Samson, and the further consensus is that she shouldn't have been given a Permit to Fly. I have zero confidence in her.

I subsequently spoke to the Fox, and if I pursue legal action he won't advise or help fix India Zulu. As a result we had a rather testy conversation in his suite of offices. Ava was sat next to me, colouring rainbows onto a piece of A4 paper, whilst the two of us bickered back and forth.

Words to the effect of, 'I told you not to buy a written off, crash-repaired aircraft' were pointed in my direction. Then he quizzed me about my route back from Holland. Why so much time over water? It was a typical school teacher admonishment.

He's a great chap, but the fact that he's always right really, really, really, pisses me off.

There's not necessarily any right or wrong answer to this, though. We could have run out of fuel over the sea or crashed anywhere. I'm not a test pilot and foolishly relied on the assessor to sign her off as a 'safe aircraft.'

Bob's view seems to be that he followed his checklist, and she passed. How she flies or whether she's safe is not his concern.

## 1st April

April fool. An offer of insurance has come through for a RTW trip. Only £8,000 covered on the aircraft. i.e. I'll lose £47,000 if I crash. They'll offer £750,000 as third-party liability though. Go or no go?

Big dilemma... Fuck it, I'm going... Have I got enough time to properly organise matters? Probably not.

Mark Twain said, 'Twenty years from now, you will be more disappointed by the things that you didn't do than by the ones you did. So, throw off the bowlines. Sail away from the safe harbor. Catch the trade winds in your sails. Explore. Dream. Discover.'

And the writer Geoff Hill said, 'my experience is that it's always best to say yes to experience ... So, my advice would be to go for

# Phoenix

it, but see if you can get any glitches in the machine ironed out before you go.'

### 3rd April

The rudder issue has been resolved, and the binnacle has been properly secured. It's been chucking it down for weeks, and there's been no chance to fly significant distances in order to sort the trim problem or the roll issue. We think we've figured out the problems, though. The engine's been opened up and examined. The previous issue with the Cylinder Head Temperatures overheating was simply a sensor failing.

In the interim I seem to have picked up food poisoning / irritable bowel syndrome. You haven't lived a full life 'till you've found yourself sat on the loo at 3am, with a duvet wrapped around you, being uncertain from which end the action will take place.

Later that morning I told Nigel, by text, about my RTW ambitions. He replied with, 'it's suicide.'

### 5th April

Email from a work colleague, *'This does not, nor is intended to, signal a lack of confidence in your ability to take the smallest aircraft in the world, around the world. Your "L" plates are off, having crossed the Atlantic twice. It does not touch upon mental stability or inclination to live longer, merely upon the welfare of your staff and off-spring. So probably best to sort out your Will BEFORE you fly away - whether that be for a few weeks or eternity.*

*Your loyal fan and eternal optimist.*

*Nick Parker*
*Principal Consultant*
*LEGAL BROKERS LTD'*

He then sent, bless him, a follow-up email, *'How incredibly exciting. However, without being funny or morose, what is your succession plan?'*

It seems that courtesy of Eddie's contacts the Russians will let me through. The Japanese are saying no, but a chap on the ground is trying to help and lots of paperwork is being passed around.

One of the oriental preconditions is that I lose weight, why ? Because by Japanese standards I'm a porker at 13 and a half stone, and that doesn't play well with flying a 'weight restricted aircraft.'

In general I'm getting twitchier by the day, and Cin still thinks I'm having an affair. And for some reason I've become properly fixated on playing Patience on my iPad.

I'm currently struggling to get my head around certain things that commercial pilots take for granted. There's more reading needed, and I've been asking lots of stupid questions of anyone I can think to contact.

It's also frustrating that Sky Demon is so much better than Garmin, and Sky Demon isn't supported globally.

Some of the legs I need to complete will test the endurance of the aircraft. Hence I'm looking to add an extra fuel tank, somehow. Maybe we could remove the seat and put in a rigid container? Something slung under the aircraft, maybe? Get something made locally? Or buy some form of commercially available fuel bladder?

And I need the dolts at the Royal Bank of Scotland to get their finger out of their arses. The 'bank authority' details need to be in place to allow the business to trade if I pop off, and they're dragging their heels. And I still need to resolve my Will.

For reasons I don't understand, I'm doing an hour a night playing Patience on my iPad.

Time's ticking away.

I subsequently called the Royal Aero Club and asked for their support with the Japanese. Then contacted the UK Embassy in

# Phoenix

Japan, and called my local radio station, regional TV broadcaster, and various papers.

I've been trying to build a coalition of people who'll help with the Japanese. Ultimately, I'm trying to raise money for charity, so any publicity is good, I guess.

And with the aircraft being named after a highly flighty female, I emailed the charity she works for. I've not seen the evil genius for 6 or 7 years but having provided her last two job references, I wasn't expecting a problem. I emailed the generic info@ address asking for help, only to be told, and I'm paraphrasing here, 'ok, we'll write an email on your behalf, but please don't contact us again.'

Later that same day Samson requested my 15-year-old niece be her friend on Facebook. Why on earth would she do that? There are a lot of things in this world I just do not understand.

We've gone past the day I wanted to leave the UK, and my window to enter India is closing. A voice in the back of my mind keeps telling me there's still time to back out.

It looks like Nigel's fixed most things on India Zulu. Separately, I bought a Turtlepac fuel cell from Australia. I emailed the BMAA and asked for their thoughts about my plan to use the Turtlepac during my flight…

*'I'm looking to take India Zulu round the world if I can get clearance from the Japanese.*

*It's been suggested to me that carrying extra fuel / having an internal fuel cell would be handy along the Japanese / Russian parts of the route.*

*Hence I've purchased the Turtlepac 'Little Buddy' that has been previously used in a CTLS. Norman Surplus used a Turtlepac in his Autogyro, too.*

*Can I have your thoughts please on using the kit as either an additional 'operable' tank or a stand-alone container.'*

# Jon Hilton

Their reply was, '*In principle we could approve this... If you want formal approval for this, you'd need to apply on a form AW/002a with a description of the proposed installation, demonstration of compliance with any requirements that are not obvious from the description and No Technical Objection from the Importer.*'

My reply was '*Thanks for this. With the CTLS, Cessna's & Citabria's I'm told the kit is plumbed directly into the fuel line via a T junction. Hence a 12v pump is used in this situation (as opposed to a bigger pump forcing fuel up into the tanks of different aircraft).*

*The Turtlepac is intended for flights through Russia & Japan (if I can get clearance) to extend the range. It may not ultimately be required... but I'd rather have it & not use it than vice versa.*

*Filled with Avgas the 'Little Buddy' weighs 33.3kg. It's been developed for the FAA Light Sport & Experimental Category (CASR Part 21.191).*

*In terms of mounting, it has four mounting points that wrap around the seat (i.e. Underneath and around the back), and that secures it in place. The aircraft's existing seatbelt is an additional securing mechanism.*

*I'll fill it with fuel and see if there's a discernible odour or vapour. The manufacturer 'sniffed' at me when I asked that question, 'We sell hundreds of tanks a year and know what we're doing', he said.*

*They do recommend that the kit is wiped clean after being filled, so 'spillage' may be an issue, but I'll investigate that.*

*Regards & thanks for your help so far.*

*Jon*

*P.S. This may be unfair, but I feel that I'll end up being 'manipulated' for financial gain if I contact the Importer. i.e. I had that experience a month or two ago and would rather not go through that process again.*'

My interpretation, rightly or wrongly, of, 'In principle, we could approve this' is... we're trying to help, the Turtlepac is a

# Phoenix

commercially available solution, and as long as you don't want formal paperwork, then you can use it. Although I may be completely bloody wrong.

And without formal approval I could be grounded anywhere along the route. And the fuel tank could kill a pilot in various ways. Disorientation due to escaping fuel vapour. Leakages causing a fire. Any 'initially non-fatal crash' would mean sitting next to a highly combustible bag of fuel.

By preference, I'd rather not burn.

Both the bank authority, for the business, and my Will have both been finished. I know I should do a decent long-distance test flight, but time is running out for my Indian Visa. And the temperatures are climbing the longer I faff about.

I'm going on the 6th of May, come what may. Whatever happens, I am going on an adventure.

I spoke to Ava's Mum about the leaving date and she was not impressed. I subsequently took Ava to the Trafford Shopping Centre where we bought an illuminated Globe so she could track my progress. I typed out an email to the school and gave them my Flight Tracker details, courtesy of the Spot GPS device, hence they'll be able to follow the flight, too.

I bought Ava a few presents and hugged her as tightly as I dared before dropping her at her Mum's the weekend before the flight.

For the most part I understand flying. I acknowledge it's dangerous. I respect the fact that people die, and I'm comfortable that what might be safe one day might be deadly the next.

In summary, I accept that shit happens.

# Chapter 9. Take off. Day 1

Thursday 5th May, 6pm, and I find myself sat in the office printing off dozens of airfield plates. Plate after plate, hour after hour. The printer has started to run out of ink and a creeping anxiety is nibbling away at me.

For each plate there's a screenshot taken from Google Maps showing exactly what the bloody airfield looks like in real life. The worry is that I won't get them all printed before 9pm.

Cinders is at home, waiting, and I need to spend time with her. She needs me to show more love, and all this is tough on her. There's still time to back out…

I manage to finish three-quarters of the plates, and email Eddie in Egypt asking if I can do the rest on arrival in the Middle East. He's fine with that, and I'm ready to leave the office. I slowly pull the wooden door closed, and stand outside staring at its blue gloss wondering when I'll get back to Bolton.

Arriving at Cindy's place she opens the door and looks tired. We have a bite to eat and she nods off on the leather settee. I lightly kiss her on the cheek and carry her to bed.

At 5.30am light is slowly creeping around the gaps in the curtains, and my girlfriend is blissfully snoring away. I'm half-awake, staring at the ceiling, wondering what the future holds.

As six o'clock dents the day I'm sat Skyping Japan asking about progress on flight clearances, but there's no news yet. What the hell will happen if they say no? A trip to New Zealand maybe? Would all that time over water be wise?

Cind and I get ready and make our way to Barton. She helps pull India Zulu out into the fresh air and we both stand there looking at

# Phoenix

my airborne lifeboat. I gently reach out and pull my 5' 4" tall girlfriend to me. Then wrap my arms around her, lightly kiss the top of her head, and my mind wanders away from me.

Reluctantly, I find myself letting go of her and start bundling my collection of paperwork into the cabin. We both check over the Black & Orange Turtlepac and sniff the air for the smell of fuel.

Looking around the cabin everything is safely wedged onboard and there's just enough space for me. Is this the journey of a lifetime? Or the final journey of my lifetime?

I slowly check through all the paperwork in my battered blue file. Permit to Fly. Insurance documents. Transponder paperwork. Details for the radio. Flying licences. Weight and Balance paperwork. Forty sets of airfield plates and overhead shots of the runways and surrounding ground. Some huge airports, and others simply tiny airfields. All of it intimidating.

One thing missing. The Radio licence. Do I really need one? I have all the paperwork I was ever issued, but is that enough? Cin's sat on a bench by the Tower building watching Aircraft take off and land. I pull out my phone, Google the CAA, and find myself speaking to a very friendly chap at Gatwick.

Simple process. Give him the radio details, pay £20.00, and get an official Radio document issued by email. I can't see I'll ever be asked for it, though. My beautiful girlfriend looks nervous and I know this isn't fair on her.

I walk over to India Zulu and slowly move around her checking for anything unusual. My gaze spans all the flight surfaces, transponder antennae, and the wheels. I slowly take the engine cowling off and poke my head around the innards of the Rotax. Simon's given her a full service and the plan is to get her taken apart in India.

I grab my life jacket from off the seat in the cabin and struggle into it. My eyes linger on its blue shoulder straps and my focus moves to the red thermal shirt I'm wearing.

Then find myself looking over at Cindy. My focus extends into the distance, and I know there'll be problems galore. How will Ava react if I don't come back? In the long run would that be better for her? The inheritance money will set her up for life.

In slow motion I pull myself inside the cabin, settle into the deep cockpit seat, and feel insignificant and lonely. Cindy will be at the end of a phone; Eddie will be available by Facebook Messenger, and Nigel and Simon will be available if I can get a text through.

My stubborn headspace tells me to confront my flying demons head-on. And simply accept that whilst we've tried to fix all Samson's faults, that there's bound to be headaches. My head aches and I silently acknowledge that Eddie was right to say this is a mental challenge.

My slim strawberry blonde girlfriend slowly walks to the cabin door, and I force a smile as my hazel eyes focus on her lovely face. She starts talking, but my mind wanders away again.

The first couple of legs into Europe should be fine, and the plan is to aim at a Customs airfield as far as possible into France. With 25 litres of fuel in the Turtlepac that's potentially a thousand miles or so.

But who the hell wants to do that in a CT? Serious brain fade will kick in sitting cooped up in India Zulu for anything more than 5 hours. And bucket seats are not designed to aid peeing uphill into a little plastic bag.

Cindy's still talking and I slowly reach out, gently pull her towards me, hold her one last time, and whisper my goodbyes. When will I see her again? Two and a half months?

Looking up at the skies, it's an ok day, but not great. It should be clear down to France. Maybe a routing via Wales, then Exeter, clear the military danger areas over the Channel and head through France.

# Phoenix

Cindy moves away from India Zulu, and my left hand reluctantly starts pulling the door shut. It's time to focus on the job in hand. A bluebottle catches my eye as it flies into the cabin. I stare at it and then raise my hand like a conductor and start trying to shoo it out, but the fucker is being stubborn and wants to stay.

I offer a cheery thumbs up to Cind, then shout, 'Clear prop,' and my right hand turns the ignition key. The top propeller blade throws itself to the right, and its two friends blur away in front of my pale face. With a deep breath, I key the microphone, call the Tower, and ask for clearance to taxi.

Samson and I slowly, reluctantly, start moving forward. I awkwardly give Cindy one last nod, fake a happy smile, and we clear the apron and head off.

Why am I doing this? This is stupid. We taxi towards the Bravo Hold and, with all three wheels tracking along the curved tarmac taxiway, everything seems fine. Nigel's played with both wheels and she's good to go.

It's overcast with clouds at 3,000ft. She'll be right, Jonathan, she'll be right. Don't overthink this.

Clearance is given to takeoff, the throttle lever gets pushed forward, and the noise in the cabin increases as we pick up speed. The wheels are moving freely, we're speeding across the grass, and we climb into the skies.

I key the mic' again and ask for clearance to change frequency to Manchester. The reply comes back, 'Freecall approved, have a good flight, and we'll see you in a couple of months.'

Looking around the cabin, all seems well. Cocking my headset to one side, so one ear is exposed to the throb of the Rotax, she sounds good. Then a hand pulls the headset back on and we start flying the SkyDemon route.

An hour later and we're over deepest darkest Wales. Mist hangs from the skies and it's not the prettiest of views. Then it clears, and sunlight batters the cabin. Ten minutes later the iPad goes blank and stops working. That creates a momentary sense of loss that leads to my butt cheeks doing an involuntary clench.

No need to panic, Johnny; this is why you have three GPS's. Just relax and carry on. Leaning forward I double-check the details on the Garmin 795. The Garmin is supposedly a rock-solid device, but it's not the future. Heavy, clunky, and not internet connected.

The clouds gather, and the sky is obscured. My mood and sense of humour improve as the iPad comes back to life. Navigation then switches back to SkyDemon.

The weather gods are playing games, though, and it starts to rain. A thousand individual droplets ping against the cockpit. And streams of water create translucent lines against Samson's carbon fibre wings.

I take a glance over at my mate, the Bluebottle, and it looks like he plans to stay still for the duration. Twenty minutes later the rain dies away as the murky clouds keep hold of their cargo.

My left hand has been tightly holding the stick. I let go for a second, and she starts to pitch left. The left wing dips, the right wing slowly climbs into the sky, and my stomach lurches.

My left hand pushes against the stick again and rolls the wings level. My right hand tries to gouge chunks of skin from my forehead as a million scenarios float by. Should I abort the trip?

Looking up at the sight gauges it looks like the Rotax is only pulling fuel from one tank. What the hell is going on? The glitch Nigel and I thought we'd figured out is still there.

My gaze takes a trip around my tiny cocoon in search of answers. Is the wind direction a factor? Has she been flying out of balance?

# Phoenix

Is there some kind of partial vacuum in one of the fuel tanks that's stopped fuel flowing equally?

I tell myself not to overthink this. You're committed now. Get on with it. Just listen to the beat of the engine and try to relax.

My headspace suggests putting her into a turn to the right to see if the tanks balance themselves out. A gentle move of the stick to the right and the scenery comes and goes for five minutes. We orbit a fixed point on SkyDemon and the Welsh coastline, the sea, the coastline, and the sea, all move around us. There's still time to turn back.

Peering up at the sight gauges the fuel levels seem to fluctuate up and down, but both tanks look roughly equal. Letting go of the stick, she flies true. The Bristol Channel is below the wings, and the sea looks rippled and hard. Go or no go? Back to Manchester and safety?

A scan around the cabin picks out all the kit tucked onboard. My red rucksack is clinging from the headrest, and the orange and black Turtlepac is covering the passenger seat. The yellow life raft is sat in the footwell below it, and the Emergency Beacon is slowly flashing its green light on and off. What to do?

How about trying to keep the tanks equal and engage the Turtlepac? That should keep the weight balanced in the wings. Twenty-five litres of Mogas will give 90 minutes or so. Maybe a change of destination? Rob from Skyferry has a holiday home in Quimper… Maybe an overnight stay, there? A friendly face and advice from a professional pilot?

I awkwardly lean across to the passenger seat, trying to keep the stick centred, and turn the nozzle on the Turtlepac. Then flick on the auxiliary fuel pump with my right hand.

India Zulu wobbles in flight as I try to regain my seating position and get my arse cheeks back to their preferred spot. Was there a change in engine tone just then?

The fuel flow readings spike on the Dynon and flash a warning. Will something blow if the auxiliary pump stays on? Will the fuel hose connection rupture and spray fuel everywhere? We didn't have problems when testing the bloody thing. Should I just use the pump in a climb?

With my right hand I flick the switch on the pump to 'off,' and the fuel seems to flow properly. Maybe gravity is enough to feed the engine. Stay calm, Jonathan. These headaches are the new normal, just keep breathing and relax.

The English Channel is below the wheels as we coast out. I cast an involuntary glance over at the Turtlepac, and I can see small bubbles in the transparent hose as fuel makes its way to the engine.

I tell myself that everything's good and order my imagination not to run riot. My gaze simultaneously alternates between the horizon, the dark blue of the Channel, and the Dynon screen.

Time inches by and the sun-kissed French coast hove's into sight. And my head tells me to head home, back to Blighty.

The sea offers a palette of dark blues, light blues, and emerald greens. The sandy shoreline is irregularly shaped and tiny islands sit off the coast. The view is made glorious by the warm sunshine.

My subconscious thinks it's a beautiful sight, but my inner aviator says there's no viable landing spots.

My wide-awake eyes take in Brittany as we press onwards and eat up the miles. Another glance around the cabin absently takes in the repaired section of carbon fibre between my legs. There's a slightly different colouring to the repairs that are hard to ignore.

An hour later more bubbles appear in the fuel hose, bigger bubbles. I find myself staring at the horizon without attempting to focus on anything. What would Nigel think? I reach for the phone and single-handedly tap out a message, 'seeing a lot of air bubbles in the hose… thoughts?'

# Phoenix

His reply is instant. 'I would expect it because the hose is such a big diameter.' Glancing at the fuel flow readings on the Dynon they seem to fluctuate, up and down. The gauge is wavering between the Rotax receiving either too much fuel, or too little fuel. And it's disconcerting.

My right hand slowly reaches over to the Turtlepac. It's basically a bag of fuel attached to the passenger seat, and my hand lightly rests on it. And begins pressing down on the cool surface, and then letting go.

As if using an old fashioned water pump I begin slowly, evenly, forcing fuel through the clear tubing into the engine. The Dynon readings seem to settle, and that offers an easy fix. Fly with one hand, manual labour with the other.

The throb of the Rotax is giving me a migraine, and my mate the bluebottle doesn't seem happy either. He has a foray around the cabin and wants out.

The phone vibrates in the centre console, and a follow-up text from Nigel appears saying I'll be fine. The inference being, not to worry. My reply reads, 'I do wish you were sat here instead of me, WTF was I thinking?' His response comes through after a couple of minutes as, 'Lol.'

You can do this, Jonathan. Whatever is thrown at you, you can handle. Just stay calm and let the aircraft eat up the miles.

France is beautiful. Little islands and sandy coves sit along the coastline as we track southwest. The view from 3,000ft is stunning, and the sea twinkles in the glow of the sun. And I'm augmenting the flying experience by pumping the bloody bag of fuel sat next to me.

Push down, release, push down, release, and for good measure my inner weirdo asks how many calories I'm burning.

Clouds gather, and it starts raining. A cascade of water attacks Samson and loneliness takes a swipe at me. My eyes absently roam around India Zulu's interior and settle on the life raft. Then I find myself texting Rob to say I'd like to accept his hospitality.

I make a quick radio call to the French Information frequency and ask them to close my Flightplan in favour of Quimper. I need a friendly face and an Englishman to chat to, and he's down there somewhere.

My right hand reaches over and switches off the fuel valve on the Turtlepac. And all I can do is sit still in the silent hope that the wing tanks will start draining without pause, whilst simultaneously scanning for emergency landing sites.

Ten miles to Quimper and I'm trying to get my head round the joining procedure. My eyes shift from the horizon to the iPad, back to the horizon, and then back to the iPad again. Each glance at the airfield plate is an attempt to build up a mental image of the 2km long tarmac runway and its surroundings.

The clouds descend in unison, and there's an impenetrable ceiling above us. The ground starts reaching upwards, and hills appear all over the place. The visibility could best be described as muggy, and we can't maintain a direct track to the runway without flying at less than 1,000ft.

That's no big deal in England, but overseas every non-standard thing seems amplified for some reason. I tell myself to stay calm, but the surrounding clouds are making me feel claustrophobic again.

My right hand picks up the blue chinagraph pencil, attached to my tatty black kneeboard, and I scribble down what I want to say on the radio… then make the call to the Tower requesting Joining Information.

My eyes are continuously scanning the rural French countryside looking for emergency landing sites in case the engine folds. The

# Phoenix

scenery comes and goes, and I reach for the phone to text Rob and let him know my ETA.

A message is already sat on the screen from Ava's Mum. 'Ava's overnight bag is at the school reception.'

What? Why the hell has she sent me that? The cloud is descending and forcing us lower. It's misty, the vis' is coming and going, and Samson's getting nudged around the skies by the weather gods.

The throb of the engine is becoming unpleasant as my headspace is struggling to catch up with the latest text.

With an unsteady hand I text Ava's Mum to remind her I've left the country. An instant reply tells me that, in that case, Ava's been left waiting at the school gates. A follow-up text from her reads, 'you absolute dick.'

The radio cackles and the Quimper Tower ask me to join right base for runway Two Eight. My head starts spinning. That can't be right. If the wind is from the East, shouldn't we be using the other runway?

I take a look down at the airfield plate and try to understand which runway should be in use. Where am I going wrong? Have I got this wrong? Is there a language difficulty kicking in?

An inner voice tells me to just fly the bloody aircraft. My eyes scan across the misty skies, then dip down to the Dynon, and then take in the dozens of irregularly shaped French fields outside the cabin.

A glance up at the fuel gauges suggests both tanks are draining equally. I let go of the stick as a double-check, and she's stable. Will we be landing with a tailwind? Maybe I misunderstood the Towers information, but I'm sure I wrote down their instructions correctly. I did, didn't I?

My right hand sits atop the blue handle on the throttle lever, and I gradually reduce the power flowing from the Rotax.

Scanning the skies, a hazy mist and claustrophobic clouds sit above the wings like a canopy. Five nautical miles to run and I'm searching the ground for the airfield, but can't see it. My eyes skip over fields, houses, villages, and roads. Everywhere's green, rural, and foreign.

How's Ava? How long was she waiting to be picked up? How's she feeling? An image of her usually happy smiley face looking abandoned sits with me.

I key the mic' and make a base leg report to the Tower but advise them, 'not yet visual.' My eyes are flicking up from the iPad to the view outside, but can't pick out any sign of the airport.

SkyDemon says to turn right and stick and rudder send Samson into a nicely coordinated bank. The noise in the cabin decreases as the throttle gets pulled back further, and there's a whining noise from the flaps as they extend.

All of a sudden the Municipal Airport appears straight in front of Samson, and it's bloody massive. How the fuck-a-doodle-do did I miss that?

My right hand reaches forward, nudges the flap lever to 30 degrees, and I take a quick glance left and right to watch them extend. The Tower reports the wind is scurrying along at 5 knots. Will it be a tailwind? Am I landing the wrong way?

Do not fuck up, John Boy. Stay alert and keep scanning the skies for aircraft. I'm getting her down one way or the other. Five or so hours of a numb arse and I seriously need to hug a tree.

Half a mile from the runway, and my eyes are on stalks. Samson floats over the threshold markings and flies along the tarmac, slowly descending. A quick glance over to the large windsock, and something's not right.

The main wheels touch down. She's going too fast. My heart's pumping faster. The wheels don't sound right. You're alone, deal

# Phoenix

with it, keep your cool. A light pull on the brakes and Samson slows, but immediately pulls to the left.

A thin veneer of sweat spreads across my forehead. Fuck. A pull on the brake again, and more right rudder is needed to keep her tracking along the centreline.

The yellow runway markings turn left onto the taxiway. A gentle left turn. My right hand tentatively releases the brake lever, my feet relax on the rudder pedals, and India Zulu starts to take the turn all on her own. For fucks sake, really? Why the dicking-fucking-cock is she turning left?

Has the rain locked one of the brakes and washed off Nigel's grease? Was one of the brakes a remnant from the crash and it's just died? I've no headspace for this. I keep jabbing at the brakes and rudder pedals to keep her away from the commercial light fittings standing by the side of the taxiway.

There's no other aircraft around and the apron is empty. My eyes are swiveling about and spot that Rob's made it airside. He appears in the distance and waves. There's light rain spitting against the cabin. I key the red mic' button and ask the Tower where they want Samson.

I slowly edge India Zulu to her lonely parking slot, power down the aircraft, and open the gull-wing door. A confused Bluebottle exits the aircraft, and the wind whips up and pulls my papers from the cabin. Stressed and tired I undo the harnesses, climb out, and reluctantly give pursuit.

Rob gets closer and helps secure the dozen airfield plates that have escaped my file. A glance at the skies and my mind wonders what the winds will be like tonight.

I lean inside the aircraft, turn on the Master, and power up the radio. 'Golf India Zulu to the Tower.' A female voice gives an acknowledgement, and my voice explains that I want to tie Samson down for the night. The reply is to pull her onto the grass 50 yards away.

I reluctantly grab the prop', whilst sweat crawls across my spine, and tug her away from the Tarmac. For twenty minutes a light rain settles on my head and body as I screw the ground anchors into the grass, tie them to the wings, and secure her for the night.

All the while Rob stands next to Samson and is happily chatting away about the airport and general protocols. I multi-task and both listen to him and text Nigel. 'Really bad pull to the left on taxiing. Ideas?'

Nigel texts back, 'check the brakes are fully off by pushing.' The next text suggests one brake might be sticking.

A wave of friendship flows through me as I'm grateful that he's taking the time to help. Two more messages find my phone. 'Check tyre pressures look even.' Then he raises a question, 'Taxiing in a crosswind?'

I'm too tired to think through this and need to switch off for today. But I did land with a slight crosswind and tailwind. For fucks sake, is that the problem? Am I overplaying things?

An hour later Rob's driving us through quiet country lanes to his holiday home in a secluded, wooded, park. I absently listen to him and simultaneously text Cin to tell her I'm in good shape. I can't explain that I'm stressed to hell, or she'll worry.

Keep your shit to yourself, Johnny, no need to upset anyone. And don't put extra pressure on yourself or you'll fuck up.

A quick shower follows, and I find myself leaning against the bathroom sink staring at myself in the mist covered mirror. My eyes can't help but notice big creases etching their way across my forehead. I absently run my fingers around my head and draw a smiley face in the condensation clinging to the mirror.

# Phoenix

There's a change of clothes and I make my way to Rob and his partner in the lounge. I pointedly ask Rob a host of stupid questions about jet airfields, general airspace and instrument flying, and an inner voice tells me I'm way out of my depth.

I ask about the downwind landing and the casual reply is, 'they make you do that sometimes.'

Two bottles of beer and a glass of wine come and go, it's the French way, and through a tired haze we chat amiably for a couple of hours.

I'm dog tired, exhausted, and fast asleep by 9.30pm.

# Chapter 10 - 7th June. France. Day 2

Didn't sleep well. Tossed and turned. I don't generally sleep well in strange beds and am fully awake and out of bed by 5am UK time.

Rob's partner is still asleep but he's up and enjoying life in France. All I want to do is go back to sleep. Rob offers a croissant, and I can't help but think they're a crazy waste of dough.

He generously drives me to the airport and helps with the customs procedures. Everywhere looks alien to my tired eyes. There's a big Turboprop waiting to fly to Paris, and bored nondescript passengers are milling about.

We get airside and Samson needs fuel. The hope was Mogas from the flying school, but no one's there. The next option is Avgas from the bigger commercial operation.

Rob and I find two guys skulking around and we ask for fuel in English. There's to-ing and fro-ing whilst both paperwork is sorted out and the procedure gets explained.

Heading back outside into the spitting rain I look up at the dark overcast skies, and feel lonely. Rob wants to get back to his partner and we say our goodbyes. I head to Samson, untie her, and reluctantly pull on cold propeller blades to manhandle her to the self-service fueling area.

I manage to fill up the wing tanks and gently, carefully, pour 30 litres into the Turtlepac. The plan is to only use it for emergencies, but fuel keeps an aircraft flying, and my headspace wants that extra flexibility. Everything is a risk. The fuel guys are milling about, and they wave, walk away, and go back to their dry office.

# Phoenix

There's a long day's flying ahead as my numb fingers start taking off the cowling to look over the Rotax. Standing in the light rain my gaze scans the naked engine. Oil levels fine, antifreeze levels ok, no leaks.

I find myself kneeling down on the cold, wet, grass and begin removing the carbon fibre wheel spat on the left wheel. It's too early in the morning for this and my fingers seem clumsy as they grasp at the tiny screws.

I tilt my head upwards to watch the skies as myriad clouds roll past. The rain is settling on my jeans, seeping into my red thermal shirt, and my ears feel cold.

Looking down again, the calipers are locked together. No wonder she was pulling left. I reach for my phone and text Nigel.

What can I do? Simply force them apart? Where along the route can I get them checked over or replaced? Back to England, or push on? My fingers are covered in dirt and oil, rain's slowly soaking into my back, and there's wet patches on my jeans from where I've been kneeling.

I stand up and root around in the footwell looking for my WD40, and it's not there. Fuck. I pick up a small bottle of oil, kneel down again, and lightly rub oil onto the caliper, then stand up, lean inside the cabin and pump the brakes. They seem to work properly. If the brake caliper is catching, should I rub oil on the disc? Is putting oil on a brake pad ever a good idea? Can Eddie help in Egypt?

I lethargically walk away from India Zulu, stretch, and forlornly look up at the grey sky. Then walk back and start reattaching the cowling and wheel spat. Time to fly. If I head home now, I'm a complete failure. Simply push on and do your best, Johnny Boy.

I secure my big red sailor's holdall in the back of the aircraft and suspend my red rucksack from the headrest on the passenger seat. There's a towel draped over the Turtlepac to confuse prying eyes, and I stow that behind the seat.

My red wetsuit is wedged in, as is my lifejacket, green file, yellow dinghy, and a range of flying equipment. It's cramped, and most everything is a vivid colour. The logic being that it's easy to find debris if the bits and pieces are brightly coloured.

The ATR-72 Turboprop starts to accept 50 or so passengers. Sitting inside India Zulu, I'm anxious. I'll let him go first, stay out of the way, and see if he manages to clear the skies in front of us. More importantly I can listen to his radio calls and watch where he taxies.

My mind starts to turn over a number of issues. Ava's face surfaces in front of me and I feel terrible. If her Mum forgot I was going, how the hell is that my fault? And how could she forget something like that? But an image of my beautiful little girl stood at the school gates, waiting to be picked up, makes me miserable.

I force myself to complete the Flightplan via SkyDemon, and fifteen minutes later I'm ready to move. Then make a call to the Tower to ask for engine start, and crank her into life.

Having kept a wary eye on the Turboprop I'm pretty certain I can't fuck this up. I deliberately pull the brake lever and my right hand slowly edges open the throttle. With full power resonating through the airframe, she stays put. Good stuff. At the very least one brake will hold.

My hand slowly pulls the throttle back to idle, and my fingers spider across the console to release the brakes. We slowly inch forward across the tarmac and she seems to track true. I nudge the throttle open a little and aim at the yellow centreline on the taxiway, and she immediately starts pulling left. My heart sinks knowing she's still fighting me.

An uneasy tingle runs its way through my body as we enter the active runway. Don't embarrass yourself, Hilton. The nose wheel is faithfully following the white centreline courtesy of a heavy foot pushing against the rudder. A languid French voice gives permission to fly, and up we go.

# Phoenix

Up at 1,000ft the weather gods are throwing the kitchen sink at Samson, and my cold wet torso is being bounced around the cabin. A swift glance down at SkyDemon confirms a 20 knot or so headwind is slowing us down. Flying feels uncomfortable and my mood is grim. But there's a fixed timeframe to get into India before the Visa expires and, headwind or not, we're going to fly.

France has complicated airspace and that means constantly speaking to someone or other on the radio. And I find myself trying to understand different accents and make my replies without any hint of a regional British accent.

Two hundred miles later and it's boring in the cabin. The winds and buffeting have subsided and straight and level flight is easy. There's the sound of the engine. The green countryside below the wings. The sound of the engine. Nothing specific to look at. The sound of the engine.

There's regular radio chatter with different authorities, but nothing too exciting. 'Flight Design CT, from blah to blah, at 3,000ft on QNH of xyz, request Basic Service,' etc., etc. And then the same spiel on the next frequency.

My tired eyes take in a beautiful chateau nestling amongst trees. There's nothing else around but greenery and pastures, and I can't help myself.

My left hand pushes the stick forward, the wings roll to the left, and we dive down for a closer look. The noise levels increase inside the cabin, there's extra G force pushing at me, but I'm blissfully happy in my little fighter on a reconnaissance mission.

The radio wakes up and a foreign voice says, 'Golfe Indiaa Zuluu, do you have a problème?' Someone's been watching his screen, bless him, and is looking out for moi. But really, I'm not allowed any fun?

Sensible head back on. Wings level, feed in more power, back on heading, and we climb back to where we belong. Don't upset anyone Jonathan… but for a moment, I'd been truly happy.

I look across at the Turtlepac and make the decision to plug it in for an hour. The intent being to get rid of the bag of flammable liquid sat on my right. Everything's going to plan.

The sun seems to get brighter as the few lingering clouds dissipate. The big red ball pours it's brightness through the skylight and starts pummeling my head. The iPad on my knee dies. The screen goes blank, and it's too hot to touch.

Has the iPad got a problem? Is it just the direct sunlight and heat in the cabin? Or is something material failing? My right hand hides it away beside the seat, and I reach for my iPhone intending to take a snap of something miles away. There's a message from Ava's Grandma on the screen.

'Hi Jon, sad to hear Ava was left at school not knowing her Daddy wasn't going to turn up. School were shocked too. You need to text or phone in advance for someone to collect Ava. It's not difficult to do this. Have a safe journey around the world. Love Diana.'

What am I supposed to do? How is this my fault? Ava's Mum knew. The school knew. Is she just trying to deflect the blame? My eyes close for a second, and my right hand rubs its way slowly across my forehead.

That poor little girl, how will she grow up knowing her parents are bickering with each other all the time?

Samson approaches the Gap Tallard region of the French Alps and starts to take a kicking. My right hand instinctively pulls the throttle back to avoid losing the wings. Every couple of seconds we're thrown upwards. My insides start twisting around my colon as my head keeps hitting the bulkhead.

# Phoenix

My right hand reaches forward again and awkwardly disengages the Turtlepac, and then moves to select fuel from the wing tanks.

I pull my iPad out and it's cooled down, it restarts, and SkyDemon gets fired up again. The planned route stares back at me. It's hemmed in by both complicated airspace and mountains leading to the French coast and on to Cannes airport. Eddie and I discussed landing there. And courtesy of the aircraft's universal identifier, FDCT, there shouldn't be a problem.

We're still being bounced around the skies and the weather gods are kicking Samson six times every minute. The Controller from Marseille calls and says the flight plan destination of Cannes has been rejected. I try to reply, but my words barely make it to the mic' as we take another hit.

I make a bare minimum acknowledgement and Marseille reply, 'Carnnes will not accept Microlights arnd we harve changed youre destinashion to St Tropez.' Ok, so having prepared for Cannes I know cock all about St Tropez. Where is it? What does it look like? Who do I have to call? How can I sound professional when the shit has been kicked out of me for the last hour?

We're overhead mountains and struggling to climb above 6,000ft. My head and torso are constantly being thrown around the cabin, and the side of my head keeps hitting the door as we take jolt after jolt. I'm tired, drained, and my ears are numb.

Will St Tropez definitely let us in?

Foxtrot Delta Charlie Tango was used on the Flightplan and that's a general identifier for aircraft up to 600kg. They'll only have found the word Microlight if they've checked the UK register. The miserable, cynical, buggers have looked me up and decided that riffraff can't mix with the Cirrus and small jet brigade.

My right hand grabs at my phone and taps out a text to Eddie, 'The controller's changed my Flightplan to LFTZ but won't confirm they'll let me in.' He immediately replies with, 'Pretend you are a playboy.'

That's a damn useless comment and there's an involuntary period of swearing that gets lost behind the beat of the Rotax.

India Zulu wings her way to within 5 miles of St Tropez and we're still being beaten about by the conditions. Each whack the aircraft takes physically hurts. I key the microphone, call the Tower, and ask for joining information.

'St Tropez Tower this is Golf Charlie Golf India Zulu inbound from Lima Foxtrot Romeo Tango 5 miles north, squawking 0501, at 6,000ft on 1026 Hecto Pascals request Airfield Joining Information, please.'

A gilded French voice says, 'India Zulu, doo you harve anee spetial qwalificashions.' What? What the hell? Has this bugger been on the Brandy? I'm too tired for this and confirm my UK GA licence.

The reply is, 'Without a mownteen qwalicashion we can not accept you.' Oh, bloody brilliant, really? My aching body feels wearied, but the buffeting has stopped for now and that's a welcome development.

The coast appears and glancing down at SkyDemon the airspace looks damned complicated, and there's way too many chances to muck up.

I want to shout at him that I'm British and that's enough of a bloody qualification to let me into his sodding airfield. My reply is, 'Acknowledged, changing frequency to Marseille Information on 111.000.'

Holding the stick with my left hand, I text Eddie with my right. Other Microlights have landed at both airfields, but seemingly not anymore. I get an instant reply from Eddie and he suggests Cuers airfield. One of his last flights, an Autogyro, landed there.

# Phoenix

If they've let a Gyro in, as long as he didn't muck up, we should be fine. Another message pops up from Eddie to say he's called Cuers, but no one's answering the phone. My stress levels are increasing and I'm in serious need of a Mars Bar.

Samson's 10 miles North of Cuers, at 4,000ft.

We're surrounded by hills, there's lots of greenery, and the sun hangs from the sky. I need a drink and my stomach feels hollow. My left thumb presses down on the red mic' button and I transmit to Marseille and confirm my change of frequency to Cuers.

Then lean forward and flip over to their radio channel. French voices are chattering away on frequency. Maybe no one's answering the phone, but they're flying.

I relax my left hand, let go of the stick, and she immediately slides into a tight left turn. Within seconds one wing is pointing down and the other is heading skyward.

For fuck's sake this is uncomfortable. Stay calm, Johnny Boy. Without great thought I just roll the aircraft the opposite way and try to balance the tanks.

The green hills and coastline come and go as I'm pushed into my seat. My back starts aching as round and round we go. My hand moves to the iPad and it has a 3G signal. Over the course of sixty seconds, it manages to download the Cuers plate.

Samson is hanging from the skies at a 45-degree angle from the horizon. I try to read the plate whilst being pushed into the seat. On the third page there's a warning about 'severe pulling downwinds.' What the fuck does that mean? Wind shear? Really? Just fuck off, will you. I'm fed up with all this and my headspace just wants to land.

Squinting up at the fuel gauges, by each wing root, the tanks look level. Maybe 10 litres in each. And 10 litres in the Turtlepac. A scared little voice in the back of my conscious mind warns me about the consequences of crashing.

Wind shear? Memories of Barton come back to me, the grass rushes towards my face, and there's a feeling of being pushed down. And then I try to dismiss the memory.

I grab my blunt chinagraph pencil in my right hand and write down what I want to say on my kneeboard. Then key the mike and repeat it. If I fuck up, and there's a recording of my RT transmission somewhere, my voice will at least sound professional on tape.

My head's hurting. Am I dehydrated?

A response in heavy English confirms the runway in use and gusting winds. I spot an aircraft and thank the heavens that all I need to do is follow him in, and don't need to think through the joining procedure.

My eyes are scanning our surroundings as we join overhead the airfield and slot in behind the lead aircraft. I announce our downwind position, and make an additional base leg call to hear my own voice one more time.

The Jodel in front touches down as Samson turns onto final. Looking around, the skies are blue and a motorway is beneath us. Assorted green colours are painted onto the landscape, and there's stretches of cultivated land complete with brown furrows.

Directly ahead there's a 2km stretch of runway with airport buildings and facilities on either side of the tarmac. My voice wearily calls out, 'Golf India Zulu, Final to land.'

I slow Samson down but still want speed on our side in case we get taken by a downdraft. My right hand flicks the flap switch, and I swiftly glance left and right to watch the flaps extend to thirty degrees.

# Phoenix

We pass beyond the motorway and over the displaced threshold. Everything normal, throttle closed, inching lower. She won't land, and she's not for losing the last meter.

Stay calm. A swift scan left and right and we're 100 meters beyond the threshold markings, and still floating. Just fucking land, will you.

Both main wheels touch down. My left hand holds the stick back to keep the nose wheel off the deck as long as possible. Our speed slowly dies away, and my heart starts beating again as the remaining wheel gently embraces the tarmac. I lean forward, flick up the flaps, and listen to the whining noise made by the motors.

There's an immediate pull to the left.

Relax, handle it. I keep her tracking along the centreline and just focus on the painted white line and try not to think too much.

We've passed the turnoff to the taxiway a while back and Samson trundles to the end of the runway. We turn right and slowly travel the full length of the runway back to the Apron. There's Jodel's, Cessna's, and General Aviation aircraft sat all around.

A thickly accented voice sparks up on the radio and my forehead creases as I try to decipher what the hell he's just said.

We pull off the taxiway, head to our grassy parking space, and I shut down the engine and take the key out. Then open the gull-wing door, take my headset off, and slap my ears to rid myself of seven and a half hours flying.

There's a fueling area 20 meters away with a few sophisticated looking people milling around. Fill up now or wait 'till the morning? Slowly, very slowly, I climb out of the cabin, grab the propeller blades, and laboriously drag her to the pumps.

In Star Trek, isn't it always the fellah's in red that die first? I look down at my red shirt and tell myself to forget all things fictional.

I carefully fill her up and pull her back to the space we were given. Then get the corkscrew ground anchors from the side of my seat and try to screw them into the ground. No joy. The surface is too hard. For fucks sake, really?

I awkwardly communicate my problem to the fueling agent. He suggests pulling her over to another line of aircraft where there's a taught securing wire running across the parched earth.

I slowly drag Samson to her new home and my fingers hurt as I tie her down, cover the Turtlepac, and secure her for the night. My rucksack gets hoisted onto one shoulder, my larger red sailors bag hangs from the other shoulder, and I trudge to the airfield exit.

The gate's locked and I stare at it in an attempt to intimidate it into opening, but cock all happens. I awkwardly climb over the five-foot tall metal fence and spot a dozen French pilots sat in front of their clubhouse. It's an archetypal French scene. Sun in the sky and everyone sat drinking either a glass of wine or expensive beer.

They invite me over and insist I sit and have a drink. I let my bags drop and find myself sat on a reclining chair with a complimentary lager placed in my hand. They all try out their English and make a lost foreigner feel welcome.

Whilst responding to their polite small talk, I check my phone and Eddie's been a hero and booked a hotel room a couple of miles away. I ask the chaps for the number of a taxi firm, and they'll hear none of it. One guy suggests he'll drive me there, and he too achieves hero status.

With a bottle of lemonade in hand my new friend walks me over to a nearby hangar. Four light aircraft are nudging against each other and my gaze rests, for a moment, on an older aircraft mounted on the wall like a trophy. We take a slalom route around the hangar's occupants and make it to the rear door where his old estate car is sat outside. I pile my stuff in the back and we head out.

# Phoenix

What about the Flightplan? Was it automatically closed when we touched down? I mention it to my friend and he gets his phone out and makes a call to close it down.

We arrive at the rustic hotel and three thoughts wander past my consciousness. Firstly, it looks resplendent basking against the wooded hillside. Secondly, they haven't finished building it. Lastly, there's a railway line just beyond the hotel boundary. I check in and my mate gives me his number, says he's flying tomorrow, and if he can help further to let him know. He drives off and his car makes a crunching noise as it compresses the gravel driveway.

I aimlessly wander into the large restaurant and am confused by the menu. When the waiter arrives I just point at someone else's food, on another table, and suggest that'll do.

Forty-five tired minutes later the serviette gets piled on the table, I take a last drink of lemonade, and push back the wooden chair. Walking past the reception desk my Spidey senses sniff out a stunning young woman sat going about her admin duties.

For whatever reason she smiles at me in an interesting manner, and it improves my mood no end. I stop and ask her to book a taxi for 7.30am the following morning. In return she explains that the local taxi driver has taken a few days holiday and I'm out of luck. No one else can help either, and taxis from the next town over won't come out this far.

Really? The taxi driver has taken a bloody holiday? And there's only one damn chap? Mild anxiety kicks in as I reach for my phone and call my new mate. He answers and says he'll pick me up at 8.30am.

I slowly walk back to my room and rehearse a speech to the receptionist. It goes something like, 'Yeah, I appreciate you find me deliriously dreamy, but I have a girlfriend and can't invite you in, soz luv.'

Facing upto my personal reality, I find myself clumsily hand washing two sets of socks and a pair of undies in the luxurious bathroom. They get draped outside on the balcony and I pass out, fully clothed, spread-eagled across the bed, at 9.00pm.

# Chapter 11. 8th June. France. Day 3

Awake at 6am as my eyes slowly crank open. Where the hell am I? A swanky, opulent, hotel room stares back at me. Just the kind of thing I was born for but can't generally afford.

At some point during the night I wriggled free of my jeans and Star Trek shirt and feel reasonably refreshed. A touch thirsty, maybe.

A raft of strange dreams surface that range from soaring the skies like an eagle, to eating out with Ava and Cindy. I absently wonder what will happen to the business and the staff if I don't make it back.

The two main reasons for the delay in leaving the UK were getting the dolts at the RBS to sort out their Letters of Authority. That particular paperwork was needed so the business can keep on trading if anything unfortunate happens. The second item needing to be ticked off was finishing my will. A voice tells me not to dwell on such things.

I slowly shower, get dressed, stow everything away, and put on another red Star Trek top. And realise I'm beginning to loathe all bright colours. Then head to reception with the subconscious hope that my lady friend is on duty again. She isn't, so I leave the key on the dark oak counter and find Jacques already waiting to take me and my belongings to the airfield.

We follow a series of quiet country roads, and the sounds of birds tweeting and crickets chirping lightly rattle around the car. I make good natured small talk and offer him my eternal gratitude.

By return, he politely tells me not to fuck up and infringe anyone's airspace. I ask what the risks are and we stand for 5 minutes, by the wing of a Jodel, as he talks through flying the French Riviera.

It's a lovely sunny day in southern France.

We part ways, and I slowly find my way to Samson and start the preflight process by checking the oil and taking off both the wheel spats and cowling. My eyes take a mooch around and everything seems fine with the Rotax, but the brake caliper has locked on the disc again. Could it be a hydraulic issue?

My hands press up against India Zulu's fuselage and I awkwardly move her forward six inches, whilst looking down at the exposed wheel. The caliper is catching the disk, not biting hard against it, but making contact.

A screwdriver gets freed from my utility bag in the aircraft footwell, and I prise the pad open. Then smear oil on the caliper, stand up, lean into the cabin, and hand pump the brake lever. She's good as gold. The break catches, releases, catches, and releases. Everything's working as originally advertised.

The sun feels stronger and a look down at my Bermuda shorts says I can cope, but the red shirt is a giveaway that a heavy day is in the offing.

I reattach her bodywork and sit inside the cabin, with one leg dangling outside and the other just chilling in the footwell. The iPad is in front of me, and my headspace is working through my draft SkyDemon route, the airspace, and who to call inflight.

I file the Flightplan electronically, then sit still for twenty minutes wondering what the day will bring. A glance around the cabin follows, and my focus fixes itself on the yellow life raft sat in front of the rudder pedals on the passenger side. In an emergency, will there be time to get it out?

# Phoenix

There's other aircraft moving around. Different types, different colours, and everyone's going about their recreational business. Time slows a little as my mind wonders what kind of lives these people lead. Businessmen, wives of businessmen, entrepreneurs, Jacques is some kind of scientist.

I slowly walk round Samson, then stand on tiptoes to check no one's siphoned fuel from the tanks during the night. And find myself sleepwalking through the preflight as myriad scenarios come and go. Am I optimistic or pessimistic about today?

Everything gets wedged into India Zulu and it's time to pull the door down. A fly breezes past and settles in behind the Turtlepac. Really? Another? I make a half-hearted attempt to get the bugger to sod off, but give up after a minute or two.

Leaning my head against the headrest, my eyes close, and I take a couple of deep breaths. My inner coward doesn't want to fly, and I absently pull down the gull-wing door and am encased in carbon fibre.

On autopilot I start the engine and we taxi to the runway. Almost immediately she's pulling left again. Really? With a boot full of rudder she starts travelling straight.

The brakes hold during the power checks, and they seem rock solid when 3,000 rpm is running through the propeller. The airframe is trembling, and she wants to fly. I key the mic', make our radio calls, glance around the skies, line up on the runway, and slowly feed in the throttle.

My subconscious listens to the heartbeat of the Rotax as Samson rolls forward. The wheels are spinning faster as we pick up speed, there's a quick scan around the cabin, and my eyes focus outside.

We're accelerating and leaving France behind as the tyres leave the deck. Up, up, and away.

It's hot outside and the window vents are open to blow cooler air into the cabin. 1,000ft, 2,000ft, 3,000ft. My hand pulls the power back to cruise, the noise in the cabin decreases, and I try to relax. Then start focusing on the communication part of flying the route.

There's lots of chatter on the radio, some in French and some in English. India Zulu aims at the VOR point, 20 miles away, and I concentrate on flying the heading and maintaining altitude. Then make assorted radio calls and feel vaguely competent.

Passing within sight of St Tropez Airport, it doesn't look that difficult. It's a horseshoe type valley surrounded by tightly knotted fauna. Everywhere looks green and pleasant with the sun glinting off the sea a few miles further south.

The Rotax sounds sweet, and there's zero turbulence.

Glancing down again I can't understand why they wouldn't let me land. If you can fly in the UK you pretty much need a bravery award. It'll be a depressing morning when I can't land on 1,071 meters of tarmac when I can manage 200m's on a good day.

And it's no worse than Denbigh Gliding Club or Oban. An inner voice tells me not to obsess about being snubbed. It would have been neat to have landed there, but maybe a CT doesn't look pretty enough.

A look down at the iPad, and my eyes follow the line of the coast as it slowly arcs its way towards Italy. I mentally work through the time difference of taking the sensible planned route, versus launching India Zulu out to sea.

My thumb keys the microphone and my voice tells the controller of my intention to amend the existing flight plan.

Samson passes over the coast and leaves land behind. Life jacket on. Big bag of fuel sat on the seat opposite. Life raft in the footwell. And the throb of the Rotax sends its vibrations through the airframe.

# Phoenix

Ten minutes later and loneliness hits me like a slap in the face as the view becomes purely marine.

SkyDemon stops working. The iPad screen says, 'Waiting for Location Data.' And there's a jumble of confused lines staring up at me from the screen. My headspace feels claustrophobic, and I tell myself not to get anxious.

My focus reluctantly moves from the iPad sat on my left thigh, to the Garmin mounted on the plexiglass window.

We approach Corsica, and the sky dims. It's overcast and it gets colder in the cabin. I awkwardly shut both window vents, whilst keeping hold of the stick, and pull out the heater stem.

Light rain starts to ping against the aircraft, then the weather gods grow angrier. And all I can do is sit there and take it for 20 minutes as vast amounts of water attack Samson.

The Corsican peaks stand at 4,000ft above the waves and they're covered in dark clouds. We hesitantly edge round them, and I reach for my bottle of warm water and take a swig. The horizon completely disappears as the murk takes over and the cabin is encased in cloud.

There's zero visibility outside the cabin, and we're engulfed in clag. My right hand rubs its way around my face, and I tell myself not to let my imagination take over. The centre of my world becomes the artificial horizon on the Dynon.

The cloud slowly retreats from the cabin, but there's gloom everywhere. Differing shades of grey, with a mix of angrier colours, stare back at me. And a chest tightening feeling of claustrophobia attacks me, again.

Differing thoughts roam around my headspace. They range from how to help Ava improve her spelling, to asking myself how long I'll survive in the Med' if the engine folds.

Flying past Corsica my nerve breaks. There's a runway or two down there and my internal coward orders me to make an emergency call, land, and take the rest of the day off. My thumb hovers above the red microphone button, but stays there.

I let go of the stick to see how the old girl is doing, and she starts rolling left. The wings have become unbalanced again and I'd kill for an Autopilot. Unbidden my right hand moves from the throttle, and I start chewing on my fingernails. Just deal with it and everything else, Jon Boy.

Every time the radio chirps up, and air traffic asks for a position report, or I take an extended look at the Dynon or Garmin, Samson keeps wandering off track.

My right-hand rubs slowly against my forehead, and my eyes close for a second.

The sun returns, the skies start to clear, and I can see the horizon again. It's hot inside the cabin now and a damp towel finds itself wrapped around my head, like a turban, to cool me down.

With my left hand firmly on the stick I lean over and root around in the rucksack. Last night's hand washed clothes are still moist. An unsteady hand pulls them out and drapes them across the binnacle to dry, and the sight of my undies relaxes me for some reason.

We sidle above a few islands and the voices on the radio turn to Italian. My left-hand keys the red microphone button and calls 'Rome Information.' A soft sounding female voice replies and gives out the reporting points to hit as we slide into the Italian skies.

There's more messy airspace approaching Rome. My addled brain struggles to understand the air traffic bods. My head hurts. I keep having to ask them to speak slowly and repeat each reporting point along the route.

The plan was to land at Rome Urbe Airport, but a 3 or 4 hour flight feels like a bloody useless waste of the day. My inner voice

# Phoenix

says, 'If you're scared of flying make each day count and push on. Don't give in. Whatever you do, don't back down Hilton, hold your nerve.'

The Italian mainland comes into view and fluffy Cumulus clouds appear like an assault course in the air. Samson makes like a fighter and for ten miles we jink around the myriad bags of virgin white water vapour hung from the heavens.

A look down at my iPad and it has a 3G signal. Flying with my left hand, and with eyes alternately scanning inside and outside the cabin, I tap out a message to Eddie on Facebook Messenger. 'Where else can I go if I push on?'

Instant reply from Eddie, 'if you want to reach Egypt on Tuesday then you will have to be in Crete tomorrow, Monday. Otherwise, Egypt will have to wait till Thursday. LGST (Sitia, Crete) is a good choice in Crete for Microlights.'

Decision made, push on. My back hurts, and I feel hungry. The vibration from the Rotax is getting unpleasant and my body aches. My ears feel numb from being force-fed the harsh beat of the engine.

I ask for Eddie's thoughts on Foggia and his reply comes through as, 'We have sent GA aircraft there before including the Ikarus… just don't mention Microlights.'

Ok, that'll do, decision made. I rehearse what I want to say, write it down on my black kneeboard, and call Rome Information. 'Rome Information, Golf Charlie Golf India Zulu request change of Flightplan to Foggia, Lima India Bravo Foxtrot.'

The reply asks for my endurance, coasting in point, and proposed route. And that means another 90 minutes in the air is needed.

The ground starts to get hilly. And then the gentle hills start transitioning into mountains. A sense of foreboding starts to creep up on me as realisation dawns that the spur of the moment decision to change destination was dumb, really dumb.

Are we approaching the Apennine Mountains?

I pull my eyes from the horizon and glare down at SkyDemon. There are mountains all along the route, from coast to coast, and I try to figure an awkward transit around the higher peaks. A look up from my iPad, and we're rolling left. The ground is at an awkward angle and Samson's sliding into a dive.

There's nothing to do but grimace and slowly roll the wings level to get back on the improvised heading. A look down at my heart monitor shows the old ticker is kicking along at 25 beats per minute faster than normal.

We're still climbing, but the engine is struggling as we edge above 9,000ft. My tired ears pick up a slightly different tone to the heartbeat of the engine. Every now and again there's a different rhythm.

Patches of snow abound outside, and it's chilly in the cabin.

The Rotax is cooling. From a healthy 95c she's dropped to 55c. Much lower and she'll fail. Will she start to splutter below 50c? Outside the cabin roughly hewn mountain sides stare back at me, and there's nowhere to land if the engine caves.

The mountains are irregular and ugly. A handful offer gently sloping sides climbing to a singular tip. Others rise vertically from scree foundations and look formidable. Differing shades of dark brown fauna are clinging to life against the stone.

And Samson's gone beyond radio contact.

The mountains suddenly disappear and we're over a flat plateau. It's the kind of place weird creatures go to live a reclusive lifestyle. There's 20 miles of grey looking rectangular fields, and then the snow-covered peaks reappear on either side of us.

# Phoenix

Samson needs to climb to 10,000ft to clear them, but she can't make it. The engine temps are still dropping and it's colder in the cabin. Was there a different tone from the engine just then?

My back aches and my tired eyes stare outside at the mountainsides, and I forlornly accept that this is a test of will.

India Zulu is not equipped for this type of flight; she can't clear the top of the peaks. Outside the cabin, hard, unyielding rock faces stare back at me. Time slows as we fly a slalom pattern around mountain after mountain.

My eyes flick down every sixty seconds or so to scan the iPad and make sure no higher peaks are lying in wait. Every time I look away from the horizon, she's rolling into a dive.

No habitation anywhere. No people. No radio contact. We're on a knife-edge, and if the engine goes that's it.

The small of my back is aching and my right hand reaches behind me to massage away the lingering pain.

Twenty minutes later and my headspace is obsessing about the heartbeat of the engine. She seems to have different rhythms. Hmph, hmph, humph, hmph, hymph, humph. My right hand moves from the throttle and scrapes across my forehead.

It's frigidly cold in my claustrophobic cocoon and my ears hurt, I'm insecure, and so heart-wrenchingly lonely. My hand moves from the throttle and slowly rubs across my unshaven jaw, then works its way behind me and starts massaging the small of my back again.

The engine temperature has plateaued at 50c. Any lower and my anxiety levels will start affecting my own heartbeat. I ignore the fitness monitor on my wrist and absently rotate it so the strap is at the top.

Time awkwardly moves forward and there's a faint staccato voice on the radio. It's disjointed, but we're heading nearer to a transmitter, and more importantly, a receiver. I silently thank the almighty for that blessing.

A glance at my phone, and there's a signal. A message appears from Cindy. She's been missing me and wants to meet up in Egypt.

No, she can't do that. That'll make the timescale too tight to get into India. But she's scared of flying and is prepared to do that because she loves me. And I've just come within a whisker of an engine failure.

I'm too tired to think, but know I want to be loved. A slow lingering look around my surroundings takes in my red T-shirt, the yellow life raft, my blue life jacket, the red immersion suit, the bag of fuel next to me, and my red rucksack. My hazel eyes absently settle on the green folder complete with all the Airport plates and reams of paper. The Rotax is loud in my ears and the outside world seems uninhabitable.

My right hand reaches for the phone and sends a message to Cin, 'if you want to fly over for a couple of days, it'd be lovely to see you. x.'

We're getting nearer to Foggia and slowly eating into the miles. We descend to 5,000ft as the high ground falls away. The engine temps slowly improve, and my stomach starts to churn as hunger takes over from fear.

I switch radio frequencies and call up Foggia. In response they sound really quite friendly, and there's a professional sounding Italian voice down there doing his best in English.

Scanning the scenery, the east coast of Italy is a green and pleasant land. The sun has come out and I'm warm again.

I've been holding onto the stick for grim death, and with the airfield within reach, it's time to see how well she's balanced. My left hand relaxes its grip, let's go, and she starts rolling left into a dive.

# Phoenix

My stomach churns as my left-hand pushes against the stick and rolls the wings level again. A deep breath follows, and I roll her to the right and put Samson into a 45-degree banked turn to level the tanks.

Mild dizziness waves at me as she moves through 360 degrees, and I keep the turn going. My arse is pushed into the seat, the sound of the Rotax hurts, it's hot in the cabin, and my head feels like mush.

The wings will take this, won't they? The carbon fibre repairs should hold, shouldn't they? My eyes look up to the wings and I wonder how much stress they'll take.

And then think, fuck it, if I'm going to die, it's going to be today. My hand pushes the stick further over and tightens the bank. My head is forced against the headrest as gravity pins my body back, and every part of my body feels heavier.

Tick, tick, tick.

And my bottles gone. I roll the wings level and let go of the stick. She's a little 'left heavy,' but not too much, and very nearly flying like the girl of old, pre-crash.

Pulling the power back, the sound inside the cabin drops, and I gently nudge her into another right-hand turn. Round and round we go again as we descend to 2,000ft. My eyes keep an eye on the Cylinder Head temps to make sure the engine doesn't cool too quickly. Releasing the stick, she doesn't roll left or right, and is nicely balanced.

Flying towards the airport I'm told the runway in use, and we're asked to join downwind. There's beautifully flat Italian countryside everywhere, with dozens of wind turbines harvesting the earth's energy. A request comes through to, 'report airfield in sight.'

Five miles out, and I can't see it. 'Golf India Zulu not yet visual'.

There's Foggia in the distance complete with terracotta roofs, apartment blocks, and a chunk of civilisation in the middle of nowhere. The skies are blue with a misty look to the horizon. Can I see the airport? Nope. My eyes are scanning everywhere as anxiety starts to bite.

And then it's in front of us, huge. How the shag-a-doodle-do did I miss that? A 1,500m asphalt runway becomes the centre of my world. I click the mic' and report visual as the Tower and passenger terminal get closer.

The Tower announces a 15 knot direct crosswind, and it's gusting a further 10 knots.

I take my phone and wedge it under my right thigh like normal, it helps me concentrate for some reason. I reach forward, select 15 degrees of flaps, and listen to the whining noise as they extend. Stick or twist? More flaps or stay at 15 degrees? Stick.

We're getting closer to the runway. My gaze takes in the town to the left and then focuses straight ahead on the black strip in front of us. My mind tries to ignore the fact that fifteen knots is beyond the legal limit of the aircraft.

A swift glance at the repaired section of carbon fibre says all I need to do is make it a survivable landing. My feet lightly move the rudder to crab the airframe as much as possible towards the wind.

Fifty feet above the ground and we float over the runway threshold. Descending. 30ft, 20ft, 15ft, 10ft, 5ft, 3ft. Throttle closed. It's quieter in the cabin. I take a deep breath, and hold it, whilst my eyes are fixated on the horizon.

More right rudder is needed to kick Samson in line with the runway. The main wheels touch down, and I can breathe again. The wind is pushing against us, but she's down.

A gust, and we're lifted into the air. My forehead tingles.

# Phoenix

Don't panic, relax, let her settle again. Don't pull the nose up, and don't force the nose down. Just find a balance where she'll slowly lose the height. Do not fuck this up, Hilton.

Time stands still again and waits. And my subconscious relives the Barton crash.

Touchdown. My right hand quickly pulls on the brakes. A foot full of right rudder keeps her straight. I quickly reach forward, flick the flaps up, slow her to a fast-walking pace, and tell myself to relax.

A quick look around and we're in a good looking well organised provincial airport. Large blue signage hangs from the silver backdrop of the terminal building, and it serves to advertise the airport's name. The warm sun makes everywhere seem welcoming.

Samson slows and we tentatively head towards the modern terminal building. An inner voice tells me everything is normal, and that I shouldn't overthink the wing dropping away. We thought we'd figured it out in the UK, but no problem. And don't worry about the brakes. Both these niggles are the new normal, just deal with 'em.

India Zulu rolls to a halt in front of the terminal. There's no other aircraft about, and I shut down the Rotax and take the key out. Then slump forward, close my eyes, and start trembling.

Everything will be fine. Just deal with everything as it's presented to you. I'm a Brit abroad and will not be beaten.

I awkwardly climb out of the cabin, stretch, and very reluctantly begin taking the wheel spats off both wheels again. The securing screws make their way inside the cabin as my fingers start fiddling. Both brakes seem locked. Are there bubbles in the hydraulic reservoir? Is that the problem?

Fifteen minutes later, both brake calipers seem to grab and release when my pasty white hands reach into the cabin and pull on the lever. I squat down on the warm asphalt and try to think. Maybe Eddie has contacts who can help.

As long as I know about the brake problem I can deal with it, can't I? It's been stressful but not dangerous, just been a nuisance. Or is it a sign of an imminent failure? Maybe the left wing is having similar problems that will lead to a structural failure of some sort.

My enthusiasm for the trip is dying, and my headspace wants this over.

Two good looking Italian's approach Samson and ask in English if I want fuel. Getting up, to make the place look tidier, I say, 'yes please.' They point to a spot 100 meters away and suggest that's where to go.

I can't bear the idea of waking Samson up again, so I reluctantly grab the prop' and start pulling. They both stand there watching.

The brakes aren't on, but she's still pulling left. Can the disc have warped in some way? It didn't look like it. We finally get to the refueling area and the chap on duty starts chatting away in Italian. And I don't have the energy to tell him I've no idea what he's saying.

Through a combination of sign language and the Basil Fawlty method of communication the wing tanks get filled with fuel. The chap wasn't paying attention and Avgas sprays over the wings. Really? If there's one bloody thing I hate, it's fuel pissing everywhere.

I ask for a cloth, relieve him of fueling duties, and start doing it myself. Then proceed to slowly, delicately, pour Avgas into the Turtlepac on the passenger seat. The refueler gives me an interested look, but doesn't say anything.

One of the airport managers appears and starts talking in English. The first thing he says is that he'd like his picture taken beside India

# Phoenix

Zulu. He pulls himself up to his full height, maybe 5'6", then leans against Samson and smiles for the camera.

He asks that I take the picture both with and without his expensive aviator type glasses on. I take to him immediately and decide we'll be mates.

Normality resumes and minutes later I fish around in my smaller red rucksack to find my wallet and credit cards. Then slowly extend a card knowing I have to pay whatever they want to charge. Part of my brain says to figure out the cost into pounds, the bigger part says, 'don't bother, you'll only depress yourself.'

Twenty-five minutes later Samson's tied down and secured for the night outside the Terminal Building. The manager chap, Rafe, needs me to complete his paperwork and we head to his office. My name, address, and passport number take an additional twenty minutes to be copied onto his forms.

I sit there wearing my red Star Trek top and feel helpless. I can only leave when he lets me and my persona slowly morphs into that of the cheerful Brit, again. Anything he wants is 100% fine. Take as long as you want, fella.

He finally releases me, and with my heavy red seamen's bag over one arm and my red rucksack over the other, I'm escorted through the empty departure building out into the sun.

Eddie's played a blinder again and sorted out a hotel. A bored looking elderly taxi driver is sat in a silver Mercedes, and he catches my eye. I walk down the steps and silently hand over the iPad showing the hotel address. He looks thoughtful, nods, and we head off.

There's seemingly no rules to the road, and honking horns and repeated curses from my charioteer welcome me to the real Italy.

Foggia's buildings look impressive, but they're past their sell-by dates. Roman-era properties stand tall, but they seem to silently acknowledge that the days of Empire have drifted by.

Arriving at the hotel it looks nice, and the foyer looks ok. A few Russian sounding henchmen are milling around looking ugly and ready for trouble. I wonder why they're here, then realise that as long as they don't bother me, I'll stay well away from them.

The hotel receptionist doesn't speak English, so I just hand over a credit card. I'm preoccupied with both the pictures of naked women on the walls, and not letting the Russians out of my line of sight. The hotel Visa machine won't take my card. I try again, and it won't work.

I pass it back to the receptionist, and he shrugs. Then I reluctantly get out a new card and payment for the hotel room goes through first time. Why the hell didn't the first card work when MasterCard had been told I was travelling?

I make my way upstairs and walk into the room. It's hot inside and there's lots of road noise. The room's clean but has a slightly downbeat Travel Lodge look to it. My bags get dumped on the bed, I struggle in and out of the shower, and then head downstairs for a walk round Foggia to find food.

My energy levels are dropping down to zero, and the only place open is a Chinese. It's devoid of customers. Hard chairs abound and it's a big space with a hint of school canteen about it.

The staff are shouting at each other and don't seem to care about me. A skinny waitress appears, and she looks at me like I'm a nuisance. I point to a couple of pictures on the laminated menu and ask for a Sprite. A big fat guy, possibly the chef, comes over and seems intent on getting me to order more.

He's pointing at his midriff and suggests I need a bigger portion. My appetite has gone, but I force down the food that latterly appears.

# Phoenix

Staring blankly through the dirty window I can't help but think Foggia's a strange place. Nice buildings, but graffiti and litter, and a look of poverty. I'm hot in a T-shirt but the locals have jumpers and coats on.

Thirty minutes later I'm back at the hotel, manage to send a quick text to Cindy, and pass out on the bed fully clothed. 9pm.

# Chapter 12. 9th June.
# Italy. Day 4

Incessant road noise kept me awake during the night. The steel shutters on the windows helped a little, but not completely and I'm fully awake at 5am.

I pack everything away and head downstairs for a very quick bite to eat in the hotel restaurant. The Russians are milling around and, as a pacifist, they're really starting to piss me off. They're loud and focused on themselves. Four of them want my table but they can sod off 'till I'm good and bloody ready.

What do these people do in Italy? Security? Oil? Something involving muscles?

Twenty minutes later I'm in and out of a tired looking taxi and at the airport for 7.30am. It's not open yet, but Rafe is there and helps me airside. I like this chap, no sharp edges and just a nice amicable guy.

He talks through the military airspace to the South, and then it's time to preflight India Zulu and get ready to fly.

After a final walk round Samson, I take a couple of steps backward and sit down on the tarmac. Looking slightly upwards my eyes cast over her carbon fibre body, take in her blue and yellow markings, and try to see everything for the first time.

Standing up I slowly pull myself onboard, fish out my iPad, and file my Flight Plan on SkyDemon. My gaze extends upwards towards the clear blue skies, and I offer a silent prayer to the god of light aircraft in the hope of a clear run to Crete.

# Phoenix

Without great thought I slowly start strapping myself in, and then a vision of an emergency landing on the sea floats through my mind. Would she flip over? Would I pass out?

And without realising it I find myself climbing out of the cabin and walking around India Zulu again. Then take the cowling off in search of anything unusual.

Every time I've ever flown it's been with the expectation of a crash. And that both calms me and puts me on edge. It also leads to a jumble of unpleasant outcomes passing through my mind.

Samson seems good to go and 10 minutes later my arse is sat in the cabin once more. A moment later I get my act together and start checking everything is safely stowed securely away. With all my belongings wedged into the cabin I'm surrounded by a mix of vibrant colours.

My headspace tries to ignore the Opal Fruit theme and focuses on absorbing the route, whilst also scanning the printed plate for Sitia airport.

My right hand stows the green file away and finds the harnesses. My left thumb keys the mic' and calls the Tower for permission to start the engine. In the background Rafe waves and disappears from sight as the prop' starts spinning.

Another radio call and Samson's cleared to taxi. I inch the throttle forward, force the rudder right, and we're moving away from the terminal at walking pace.

We pull short of the holding point, and I carry out her preflight checks. Flaps down, trim set, full and free movement on the stick, check the mags, the engine is upto temperature, and we're all good to go. My left thumb presses the red microphone button on top of the stick, and I state, 'Golf India Zulu at the 34 hold ready for departure.'

A voice on the radio says, 'India Zulu return to the terminal.' Oh, for god's sake, what now? Sitia airport closes at 1pm and big delays will cause havoc. A mad thought crosses my mind to say fuck it and go without clearance.

Another thought crosses from the other direction and says, 'don't be a dick.' That's followed by a shake of the head and a facepalm moment. The throttle gets gently nudged forward, there's a push on the rudder, and the wheels send us through a half-circle.

Am I staying in Foggia tonight with the Russians? The radio comes to life, 'India Zulu, your Flight Plan has just arrived; you may turn around again.'

We head back to the runway hold and I feel nervous, anxious. This isn't just a test of nerve in the air, it's an ongoing stress test on the ground. I've never felt the need to be liked as much as I do now. I want friends around me, people I know and understand.

No time for this Johnny. Just get on with things, and shut up. You're a man, you're a Brit, just shut the hell up, and make everyone around you feel that this is the most natural thing in the world. In general, put a smile on your face each and every time some other fucker is watching.

Clearance is given to take off. A heavy foot keeps the extra rudder in, my right hand inches the throttle forward, and we roll on to the runway. Full power flows from the Rotax, and we're airborne.

We head south and try to stay clear of the military airspace. They have jets playing around up there and the intention is to stay low and keep out of their way. The landscape offers rolling hills, lots of greenery, and cotton wool clouds pepper the skies.

'Brindisi Information this is Golf Charlie Golf India Zulu. Flight Design CT from Foggia to Lima Golf Sierra Tango, ten miles southwest of Amendola at 3,000ft, squawking 7,000, request basic service, please.'

# Phoenix

Brindisi seem helpful, but I'm asked to descend below 1,500ft. We pass over the coastline and I move the headset from one ear to listen to the Rotax. She's beating along nicely as we leave Italy behind and head over water. My mental state dips as the view becomes completely marine.

Chance of rescue in the event of an engine failure? 50/50, maybe. A finger outlines the numbers on the window, and my inner coward asks if there's sharks circling below the wheel spats waiting for a snack.

I call Brindisi again and ask them to confirm which Danger areas are active. Then make a further request to climb to 7,000ft within one of the empty sectors. The request is denied.

Ninety miles further on I pull back the stick and we climb towards the international boundary. Five minutes later I key the mic' and make a radio call, but no one answers.

The sound from the Rotax increases as we hoist ourselves further into the skies. We're gaining height but the engine temps on the Dynon are reducing, and the readings continue spooling downwards.

An inner voice says, 'you are completely on your own.' My gaze makes its way around the cabin and focuses for too long on the yellow life raft in the passenger footwell.

What are people at home doing right now? Lunch breaks? Having a cup of tea and a bite to eat? Possibly an occasional trip to the loo? Generally nice and safe? Will I die if the engine quits?

I make repeated calls to the Greeks, but no one answers. The Dynon shows the engine is still slowly cooling, and the green readings have become yellow. My right hand picks up the phone, goes into the photo album, and starts scrolling through pictures of Ava and Cindy.

SkyDemon packs up on my iPad. It's lost its satellite signal and we're back to relying on the Garmin. It's a slap in the face moment and my cheeks flush a little.

My weary left hand pulls the stick back. My right feeds in more power, and I try to juggle the engine temps against the outside air temperature and my need for altitude. If the engine runs too cold, she'll fold, and the life raft will be needed.

Loneliness clings to me like a limpet as my mind asks whether I'm supposed to be enjoying this.

My left thumb keys the mic' and I start making a series of blind radio calls in the hope someone can pick up my transmissions. My voice sounds competent and casual, but inwardly it seems thin and weedy as I broadcast from 7,000 feet above the hard waves.

There's a cackle from the radio and someone on the Kalamata approach frequency replies. I politely ask to fly into their airspace, and the request is denied.

Time's running out to get to Sitia and maybe Samson should just stay low, below their airspace, 'till Crete? The engine will be warmer at lower altitudes, so should I just stay low with the engine in the green zone? Or stay high with the temperatures in the yellow or red zone, but maybe more cooling issues later?

Up high would mean time to get off a mayday call in the event of a problem, but there's no guarantee it'll be heard or acted upon in time. Or fly lower and just accept the prospect of ditching? What would the Fox say? He'd be polite, shake his head, and then give me that patented look that says, 'whatever you do, you are a dick.'

My gaze takes another long tour around the cabin, and an inner voice asks how Ava's day is going.

Decision made, descend, and skim past Peloponnese, then aim for Crete. My left hand moves the stick forward, and my right pushes

# Phoenix

open the throttle, to keep the engine revs up, and we descend to 800ft.

The Greek coastline is on the left and looks pretty bland without sunshine splashing against it. The sea sits passively beneath the wings. There's inlets and bays on show, but without the sun's glow it's not inspiring.

I find myself glancing through the window and staring down past the left wheel at the water below. My forehead is lightly resting on the plexiglass as the thought rattles around my mind that single-seat flying is bloody lonely.

I make a call to Alexandros Aristotle Onassis Airport on Kythira, but no one replies. A feeling of loneliness, combined with sadness, grabs at me as I realise why I've taken on the trip. How's Ava doing right now?

We clear the mainland and climb further into the skies. After three unanswered, dispiriting, radio calls Athens replies. I ask to route directly to Crete, but the request is denied, and they order India Zulu to route from IFR reporting point to reporting point.

The sun has come out to play again, and I find myself sat with a towel wrapped around my head trying to fend off heat-stroke.

I start to think more about Ava and wonder what kind of life she'll have without me if the engine folds at any point along the route. And absently find myself staring at her picture on my phone.

Each time I look down for more than a second or two Samson starts pulling left and dropping a wing. The radio work intensifies, and it's a good distraction. Every time I try to check a position or distance to the next reporting point, we're heading off course, and it's getting really fucking tedious.

Radio contact with the various ground stations is becoming intermittent, and I keep making calls with position reports, but no one replies. Plan B is to call Souda Approach and request transit through their airspace enroute to Sitia.

Clearance is given to transit their zone, and five minutes later I can't raise them again. A hand pushes the throttle wide open, and we start moving as fast as we can towards Sitia.

A glance over at the iPhone and there's a signal. I click the email function and one arrives from my Japanese contact. Our oriental friends consider me an adventurer, apparently, and won't approve flight through their airspace in a Microlight.

It's turbulent over Crete and I'm being bounced around the cabin. I switch to the Iraklion frequency, make contact, and my voice falters on the radio as we take a hit. I mumble through a position report and get cleared to fly on to Sitia.

Between Eddie, the Heraklion Tower, and Sitia they agree to keep the airport open a further 25 minutes beyond closing time. My headspace silently acknowledges Eddie's value and how much I need him.

I descend from 5,000 feet in a steep right-hand turn in order to balance the fuel in both wing tanks. My tired, jaded, eyes watch Crete go round and round in front of my face as we turn and turn.

The corkscrew motion seems to have worked well, and she's nicely balanced.

The runway appears in the distance atop a cliff face. We move nearer to the threshold and the Cretan Sea is slung below the wings. The cliff face is staring back at me, and it feels like we'll be landing on an aircraft carrier.

The Air Traffic guy announces the wind data and provides a warning not to hit any of the seagulls catching the breeze above the cliffs. There's a break in the transmission, and the radio comes alive with an announcement that the wind has swung through 100 degrees.

# Phoenix

Samson's as light as a kite as she ghosts over the white numbers painted onto the runway. Two feet above the tarmac we get taken by a gust and are hoisted upwards. I fight to keep my nerve as the wind suddenly releases us.

Time moves slower as we fly further along the runway. She touches down and the sound of the wheels going from zero to fifty miles an hour echoes in my headset.

Samson immediately starts pulling left as we slow. A hand reaches out and pulls on the brake lever, then moves to the radio and switches to the Ground Frequency.

We taxi to our destination and pull up. My right hand turns the ignition key to the left to stop the propeller, and my fingers spider around to shut off the avionics.

I tumble out of the aircraft and can't stand up without feeling uncomfortable. I sit my arse down on the tarmac and stare into space. After six hours flying my bum is numb, I'm deaf, absolutely trucked, and my head feels like it's full of broken biscuits.

Five minutes later, I get my arse off the deck, tie Samson down, and am escorted off the apron and through the expansive terminal building to the taxi rank beyond.

Eddie's organised a budget hotel by the seafront, and upon arrival I dump my stuff and head out for something to eat. I take a red plastic seat in an open-air restaurant nestling by the beach and feel lonely again.

A pretty brunette waitress approaches the table and seems a little over-friendly. I just sit there, trying to look innocent, whilst she practices her English on me.

Fifteen minutes later my cheap steak arrives as a solitary mongrel dog ambles past my chair. I feel his pain, cut off a piece of sirloin, and drop it on the tarmac. And a minute later half a dozen of his skinny mates surround my table seeking their supper.

# Jon Hilton

My waitress tells me off for feeding the strays. I try my best to look abashed and find myself staring at her pretty face, wondering why the population of Crete seem so distressingly good looking.

After she's finished her gentle rebuke, I start typing out a message to the couple of hundred people on Facebook following the flight.

*'Can I ask a favour please… Had an email from my contact in Japan… The Japanese aren't willing to let me through as an 'adventurer'… I am & have been raising money for Clatterbridge Cancer Charity, and if everyone on here could donate just £ 5.00 (or even a £ 1.00 - it's the thought that counts) to my www.justgiving.com/Jon-Hilton page, it may help them recategorise the flight… i.e.. As something they will want to support... Otherwise I can't go RTW & will have failed…'*

I slowly amble back to the hotel and fall asleep to the accompaniment of stray dogs barking on the waterfront, and the chap snoring in the room next door.

# Chapter 13a. Crete. 10th May.
# Day 5

My eyes reluctantly open and take in my surroundings. I very slowly remove myself from the thin bed linen and stand up. Then make my way to the window and twitch the curtains open an inch. Sunlight makes a dash into the room, and the skies are a beautiful blue.

A glance at my watch says it's 5am. I'm not cut out for early mornings, my head feels muggy, my body aches, and I feel thirsty.

I totter back to bed and, instead of climbing under the covers, fish out my iPad and try to get the route into Egypt sorted out via Rocket Route. It doesn't like my Apple device, so I reluctantly grab the Garmin and start afresh.

Thirty minutes later all the reporting points are programmed into the Garmin with a destination of Marsa Matruh Military Airport. A scratch of the head turns into an extended facepalm moment that seems to last an hour.

I manage to roll off the bed again and drag my sorry arse to the bathroom. Then make my way in and out of the cramped bathroom and put on a blue T-shirt, Bermuda shorts, and trainers.

My T-shirt has seen better days, and I feel crumpled. That's supplanted by a surreal feeling of ghosting in and out of different environments, without leaving any footprints behind.

Everything gets packed inside my two red bags and they get hoisted onto my back. I awkwardly make my way downstairs for a light breakfast and try to feel confident about the day ahead. My gaze absently casts about outside the window, and I stare at the greenery as it's being knocked about by the wind.

I check out of the hotel and walk outside into the heat. The beach is across the road, and I heave both bags on to one shoulder, cross the tarmac, and struggle across the sand to the water's edge. Then kick off my trainers and stand in the Aegean staring out to sea. The thought wanders across my mind that if the engine fails, I'll probably die today.

An inner voice tells me to shut the hell up and just get on with things. I slowly turn my back on the horizon, slip my trainers on, and trek towards the centre of the town to find the taxi rank.

Feeling hot and bothered I spot a taxi and get my kit onboard. Fifteen minutes later I've exhausted my supply of small talk just in time for the estate car to pull up in front of the blocky looking silver terminal building.

Then pull my kit from the car, pay up, say my goodbyes, and walk towards the airport doors. They happily move apart to reveal that the lights are off and no one's home. White walls and tiled floors welcome me and my belongings inside the terminal.

I heave both bags onto one shoulder and make my way over to the row of offices exposed to public view. A man and woman eye me suspiciously from behind their counter. I take a deep breath and try to explain that I'm a pilot and my aircraft is parked outside. The look pointed in my direction says, 'you're going to be a nuisance' and they ask me to wait.

I amble away and sit down with my back against one of the large white concrete pillars facing them. My arse recognises the cold marble floor and isn't impressed.

It's windy in Sitia, mid-twenty knots, and that's borderline for a light as a kite microlight. There's no time to sit out the weather and the Indian Visa runs out soon. I pull my knees up, rest my head on my chin, and close my eyes.

Minutes later one of the Greek types makes his presence known. He looks down and I can tell his 'Spidey senses' aren't impressed. I

# Phoenix

look up at him and can't help but wonder why these people are so bloody good looking.

I smile a tired smile and pull myself to my feet. Then get that guilty warm feeling that comes from knowing that someone who's just looked down on me, is shorter than I am.

He backs away ever so slightly and invites me to complete a bunch of paperwork. The airport terminal lights come on as the business day starts and I'm led outside. Samson's at the far end of the airport complex and we jump in a small white car and head off. My aircraft is where I left her and is shielded from the winds.

There's a quick walk around the fuselage, and I unlock both doors and start putting my bags on board. Then begin the process of untying her from the concrete securing points. Every action becomes draining as the day seems to be getting hotter.

Both hands take hold of a propeller blade each and I pull Samson towards the refueling area. Another couple of good-looking fellah's appear, both with thick dark hair, designer stubble, expensive sunglasses, and a touch of the George Michael about them.

After the earlier feeling of being a hassle for everyone, the sight of a tiny India Zulu seems to have put smiles on their faces. She's endearingly small to them, and I'm seemingly a plucky Brit.

I tell them I need fuel and the shorter chap seems happy to help. I stand on tiptoes and undo the fuel caps on both wings. He pulls over a step ladder and climbs up above the left wing with the fuel hose in hand. The nozzle is too big for the tank, and it won't fit. There's a pause whilst he looks at me.

Then he looks off to one side and asks, 'can you take Avgas?' My reply is yes, of course. He says, 'it doesn't say so on your wings.'

No one's ever asked me that before. She can take Avgas, just not for extended periods. But isn't that supposed to be at my discretion as Pilot in Command? What's he bloody well playing at?

# Jon Hilton

My tired right hand rubs its way around my cheek, and I hear myself utter that unless he can get Mogas then it needs to be Avgas. He stares at me. I stare at him. The sun is getting hotter.

He keeps staring at me as if I've got something else to add, then shrugs and turns his back. I'm deflated and don't know what to say. He climbs down from the step ladders, walks into his cabin, and starts rooting through his desk. I follow him inside figuring I need to say something.

He blanks me, and won't engage in conversation. A moment later he pulls out two stickers and a funnel from a drawer, brushes past my shoulder, and heads outside into the sun.

I awkwardly walk after him feeling both bemused and bugged that I'm dependent on him. He climbs the step ladder, again, and carefully puts a red sticker on the wing. Standing on tiptoes I can read the word, 'AVGAS.'

My good looking friend then pulls a slim digital camera from his pocket and takes a picture. Putting away the camera he seems happy to start filling her up. My face gives off a confused vibe. By return he casually mentions that now he has photographic evidence that India Zulu can take Avgas, he's able to help. Then volunteers that the Greek economy is in trouble and jobs are scarce.

Twenty minutes later the tanks are full and thirty litres have been gently poured into the Turtlepac for good measure.

India Zulu is starting to rock in the winds. It's gusting to 24 knots and I want to be safely back in Bolton. The people might be fuck ugly compared to the Greeks, but it's home.

Shaking the fellah's hand I say my goodbyes and climb aboard. The red immersion suit is wedged into the corner of the passenger seat, but it's too bloody hot for that. My absent gaze stares at it and starts asking questions. Would it save my life if I wore it? Possibly, probably.

# Phoenix

Sitting in the bucket seat I can't bear the thought of putting on such a bloody heavy monstrosity, though. I want to be alert and being cooked inside the immersion suit won't do.

Instead, I pull off my T-shirt and put on a red Star Trek top, then claw on my blue lifejacket, and find my train of thought wandering away from me. There's sea on one side of India Zulu, and mountains on the other.

I put on my headset, push in the Master Fuses, and turn on the radio. Then ask for permission to start the engine. The Tower give approval and make a couple of further comments.

They expect a straight-out departure and confirm that the wind is at 45 degrees to the runway. Additionally, they report that large seagulls have been seen loitering around the skies and they're expecting a commercial jet soon, so could I hurry up, please.

Nothing to be said. I just repeat back the pressure settings, confirm clearance to taxi to the 05 threshold, and silently acknowledge both the threat of a bird strike and that there's no time to change my mind.

The engine cranks into life and she sounds good. The propeller is blurring away and it's hot in the cabin, maybe 25 degrees. The window vents are open, but all they're doing are circulating hot air around my head and torso and the heat is starting to abuse my body.

The thought of fucking up at an International Airport puts me on edge. I carry out my takeoff checks, enter the runway, and sit there for a second staring at the long white threshold markings painted onto the tarmac.

Then lift my eyes to the hillside at the end of the runway, maybe ten miles away, and maybe 4,000 feet up. It's hot and that affects Samson's climb rate, but there's plenty of distance to climb above them and continue over the sea. The heat shouldn't affect the rate of climb too much, should it?

Breathe, relax, breathe, relax, everything will be ok. The Rotax sounds healthy and the last service was a biggie. There may be problems with the brakes, and there's the roll problem, but they're both manageable.

Time to head to a new continent, John-boy.

With my left hand lightly touching the stick, my right releases the brakes and slowly pushes the throttle forward. The engine noise builds and we're rolling forwards. A heavy foot on the rudder pedals keeps her centred, and fifty meters later she's pulling herself into the blue skies.

We immediately weathervane to the left and she wants to do her own thing. I try to keep her tracking straight along the centreline of the runway by kicking in a boot full of rudder. A glance around shows brown countryside that could do with a downpour, and either small mountains or bloody big hills in front of us. We're climbing and the Rotax is loud in my old Dave Clark headset.

A look inside the cabin and everything seems secure. All the systems on the Dynon seem good and she's gently pitching up. Do I need a wee? A quick clench confirms I haven't drunk too much, and all is well.

Another look inside the cabin and the Dynon catches my eye. The engine is overheating, and my hand pulls back the throttle a touch. Don't panic, stay calm, relax. We're still climbing, and we'll clear the top of the ridge line with a thousand feet to spare.

It looks greener outside as we push on. A glance down at the Dynon and the engine seems healthier as the temps move back to where they should be. I smile and shake my head.

The stony looking mountainside is getting closer, and there's patches of dark green grass peppered with rocky outcrops. Was there a very slight change in engine tone just then? A glance down from the ridge line to the instruments and a red banner is flashing on the Dynon saying, 'Low Fuel Pressure.'

# Phoenix

The fuel flow to the engine has dropped off a cliff. It's down to 0.08 bar. Will the prop' stop? For fucks sake, really? Deep breath, exhale, deep breath.

We're too near to the hillside, and she won't be able to turn back without stalling. Is the engine ok? A nervous glance inside the cabin and everything's tied down and secure.

A look outside and my gaze takes in rocks embedded in the landscape. The skies are blue and there's no clouds in the firmament. It's just me and Samson.

Vapour lock in the engine? Can it be? Is it so hot that the fuel is turning into a gas and she'll stop? I have Avgas in the tanks so the engine shouldn't falter, should it? Is there a little Mogas screwing things up?

Don't panic, stay calm, my forehead feels tingly, and my scalp is itchy. Make a mayday call to Sitia? Is there time? What's the solution? Should I reduce the pitch angle to increase the fuel flow?

Our stall speed will increase in a turn, so she can't turn back. Time's slowing, and the air feels cooler as my skin bristles.

My left hand gently pushes forward on the stick to flatten out the climb. My eyes cast an involuntary look between my legs at the repaired section of carbon fibre, then flick up towards the approaching landscape.

A glance at the Dynon and our airspeed has dropped to fifty knots, and we're on a knife edge.

There's a slight crook between two peaks on our left, and maybe we can squeeze through the middle. My left foot gently adds in a little rudder and time slows as my eyes move between the Dynon and the landscape.

Reducing the pitch angle seems to have helped, and the fuel flow seems better.

Samson's 200ft above the ground and stones are littered everywhere as we inch towards safety. There's no sign of life outside the cabin and terra firma looks bleak and barren as it gets closer.

Minutes seem like hours and seconds seem like minutes as my consciousness sits with me wondering if we'll clear the ridge. And all I can do is sit still and watch what happens.

And a thought pops into my mind. I calmly pick up my phone, switch it to camera mode, and start taking pictures.

A handful of moments later we crest the ridge with 100ft to spare, and slide beyond reach. And an immense feeling of relief floods through my body, as the hillside falls away and we're thousands of feet up with a beautiful view of the coastline.

What the fuck just happened? Vapour lock? Really?

It feels cooler in the cabin and the outside air will be cooler. Will the fuel revert to being a liquid now? Had Samson just been sat outside with the sun beating down on her for too long? Should we go back to Sitia? Or maybe Eddie could find help in Cairo if we go on?

The engine sounds solid, and that makes my mind up. I am not fucking giving up. Simply follow the reporting points, sound relaxed on the radio, and fly across the fucking Mediterranean. This has just been the consequence of Samson sitting in the sun too long. No need to get stressed.

My view takes in everything outside the cabin, then focuses on the Dynon screen. Everything is in the green. The cabin seems cooler, and my mindset improves a little. Relax, old fella.

My right hand rubs across my chin and then heads back to the throttle. I make my radio calls, change to the departure frequency, then head out to sea.

# Chapter 13b. Mediterranean. 10th May. Day 5

The Rotax is humming along nicely and there's sixty minutes of relatively glorious boredom. The sun is beating against the cabin, but the window vents are open and circulating a stream of cooling air.

The panorama offers azure blue skies complete with a cotton wool haze sitting on the horizon. The sea has a cobalt blue tint and it's beautiful at 8,500ft. I look up through the skylight at the ball of heat in the cloudless sky, and a wry smile crosses my face.

And the engine shudders for a moment.

My right hand involuntarily twitches against the throttle. My eyes dart from the horizon to the Dynon. We're straight and level. Vapour lock again? Is there too much heat under the cowling as the sun plays havoc?

We're out to sea and in no man's land between the Greeks and the Egyptians. My eyes make their way to the immersion suit, and then focus on the little yellow life raft in the passenger footwell.

The engine tone is wavering. The fuel flow readings are dropping. The warning message has flashed up again on the Dynon and we're seconds away from the engine stopping.

A quick glance to the horizon and it's beautiful outside. This can't happen on such a bloody lovely day. I tell myself to stay calm whilst wide-awake eyes search the cabin seeking inspiration.

If the fuel is turning into a gas, how can I get it back to being a liquid? The Turtlepac is securely attached to the passenger seat and my right hand reaches for it. The thick nylon material has been covered beneath a towel and her skin feels cool.

To prevent awkward questions in Crete all the hoses and connectors were kept out of sight below the seat. Likewise, the fuel line into the Rotax is hidden in the passenger footwell. And neither are joined together.

The two ends of my lifeline are separated by a meter. My knees clamp around the stick and both hands reach forward. I make a fumbling attempt to attach the Turtlepac valve to the Rotax fuel line.

I can't reach. Stay calm. Try again. I relax the harnesses strapping me to the seat and lean further forward. The stick shifts position between my legs and India Zulu starts a right turn.

I take a deliberately deep breath and order myself to relax. Then lean back and roll the wings level. An anxious inner voice asks how much time there'll be before the engine folds, and time begins to slow again.

At what point should I give up, activate the emergency beacon, and plan for a damn gentle touch down on the ocean surface? A vision crosses my mind of the wheels touching the water, and flipping Samson upside down.

Would any impact knock me out and lead to drowning? And how cold is the water down there? How much of a shock to the senses will that be? How much time will I have to exit the cabin with the life raft?

I hunch forward in another attempt to hook up the fuel hoses. The bucket seat isn't helping, and my butt is sat on the edge of the seat. Both hands are awkwardly reaching out and Samson starts falling from the sky as she twists and turns into a spiral dive.

Nausea starts to bite as time takes a breather and watches what happens.

# Phoenix

I can't fly and hook up the Turtlepac. It's one or the other. I release the harnesses completely and pull myself downwards into the passenger footwell. My midriff is straddling the centre console, and my head is underneath the binnacle whilst outstretched hands grapple at the hoses.

India Zulu is pitching down and rolling right. A corkscrew motion. Our speed is increasing, and we're heading towards wings coming off time. The hoses reluctantly click together and numb fingers fumble to attach the electric pump.

A feeling of light headedness coupled with a horrendous dose of loneliness pulls at me. I'm fighting gravity and trying to pull my head and torso out of the footwell. We're spinning around like a sycamore seed falling from a tree.

I awkwardly straighten my body and peek above the binnacle. Wide awake eyes look towards the horizon as we twist and turn towards sea level.

I force my arse upwards back into the bucket seat, and both hands start pulling back on the stick. A swift glance around the cabin reassures me that everything is still where it's supposed to be. There's nothing outside, except the royal blue of the Mediterranean.

My skin is tingling as the dive slowly flattens out. A quick scan of the Dynon says we've gone way beyond Samson's VNE figure. Hold together, baby, please hold together. An involuntary glance at both wings leads to a detached inner voice asking which wing will fold first.

Our speed slowly bleeds away, and I tell myself to ignore what I can't control. Will the Turtlepac solve the fuel pressure issue? I shimmy into the harnesses again and my right hand flicks the switch on the auxiliary fuel pump, and I hold my breath.

What's Ava doing right now? Is she happy? Will she live a long full life? Where's Cindy? What's going on in everyone's bubble?

Wide awake eyes keep moving from outside the cabin and back to the Turtlepac. A bubble filled liquid starts to flow, and it disappears towards the engine. Deep breath, exhale, deep breath.

I focus on the Dynon and watch as the fuel flow readings start coming back to life. The digital finger slowly moves right towards the green zone, and the warning message disappears from the screen.

What the fucking hell was all that fucking shit about?

Thank Jehovah for the bloody Turtlepac. At least the engine didn't stop. She just teetered on the edge and scared the crap out of me. I reach across and root around behind the passenger seat. There's a dirty towel there. I grab it and wrap it around my head to fend off the sun.

The view over the sea is beautiful, and we slowly start climbing back into the skies again. I'm walking a tightrope, but the beauty on show blows me away, and a megadose of adrenalin tells me I'm alive.

The main fuses pop.

Deep breath. Deal with it. My head feels clearer now and I might have been getting a touch of sunstroke earlier. The towel is helping and a smile crosses my lips as I realise how bloody silly I must look.

Without electrics, there's no flaps, radio, transponder, and the nav' kit will die. My head swivels left and then to the right. Everything is still stunningly beautiful outside the cabin.

The engine should rumble along without electrical power, shouldn't it? How long does it take a CT to glide from 7,500ft to the sea? My head tries to work out the maths. The rational me thinks fifteen minutes or so. The hot head says, 'who the fuck cares.'

# Phoenix

I close my eyes, take a second, and slowly open them again. Just too many devices being charged? Two Garmins, iPad, Extra fuel pump, iPhone charger.

My right hand unplugs the iPad and pushes the fuses in again. They stay in.

A look at the Dynon and the fuel flow readings are spiking. Really? All this is getting too fucking tedious. What does that mean? This damn well didn't happen when testing above Lancashire...

What does too much pressure mean? Will the fuel pump fold in some way? Will the hoses break free and spray fuel around the cabin or start a fire elsewhere? Is it time to switch back to the main tanks?

A glance up at the sky and a sideways look down at the sea to my left helps form a new plan. My right hand flicks the fuel pump off, and then reaches over to bring the wing tanks back online. There's no discernible pause from the engine as the main tanks pick up the strain immediately.

My left thumb keys the mike, and I try to exude confidence as I call the Egyptians in the hope of hearing someone else's voice. But no one replies.

It's hot inside my bubble and my right hand reaches for my phone. It's too hot to touch, and the screen is dead. My right hand rearranges the towel on my head in an effort to keep me cool. The phone is my canary and when it picks up a signal it makes me feel better; without it, I'm on edge. I put it behind the passenger seat to keep it away from the direct sunlight blasting the cabin.

Then start making continuous calls trying to find a ground station that can hear me and record my position. I don't want to be alone. 'Alexandria Radar, this is Golf Charlie Golf India Zulu, come in please.' There's no reply, and I keep repeating the same mantra over and over.

Ten minutes later, a voice replies and asks for a position report.

There's a faint horizontal line on the horizon and I can't make my mind up whether being over Egypt is a good thing or a bad thing. My inner comedian says at least it's dry land, very dry land.

The Air traffic guys want India Zulu to fly from reporting point to reporting point. The thick Egyptian accent asks that we climb back to 8,500ft. My reply says that I'd rather stick at 7,500ft thank you. The response is, 'negative, climb to flight level 085.'

We're over the desert, now. A reluctant hand pulls the stick back, the nose pitches up slightly, and she starts climbing. The Dynon flashes a warning about fuel starvation and my heart misses a beat. Could the main fuel pump have died? Is this just a problem on climbing?

I move my right hand from the throttle, look around the cabin, and reach for the phone behind the seat. The screen comes back to life and it's picked up a signal from somewhere on the ground. My right hand taps out a text to Simon, my mate the Rotax engineer, in deepest, darkest, Lancashire.

'Hi, how much would you charge to come out to Cairo for a couple of days?'

There's a nearly instant reply and I thank the gods for whichever unidentified mobile phone mast is helping me reach England. Simon says, 'why what's wrong, mate?'

'Couple of fuel warnings. Not sure if the engine pump is struggling. Think the Turtlepac pump has died. The fuel warnings have come on climbs.'

Then I wonder if I've caused the fuel problems. Could one pump have overwhelmed the other? The manufacturer said that wouldn't be an issue. My bloody head hurts as the noise of the Rotax is going through me like a drill into a tooth.

# Phoenix

Simon texts, 'I've just ordered a fuel pump this morning but they are out of stock for 4 weeks mate. You may be getting vapour lock if it's extremely hot.' I reply with information on the fuel flow in level flight. Si thinks that's a bit low. He asks, 'Is the engine struggling at all?'

My reply is, 'Fook, this is stressful. Engine seems fine, at present.' The text back reads, 'Ok, when you land I'll try and talk you through some checks.'

What's my status? Am I struggling? I'm sat thousands of feet above a bloody desert with a towel wrapped around my head and been sat in the same damn spot for hours. I'm hot, dehydrated, and tired. The engine has bitched a few times, my ears hurt, and I've had better days.

Then find myself asking how much shit will hit the fan if we don't climb as requested. Will they send up a jet to intercept us? My left hand lightly pulls the stick back, we pitch up, and start climbing.

The propeller stumbles, and comes to a stop.

One vertical blade stares at me, and there's a rough silence hanging in the air. Looking outside the cabin everywhere is either blue sky or yellow desert. No sign of roads or habitation.

Relax, try to relax, take a deep breath. Think. You have height on your side. What's the best glide speed, 65 knots? Change from the wing tanks to the Turtlepac? Don't use the pump? Try to squeeze fuel from the bag into the engine to manage the fuel flow?

I don't want to be alone and text Simon with a glib comment. 'Funnily enough, the prop just stopped.' Another deep breath, exhale, another deep breath.

Then send a follow-up text saying, 'Changing tanks. Fingers crossed, old chap.'

I'm shitting myself and trying to sound relaxed? What a bloody idiot.

It's quiet in the cabin and a facepalm moment heads my way as my gaze takes in the repaired section of carbon fibre. Unbidden my left hand nudges her into a shallow dive, whilst my right hand moves back to the bag of fuel and starts a bellows type action.

Press down, release. Press down, release.

Then wedge the stick between my legs and reach forward with my left hand. My right is continually pumping the Turtlepac. I take another deep breath and hold it. Then turn the ignition key to off, then turn it right again.

The Rotax restarts, and the propeller starts spinning.

With my left hand back on the stick again my right keeps pressing up and down on the Turtlepac. With a steady pumping action the fuel flow readings on the Dynon are back in the green.

Will the Turtlepac get me to Marsa Matruh? It'll be touch and go. There's no way I can make it back to 8,500ft and there's no way I'm going to bloody try. They can send up a bloody jet if they want to harass me.

Is it time to make a Pan or Mayday call?

Simon will be worrying. My right hand takes a breather from pumping the bag and lifts up the phone. Then quickly taps out a simple text. 'Flying again.'

A couple of minutes later he replies with, 'My Arse was twitching like a rabbits nose for you then!' My bravado has gone walkabout and I just want this over. I text back with, 'Yours was?'

Then feel a pang of guilt that I'd no right to message him about my strife, I just didn't want to be alone. Realisation dawns that if the engine hadn't restarted, if we'd crash-landed in the desert, if I'd

# Phoenix

died, then Si would have been the last person I'd have been connected too.

A deep breath, exhale, deep breath. My left hand picks up the phone and scans through pictures of my girlfriend and daughter, then moves back to the throttle.

In a shallow descent the fuel flow readings are back in the green, at 0.3 bar, without needing manual labour. I pick up the phone and single-handedly text Simon to put his mind at ease. I want to let him know Samson can land, unless something else goes wrong.

My inner comedian feels the need to lighten the mood and my fingers tap out, 'Bloody towel on my head to stay cool. Look like a dick.' His reply is all business, 'Your fuel may be slightly vapour locking with the heat.'

I make a scheduled radio call and get passed over to the Marsa Matruh Military frequency.

Another thick accent asks for a position report. I call out our location and request a descent to 4,500ft. That gets approved, and the voice says that a military cargo aircraft is on a converging course. My right hand leaves the throttle and rubs against my jaw as my eyes wearily cast about.

I report in again at 5 miles out and the Controller asks that we orbit to allow the military types to land.

That's easy. I put her into a shallow turn to the right and watch the sand move past the horizon. The radio cackles and confirms clearance for a very long final approach.

The engine sounds strong again and she's nicely balanced courtesy of the request to hold. I'm fucked, though, and my head's taken too much of a beating.

The airport is in the middle of nowhere and there's a sandy panorama staring back at me. It's home to military jets and transport aircraft. It's our entry point into Egypt where the authorities will cast their eyes over us and search for weakness.

A mile to go and the flaps extend, and she slows. The airfield hoves into focus and there are military bunkers to the left of the runway protecting Egypt's deadliest jets. The tourist in me wants to take a picture, but Eddie's warned against that kind of thing. Taking such happy snaps is frowned upon in North African military circles.

Half a mile to go and I wedge my phone under my thigh, like normal.

We pass over the threshold markings, still descending. The main wheels touch down and I keep the stick back. The nose wheel lightly touches down and she starts pulling to the left, but I'm ready with a boot full of rudder. We slow and my gaze takes in the military airport.

Don't think about the past Johnny, just focus on the present. I key the mic' and ask where to pull off the runway. The military transport has vacated left, and I can see the Hercules moving away in the distance. A heavy Egyptian voice says to turn right and continue to our newly allocated parking space.

I repeat all the instructions back in my best English accent. If I'm lucky they'll think I'm a corporate jockey having a midlife crisis in a Microlight.

It's hot outside the cabin, very hot. There's a light pull on the brakes, we come to a halt, and I stop the propeller. And feel well and truly trucked.

A big sandy coloured fuel bowser drives up beside India Zulu, and I find myself awkwardly climbing out of the cabin to meet half a dozen locals. Some military, some civilian, and all the faces merge into one.

# Phoenix

My anxiety is that a bully of some description makes life difficult. This lot look confused by Samson so we're being given the cheerful, benefit of the doubt, approach.

A senior military officer appears and I recognise the authority figure as someone not to fuck with. My bully has appeared. By return I pull my shoulders back, push my chest out, smile, and project my cheerful Brit abroad persona. Easy going, friendly, relaxed.

The undertone being, 'I'm in your country, I respect you, and we can all be friends, so let's try to make this as painless as possible, shall we.'

A military bus appears and one of the civilians says, 'This way, please.' Half a dozen steps and I'm on board with both of my red bags. It's a tired looking vehicle. No air-con. Shabby seats. A troop carrier.

Thirty seconds later and I'm in the main terminal building. It's a sterile-looking affair and I stand there surrounded by folk who don't know me, and feel insignificant and lonely, again. Eddie's my lifeline now.

Looking down my eyes scan my red rucksack, the big red seaman's bag, red shirt, life jacket, Bermuda shorts and trainers. With hindsight the shorts might have been the comfy approach to a sea crossing, but they're not making me look competent in front of the military.

Then again, dressed like a halfwit, at least no one would confuse me for a James Bond type with an undisclosed agenda.

My bags are put through the X-ray machine and my belt and watch are inspected. A man with a sidearm strapped to his hip indicates I should lift my arms so I can be frisked.

There's a loud conversation going on in Egyptian to my right and a large heavyset guy seems to be arguing with the military commander. From their stances, and the looks being shot in my direction, my guess is that there's a tug of war going on.

There's a break in their conversation and the big guy introduces himself as the handling agent. He's arguing my corner, it seems, and winning. There's raised voices and various military types aim sidewards glances at me.

I tell my new mate I need to file a Flightplan and leave. The military wants passport details and my Egyptian contact information. I'm on edge and drained, but still outwardly projecting cheerfulness.

The handling agent brings a carton of food, and they seem like somebody's idea of rations.

I'm walked to an office where a young fellah, behind a tired looking desk, asks in faltering English about my destination, reporting points, and ETA.

The agent seems to be pulling things together on my behalf and I get pointed towards the exit. The need is to get to October Airport, near Cairo, before sunset. And the sand is falling through the metaphorical hourglass.

With a cheerful smile for all to see I hoist both red bags on my back and make my way over to the bus for the 200-yard drive. The fuel bowser is still there and so are the half dozen onlookers milling about in the unbearably hot sun. All of them have eyes on me as I disembark.

I slowly look at every weather-beaten face, take in the military aspect to the airfield, and realise that if I tell anyone about my engine problems, that's it, game over. And that would put me back into the orbit of the military commander, again.

Should I simply hope everything is ok and carry on? It's bloody insanity to fly any further and I know I'm tired and making shit decisions. The Fox would be calling the CAA by now.

# Phoenix

I walk towards Samson, stand on tiptoes, undo the fuel caps, and the fuel guy starts filling her up.

He glances over at the bowser to check how much she's taken, and accidentally pulls the fuel line out without switching the mechanism off. Fuel pisses everywhere as Avgas spurts over the wing and cascades down onto the tarmac. And all I can do is roll my eyes and curse his parents.

I want my safety net back and foolishly ask for 30 litres to go into the Turtlepac. Common sense says to unbolt the fuel cell from the seat, take it out of the cabin, and lay it on the concrete. My left hand goes to my forehead and starts pinching skin together, and I just don't have the energy for that.

I signal that he should fill the Turtlepac, in situ, and he both looks blankly back at me and shrugs.

Twenty litres go into the bag, and his hand slips. Fuel splashes everywhere inside the cabin and starts pooling on top of the black carpet in the footwell. The onlookers take a collective step back as they sense an issue.

Enough of this, that's enough fuel. I frown, shake my head, and ask for paper towels. Then start mopping up the wasted Avgas inside the cabin. It's time to bid adieu to my carpet and I pull the fuel soaked material out and start dabbing at wet areas of carbon fibre.

The fuel is instantly evaporating in the heat, but there's a lingering smell.

The agent asks for $450, which Eddie primed me for, and I slowly count out the cash as all eyes are on me.

As the last dollar is handed over I shake all the hands I can and climb back on board. The watchers move back a dozen more steps and all of them smile and seem cheerful now that funds have been exchanged.

A yellow 'Follow Me' car rolls into view and takes up position in front of Samson. I key the microphone and ask for permission to start the Rotax. The voice on the radio gives its approval and asks that we follow the vehicle in front.

A hand releases the brake lever and a foot is pressed to the rudder. My eyes focus on nothing other than tracking the yellow line on the tarmac, as the car in front paves the way to the runway.

The small car peels off and I'm on my own. The propeller blades look blurred in front of my tired eyes and there's a lingering fuel smell. I involuntarily carry out my engine checks and click the microphone, 'Golf India Zulu, ready for departure.'

This is madness, Hilton. Just find a hotel and forget about flying for a couple of days. Then leave India Zulu behind and get a commercial flight home.

The radio announces that we're cleared to take off and Samson wheels right onto the runway. I keep the power going as we straighten up, then slowly inch the throttle fully open and she picks up speed.

A last glance takes in the airport building on my right. A look left scans across the hardened, blast-proof, hangars hiding the jets. My gaze focuses straight ahead, and we're airborne.

# Chapter 13c. Egypt. 10th May. Day 5

Eddie's out there somewhere in the distance, and he's my mate.

Sitting below the wheels there's an aquamarine sea leaning against the coastline. Blocks of sandy coloured buildings are surrounding the waterfront and everywhere else has a yellow look to it. A professional sounding voice distracts my internal tourist. The controller asks that we use our VOR to fly a specific radial from our position above the beacon.

My mind flickers to the contents of the Flightplan. Someone's not read it and just assumed India Zulu is fitted with that piece of kit.

I make a mental guess that the radial is from the VOR to our next IFR intersection and head off in that direction. Minutes later the radio chirps up and my inner cynic instantly says, 'Johnny, you've fucked up. They're expecting a professional pilot with all the right kit on board and that's not you or India Zulu.'

The voice on the radio sounds friendly and says to swap frequencies to Alexandria. Then follows up with, 'you're welcome back anytime.' That sounds good to hear, but makes me feel like a fraud.

The day is running away and it's blisteringly hot inside Samson's carbon fibre cabin. A rumbling anxiety about fuel starvation is still there, but we need to make headway towards October Airport before it closes at sunset.

Eddie's previously warned about how quickly it gets dark. The day transitions into night within the click of a finger. If I'm running late the other option is to try a night landing at Cairo International Airport. Do I really want to land at a huge airport with all the bollocks and costs that go with that? Plus, I haven't done a night landing in 20 bloody years…

Time ticks by as we very slowly climb away from Marsa Matruh. The stick is angled back a little and Samson's climbing at 200ft a minute. My headspace says to pull the stick back further and climb faster, but another voice says that'll lead to fuel starvation problems again.

Looking around the cabin, I'm tired, anxious, and cocooned inside my aerial life raft. Bizarrely my flagging state of mind is finding it easier to ignore the prospect of an engine failure, and that seems to lift the pressure somewhat.

The radio comes to life and a thick accent asks. 'Golf India Zulu confirm your position and altitude.' I read back my position then take a deep breath before replying with, 'Golf India Zulu climbing to 8,500ft.'

Three-quarters of an hour later and the air feels cooler up at eight and a half thousand. There's nothing of interest to see anywhere and there's blue skies above the wings, and yellow sand below the white wheel spats.

We move closer to October Airport and should make it with 15 minutes to spare before they close for the night. My left hand pulls the headset from one ear and listens to the painful throb of the Rotax. There's a heartbeat of sorts and I'm listening for any sign Samson is labouring.

I transfer radio frequencies from Alexandria to October Airport with the silent hope that Eddie's down there, somewhere.

The airport is a municipal type facility handling flight training. A distant voice is flying circuits and making downwind calls in another heavy English accent.

The horizon starts becoming indistinct as the outside air takes on a sandier hue. A sandstorm swirls around and there's a dozen miles

# Phoenix

worth of visibility in front of India Zulu. Beyond which is a wall of sand. Looking left and right the skies are clear, but not in front.

My gaze drops to the repaired section of carbon fibre inside the cabin, then absentmindedly moves back to the view outside.

The voices on the radio sound louder and I check the Garmin for my position. Then key the mic' and try to impersonate a competent sounding pilot. 'October Airport, this is Golf Charlie Golf India Zulu 10 miles South West request joining information, please.'

The reply confirms the pressure setting, runway in use, and 20 knot winds. Ten knots faster than I'd like, but my head tells me to just keep calm and carry on.

The view beyond the propeller offers subtly different variations of yellow, as the sand filled sky churns around in front of us. Looking down at the deck there's not a tree or road in sight.

The airport is just visible in the distance and looks like a dismembered finger surrounded by sand.

Scanning the sky I see a dot which my inner radar guesses to be a Cessna 172. Someone's training to be a commercial pilot and is busting his balls to sound professional on the radio. I feel his pain and wonder what his version of the Fox is like.

My thoughts wander away from the winds and sandstorms and ask what the Fox is doing today? What's happening back in Blighty? Is everyone living, laughing, loving? Are they more than 20ft from a toilet? Is Ava practicing her reading? And why the hell aren't I home?

A voice intrudes, and I pull my headspace back to the student pilot as he touches down. Then report, 'Golf India Zulu, final to land.' A disembodied voice confirms we're cleared to touch down.

My right hand moves over to the trim wheel and sets her up to descend. Then moves to my phone and tucks it under my right thigh. The runway barely stands out against the sand and dunes, and a glance at the PAPI lights say we're too high.

She'll be right, Johnny Boy. My right hand closes the throttle, and she slowly loses height. Would the Fox want a touch of power? Do they tell you on the radio if the wind is gusting in Egypt? Is it the same procedure as the UK? It should be, shouldn't it?

I can't think properly, just too knackered. We ghost over the threshold markings and I'm lightly holding on to the stick and gently pulling back. She doesn't want to touch down, but after a few extra heartbeats the sound of the wheels going from zero to fiftyish miles an hour grabs at my senses.

My right leg kicks out, adds in a boot full of rudder, and we're both tracking along the centre line and slowing. A wave of tiredness washes over me and my body feels withered inside.

The radio orders a right turn and instructs me to park in front of the small terminal building. The sun is setting as I shut down the engine and open the gull-wing doors.

The air feels hot and dry, and it's time to climb outside the cabin and shake off 6.3 hours of flying. My tired eyes cast around and try to take in my new surroundings.

A handful of Egyptians are milling around, and there's half a dozen new looking Cessna 172's parked up. A military type appears by the side of India Zulu, and I recognise the way he's holding himself and the set to his face.

Here's another bully to either confront or appease. I find myself staring at his weathered face for a handful of seconds, then force a cheerful smile on my boat race.

I try explaining that I want to see Eddie's friend, the retired General, and park in his hanger. The staccato answer is no, you leave your aircraft where I tell you. He brusquely orders that all my

# Phoenix

kit is taken out of the aircraft for inspection in the isolated terminal building.

A moment later a distinguished-looking man appears by the side of my bully, and I guess he's the General. He smiles at me, shakes my hand, then turns to confront the younger man. And the shit hits the fan. I'm subject to a tug of war between the junior officer and the old warhorse as both of them start shouting at the other.

I just want to go to bed, and start asking myself how the fuck I ended up here.

A slim young man walks over and makes small talk whilst the battle rages around us. He tells me there's only half a dozen privately registered aircraft flying in Egypt. The rest are either Commercial or Military; hence I'm an oddity.

The General turns and begins talking to me. He tells me to keep everything inside the aircraft, then turns back and continues shouting at the bully. Other military types are standing around looking torn. He peels away from the younger officer and gives me a lopsided grin. Then points to a hanger further along the taxiway. Eddie is there.

There's more raised voices and I'm faced with a dilemma. Looking from one authority figure to the other, I make my choice. A General is a good guy to be mates with and I walk backwards and sit my butt inside India Zulu. A car appears and I'm being waved at.

I turn on the Master and call the Tower for permission to start the engine, but there's no reply. Should I just start her up? There's more waving from the General and he jumps in the car. I turn the key, start the prop', release the brakes, then follow the car at walking pace. My headset is half on and half off and the door's open and vibrating behind the wash of the propeller. There's a dry heat to the day that I can taste.

We make it to the General's hangar and I shut her down. The wind is mid-twenty knots, it's very nearly dark, and Samson's wings are rocking.

At this end of the airfield there's a collection of old aircraft littered around that look like they'll never fly again. There's twin-engined aircraft sat about without their engines and old Warriors without doors and propellers. Everything is being slowly sandblasted into submission.

Climbing out of the cabin I walk to the back of the aircraft, push down the tail, and walk India Zulu backwards into the hanger. There's fluid all over the nose wheel spat, and it starts to dribble earthwards.

With the privileges of rank the General has various aircraft wedged into the hanger. Eddie appears and my emotions start to bubble to the surface as my conscious replays the day's events.

My Liverpudlian mate has had sandwiches prepared, and I'm invited to eat up and drink a Coke. General Badran tells me about his hanger, and flying experiences, and it seems I'm to be treated as an honoured guest. I've no idea how to thank him and the best I can muster is to listen intently to his every word and try to ask the questions he wants to hear.

Standing in a rectangular room, complete with large wooden table in the centre, my gaze scans the walls. There's a picture on one wall with a plaque underneath it. Father and son, plus Eddie and the General.

Eddie sees me look at it and, with his gentle brogue, tells me how they died on a circumnavigation 2 years earlier.

I've no answer to that and try to move onto a different topic, the brakes. Eddie's man, Abdullah, volunteers to look at them and we go and hunch over both wheels. Between us we begin the process of replacing the oil in the hydraulic reservoir and squeezing out any air in the system.

# Phoenix

Twenty minutes later Eddie and I are in Abdullah's sedan driving to Cairo. It's pitch black and the air feels dry with an arid taste to it. The journey seems endless until we meet the outskirts of the city's twenty million people. Insecurity starts to bite as my headspace says this place looks cock all like Bolton.

Hard, wiry, looking men are loitering in pools of artificial light and vague figures seem to occupy the shadows. Women are peppered about here and there and they look like they're used to a tough life. Guns and security checkpoints appear irregularly, and Eddie's chatting away and seemingly at ease. My senses tell me we've no chance if we're pulled over by the wrong type of people.

My stomach's churning and it's either the sandwiches are preparing me for the trots, or I'm scared. Eddie casually points to a hotel as we get deeper towards civilisation and says how it was attacked during the last round of domestic troubles. All I can do is smile a thin smile and raise an eyebrow.

The roadway gets more congested, and the traffic slows as a multitude of red taillights fill the road in front of us. There's an abundance of honking horns and a dry heat to the night.

With eyes scanning the accumulated humanity my eyes pick out a sign 50ft above the kerb. It's clinging to an old building and there's a makeshift wooden scaffold leaning against the wall. And two fellah's are awkwardly climbing upwards with a ladder between them.

My head tells me these men need to do what they need to do to make a living, even if it's life-threatening. Life seems like a cheap commodity in Egypt and I can't help but wonder how much a tired pilot is worth to the wrong type of native.

Forty-five minutes later we arrive at a posh looking five-star hotel. There's a military checkpoint outside and inside the lobby there's an airport-style security scanner. I walk through and have my kit looked at by a serious looking man with a holstered weapon. Then sit my thoroughly abused arse on a chair next to the reception desk and go through the checking in process.

There's some form of discount that Eddie's been able to negotiate, and I feel completely thankful that I can call him my friend.

I just want to lie down and fall asleep, but Eddie mentions that Man Utd are on TV in one of the basement bars in the hotel. So I reluctantly agree to take my stuff upstairs to the room, have a shower, and then meet up for a pint.

Twenty minutes later, we're sat in a smoky bar watching the football. United lose, but a voice tells me it's not the end of the world. My eyes won't stay open, and I make my apologies to Eddie, shake his hand, give him a bear hug, and then head out of the bar.

In a mild daze I walk my way across the vast lobby area, complete with half a dozen themed restaurants on the left, and find the lift.

Ten minutes later I'm in bed typing out a tired synopsis of my day to the couple of hundred people following the flight on Facebook. I upload my notes and fall into a comatose-like sleep.

The phone rings. I slowly open my eyes and wonder where the fuck I am. Moving my wrist towards my face, I can just make out that my Mickey Mouse watch says, '11.30pm.' What the hell...

Pulling the phone from its cradle a hurried voice tells me to go downstairs to the bar. What? Why? The answer is, 'you gave your room number and signed for the drinks, but you need to pay cash, sir.'

My sleepy reply becomes, 'Can I do it tomorrow, please.' In turn, the voice says, no, I need to go downstairs now. My patience leaves me, 'I am not damn well coming downstairs. You know my room number. I paid a £300 deposit when I checked in and, if you insist, I'll pay cash tomorrow, but I am not getting out of bed now. Good night' and then I hang up.

# Phoenix

My head hits the pillow, but I can't get back to sleep. It's been a tough day and chasing me for a tenner is just too damn annoying. I reach for the handset again knowing that unless I get this off my chest it'll just fester. I get put through to the duty manager and groggily make a complaint.

Feeling like I've resolved my issues my head settles back onto the oversized pillows, and sleep finds me again. At half-past midnight the phone rings. I clumsily reach over again for the handset and a voice asks, 'Can I ask, Sir, did the Duty Manager resolved your complaint?'

I grunt a polite reply, and the voice then wishes me a pleasant stay and a goodnight.

It's dark in the room, but my headspace is coming round again and sleep won't take me back. My hand reaches across to my iPad on the bedside table and there's a message on Facebook from an infamous ferry pilot. He rambles on and uses the word, 'irresponsible' with respect to the flight.

A moment later I'm wide awake and well pissed off.

Maybe he's right, but if I don't reply, I won't sleep. I get out of bed, walk to the walnut desk by the mirror, and start typing. Without realising it the text turns into a long narrative about the current state of affairs.

Pressing 'Post' on the comment I climb back in bed, lie back on the pillow, and wonder what Ava's day has been like.

And then resolve that if any other fucker bugs me tonight they're going to get seriously bitch slapped.

# Chapter 14. 11th, 12th, 13th May. Egypt

My eyes flutter open and take in my surroundings. Twin beds sit in the middle of a decent looking room and I'm in the one farthest from the windows. There's an expensive looking telly, mini bar, and thick curtains that suggest no unwanted light will be allowed in.

A beleaguered look over at the phone and it's 9.30am. Cindy arrives today and Eddie's offered to pick me up and drive us to the airport.

My mind goes back to yesterday and it all seems like a blur. How the hell did I get through all that? I reach for my iPad, looking for a message from Cin, and remember last night's Facebook message. Then re-read the message I put out.

*'Please note. When I got India Zulu back from Germany she had been signed off by a Test Pilot. We also thought we'd resolved a number of issues that the German repairers had fluffed…*

*The Rotax is a very reliable engine. India Zulu has been thoroughly serviced and inspected. Any suspicious squeak or misfire has been investigated and resolved. We did think we'd resolved the aircraft rolling to the left (after a few tweaks) but … she still wants to turn left and dive.*

*My solution to this is to fly her out of balance for a while (which I don't like doing) and bank the aircraft through a right hand turn to move fuel (weight) to the right wing. This seems to work. I've asked a whole range of people about what I might expect on this flight. I've tried to take on board everyone's suggestions and thoughts. As far as I'm aware there are no other Rotax powered aircraft in Egypt and one pilot, yesterday, told me there are only five private pilots in the whole country.*

*This may be right or wrong, but the flying community is definitely small. People don't fly for fun here. In terms of 'vapour lock', if that's what the issue was, I*

# Phoenix

*have trained to restart the engine (on one particular flight over Carr Valley where I did it a few times), so the prop' stopping is stressful but not paralysingly so. The extra fuel cell (sat on the passenger seat) is my peace of mind / plan B. It represents an additional two or so hours flying to add to the aircraft's existing endurance of 8'ish hours. I haven't pushed anywhere near these limits.*

*From a weather perspective it's tough juggling the conditions across hundreds and hundreds and hundreds of miles. According to my sources, yesterday, it shouldn't have been quite as windy as it was at my departure and destination airports. The slight irony is that those were maybe two of my best landings of the trip... This hasn't been an easy flight so far. Let's call it 'testing'... If you're a Microlight Ferry Pilot (specifically XYZ) I'm trying my best to go round the planet with the intent to raise money for charity (www.justgiving.com/Jon-Hilton).*

*I am not the complete pilot & I take my hat off to every instructor and professional pilot... I have a lovely girlfriend and daughter, but this is something I need to do. Regards, JH.'*

I finish reading the last sentence and feel bugged that I rose to the bait by replying last night. But then again, I did take a series of stupid bloody decisions to fly on, any of which could have been fatal.

I fall out of bed and head to the shower. Thirty minutes later I've navigated breakfast and spotted Eddie walking across the expansive foyer towards me and my Bermuda shorts.

There's small talk, general pleasantries, and I find my tired eyes looking at my Liverpudlian friend realising that his advice can keep me alive.

We walk through the hotel's security scanner and head outside into the heat. Abdullah is there with his sedan and we drive through the bustling traffic to the airport. I amble through various random elements of small talk as we fight the traffic.

A large sign spelling out 'Cairo Airport' hoves into view and Eddie casually mentions how he got arrested there for plane spotting a few years before. We park up and wait inside the vast Airport terminal. Eddie needs money from me to pay a local to find Cindy and I duly hand it over. Lots of people are coming and going and everywhere is bustling with movement and humanity.

And I'm adding to the general ambience courtesy of my blue shirt, tired looking shorts, and flip flops. I find myself walking round in circles, with my mind in neutral, as my inner pilot tells me I should be flying on tomorrow instead of welcoming Cindy. But, I love her.

She appears in the distance and walks towards me. Blue leggings, matching blue top, cheerful smile, and such a beautiful face. She's blessed with blonde hair, has a slim figure, and is just lovely.

I reach out and her feet leave the deck for a handful of moments as I lift her up, and we cling to each other. We kiss and then there's a flurry of questions. She asks how yesterday's flight went, and I respond with my mantra of, 'fine thanks.' Then add a forced smile.

We drive back to the hotel and Eddie suggests we all go out for a meal. I look over at Cin and mumble that we'd like an evening to ourselves, please.

Day 7

The following morning we meet Eddie and agree to do the tourist thing. We hit the road and every car, without exception, has dents and scratches. I'm pushing out a cheerful persona but I'm painfully aware that when Cin leaves, I'll be alone again.

The four of us spend two hours driving towards the Pyramids. The sights and sounds of Cairo float by as the traffic stops and starts. People, urban noises, honked horns, and life on the edge.

Sitting next to Cindy, with my arm wrapped around her, my eyes lazily scan across all types of vehicles. We pass an irregular number of VW camper vans, and, without exception, each has its engine hatch propped open as a way of moving more air around the compartment.

# Phoenix

An inner voice tells me that everywhere away from an air-con unit is just too damn hostile.

We arrive at the Pyramids and it's both dusty and oppressively hot in the direct sunlight. The once magnificent mountains of rock look weathered and tired, but not completely beaten by the years they've viewed.

Myriad faces come and go and yet again I'm on alert for theft, violence, or deception of some sort. By contrast my girlfriend seems completely relaxed and is enjoying life as a tourist. Our appearance attracts various sets of hungry eyes and our driver, Abdullah, shouts at a collection of approaching locals and wards them away.

Strolling past the Great Pyramid Eddie introduces us to a few of his friends, Ragab and Sabry, who happen to manage a number of Camels. It seems obligatory that we go riding and, yet again, I'm out of my comfort zone.

We all dismount and a camel called Charlie Brown kisses me as one of its party tricks, and it's one of life's surreal experiences.

We slowly make our way back to a tourist type restaurant as a group of children approach. I'm bemused, until I realise they're begging. The child elbowing her way to the front of the small gang is wearing a Manchester United top, and it throws me for a moment.

Begging, but wearing a Man U top? And such a young girl? It's oppressively hot and my gaze extends to the Pyramids, and I can't help but wonder what kind of life these kids will have.

Driving off they chase after the car in the hope, Abdullah says, that we'll throw something for them.

My mind wanders away from me again and mulls over our surroundings. Egypt offers a different culture, different lifestyle, different climate, and none of it is in any way comparable to

Bolton. My hometown might be a gloomy, partly derelict, shit hole but it's where I belong.

Years ago I looked up the names of people who were Bolton born and bred. The logic being that where you come from doesn't define who you are, or what you can become.

Bolton is the birthplace of the actors Robert Shaw, Sir Ian McKellen and Peter Kay. Plus, a World Cup winning footballer, and one of the most successful British Gold winning Olympic athletes of all time.

Interestingly, the inventor of the first self-propelled torpedo came from Bolton. And so did one of the Great Grand Parents to the Von Trapp children, from the Sound of Music.

Admittedly, from what I can tell, every successful person seems to bugger off and flee the town as soon as they've made their money. But I guess compared to other parts of the world, my town ain't too bad at all.

Day 8

After a good night's sleep Cindy and I sit through an underwhelming à la carte breakfast (costing a mammoth £42.00) and then we meet Eddie by the hotel pool.

For such a big hotel it's a relatively small pool area. My thought processes suggest it's too oppressively hot outdoors, hence the Egyptians consider that burning in the sun isn't such an enjoyable process. And consequently only offer a small space for such activities.

Cin's sat on a sun lounger, and I try to gently suggest that without sun cream she'll burn in a handful of minutes. She pouts and lets me know that she'll put cream on when she's, 'got a bit of colour.'

# Phoenix

I roll my eyes, shake my head from side to side, and decide to go for a swim. Looking over at the sign by the side of the pool it says it's 37 degrees in the shade.

After my last lap Eddie appears and sits down on a sun lounger. I climb out of the pool and sit opposite him. The water quickly dries on me without the aid of a towel and we exchange chitchat. He's on edge because a flight he's been working on has lost contact with everyone. Cindy's within earshot so I try to change the subject.

She overheats in her bikini, makes her apologies, and heads indoors to cool off. Eddie and I chat about flying in general, the difficulties of using an iPad to lodge flight plans on the Garmin app, and about two other recent flying incidents in the press.

I Google the jet incident he's just mentioned and find a report in the Independent.

*'Pilot killed at Evans airshow had little experience on jets.*

*A pilot who died in a plane crash at an airshow founded by broadcaster Chris Evans had "not enough experience" flying jets after he left the RAF for the City, a report has found.*

*Kevin Whyman, 39, was flying a Folland Gnat in a display at the CarFest event at Oulton Park, Cheshire, on August 1 last year. A report by the Air Accidents Investigation Branch (AAIB) stated that the aircraft was performing a low-level roll when its nose dropped. As Mr. Whyman attempted to regain control, he carried out an "inappropriately timed" action that "made the situation irrecoverable".*

*Mr. Whyman was a Cambridge graduate who coxed the university eight to victory in the Boat Race in 1996 and' 97. He left the RAF in 2001, had not flown high-performance, swept-wing aircraft before converting to the Gnat and had a "low average annual flying rate" of 12 hours over the past five years, the AAIB said.'*

The second crash Eddy mentioned was about the self-styled, *'Bird in a biplane.'* I'd heard the same rumours he had that her 'solo flights' were made with a co-pilot hiding himself round and about.

Cindy reappears and I change the subject again as she walks within earshot. She politely interrupts and says she's tired and wants a lie down in the room. We resume our conversation and I ask Eddie if he'll run me to the local store so I can buy a new funnel, WD40, brake fluid, and then go on to exchange more currency.

Taking a swift look down at my watch, Mickey's hands are swimming, and my 30 year old water-resistant watch appears to have given up the ghost. A slow shake of the head follows and a new timepiece gets added to the shopping list

With Cin upstairs, Eddie, myself, and Abdullah head out. Eddie's clearly comfortable out and about in downtown Cairo, but I have that uncomfortable feeling again as a fight or flight sensation sits with me.

We drive round the block from the hotel and roll past a new looking BMW. The rear window has been smashed, there's a crowd, and a young woman is stood there crying. From what we can tell she was forced to stop, had the window smashed, and was robbed.

We drive on and find a local hardware store. I'm trying to put all my anxieties to one side and look like I belong. Getting nearly everything on my list I see Eddie with a funnel. I ask for it, so I can pay, but he keeps a tight hold and reaches into his trouser pocket.

'Errr, I'll pay,' I say, and he replies with, 'I'll buy it for you.' A puzzled look seems to wander across my forehead and he follows up with, 'dealing with pilots is my hobby, as well as my job, and I want to help.'

We jump in the car and head out again on a further foray to find a watch of some description. Twenty minutes later I concede defeat

# Phoenix

and mention that I'll just have to get by with the electrical devices I have, phone, Dynon, iPad.

Eddie swivels round to face me, as I'm sat in the back with my existing purchases, and smiles. Then removes his own watch and hands it over.

I utter my thanks and can't help but wonder how I've been so fortunate to meet this guy.

<u>Note:</u>

*It latterly turns out the hotel has six pools, and Eddie generally got his pilots into the exclusive VIP swimming area. Royalty, the rich and famous, and some chap called Mo Salah (who plays, or played, for one of the less well known Northwest football clubs) were regular attendees.*

# Chapter 15. 14th May. Egypt. Day 9

I'm wide awake sometime before 6am and my eyes reluctantly roam around the room. Then my focus slowly turns to the day ahead, and a feeling of regret surfaces that I didn't ask Cindy to marry me last night. But I'm scared of what's ahead and can't cling to her in order to make myself feel better, can I?

I think she'd be happy if I asked. She hates flying but got on a jet to come and find me, bless her. Was she expecting a proposal?

I gently prod her and wonder if there's time to get in a quicky before I have to get up. She's still sleeping away, so I gently nudge a bit harder. The unconscious female doesn't seem to realise that Plan B involves pretending an earthquake has hit the room.

Thirty minutes later I'm showered and trying to check through all the stuff I've thrown on the bed. Everything needs to be accounted for and then crammed into my red Seaman's bag.

We head downstairs for a swift breakfast, pay our hotel bill, and then wait for Eddie. Cindy's standing next to me but looks lost. Should I propose now? The moment passes as Eddie and Abdullah appear at reception.

There are pleasantries and small talk, and I realise I'm slowly distancing myself from everyone again - one flight at a time, one day at a time. Don't get emotional, don't hold on too tight to anything. Just go through the daily process of looking at the weather, winds aloft, making judgement calls, organising flight plans, and then go flying.

Cin wants to drive out with us to the Airport but I didn't like the trip when I did it, and I sure as hell don't want her anywhere near

# Phoenix

the seedier side of Cairo. She has to be safe. We hug, say our goodbyes, and my eyes unfocus slightly as I stare at her beautiful face, and I so desperately want to marry her.

Ninety minutes later and the car is nearing both October Airport and India Zulu. Roughly 8:30am and it is getting hot. There's a dusty checkpoint at the perimeter of the isolated airport and Abdullah speaks to the guy with the gun, and they spray words at each other.

Memories surface from previous conversations and it dawns on me that if anyone asks about Eddie's Visa status, then we're all fucked. My headspace tries to put those thoughts from my mind and my gaze scans the inside of the car, and then goes left and right.

A railway track crosses our path, and it seems to lead beyond the horizon to an infinity of sand. If India Zulu loses power above the desert I might walk away from the landing, but I'll die here.

Twenty minutes later we're at the General's hangar. The hope was for an early departure but there's headaches getting the fuel bowser over. Time seems to crawl along and I find myself sitting in the meeting room, staring up at the plaque dedicated to 58-year-old Babar Suleman and his 17 year old son.

If I hadn't had the conversation with the Fox about stall speeds increasing in a tight turn, would I have tried to turn away from the mountain in Crete? Would I have remembered that from my original flight training? Or would I have panicked and crashed?

My thoughts go back to the Fox's office and a previous conversation. Putting a figure on how much the stall speed increases in a turn has been the only thing I've ever said that actually impressed him. With everything else he just rolls his eyes and puts out that cheerful look that seems to say, 'you are such a dick, Hilton.'

Maybe all Chief Flying Instructors possess that gift.

I pull my thoughts back to the heat of the desert and tell myself to stop dwelling in the past. Poor Babar and Haris made one poor decision and died, so just put that subject in a box, learn what you can, and move on.

Time catches up with events and it's time to go check everything is safely stowed away inside Samson. I stand up and make my way towards her. It's dusty, hot, and the air has a light gritty taste to it that I can feel in my lungs.

Today's plan was to wear the Captain's shirt, but I felt like such a bloody fraud trying it on this morning. Nor could I bring myself to wear both it and the accompanying epaulettes.

With the Flightplan filed I say my goodbyes, hug Eddie, and tug India Zulu out of the hangar into the heat. I climb onboard, pull down the gull-wing door, and feel both claustrophobic and lonely.

My fingers put the key in the ignition, push in the Master fuses, press the red mic' button, and ask for permission to start the engine. Permission is given from the Tower and I turn the key to the right and light the touch paper.

The Dynon displays an outside air temperature of 40 degrees, so it'll be hotter inside the enclosed cabin. The radio comes alive and a thick Egyptian voice tells me there will be a 40 minute wait before I can go anywhere. Really? What the fuck?

My temperature's rising and sweat is oozing from every pore. The back of my T-shirt is stuck to the seat as I shut down the engine and do a cut throat gesture over towards Eddie. Then slowly climb out of the cabin and walk over to pass on the news.

The sun feels like a lead weight pressing on my head as I push Samson back inside. The heat can't be good for her. Will this lead to vapour lock again? How scared should I be? I'm bloody overheating, so she must be.

# Phoenix

With her sat back in the hangar I take a deep breath and lean forward to look at both brake calipers again. Then sit down on the deck and cast my eyes over Samson.

A lonely inner voice asks whether Cin's by the pool? It's too hot to sit outside for more than five minutes without burning. Has she got sun cream on this time?

Time slowly ambles by and it's time to move again. There's one last goodbye to Eddie and Abdullah, then I pull Samson by the prop' back into the harsh sunlight. Looking to the right of the hangar the desert offers a fine yellow sand, and it presses against both sides of the tarmac taxiway.

I pull the door down, spark up the Garmin, look around the cabin, then check everything electrical is properly hooked up and charging. The Garmin has all the reporting points programmed in and we're ready.

Straight to Sharm and then onto Amman. Time's drifted away and there's no extra meat on the bone, plus the Indian Visa is about to run out and I need to fly. Will Cindy be ok getting home?

My left thumb presses the red button on the stick and my distracted voice says, 'October Tower, Golf Charlie Golf India Zulu at General Badran's hangar requesting Engine Start, please.'

A voice replies and confirms the Rotax can be fired up. Here we go. I wave goodbye to Eddie one more time, release the brakes, and we start rolling. The 'Follow Me' car swishes past and I push the right rudder pedal, and we move away from the dusty hangar and follow it.

Samson's still pulling left, but weirdly it feels like a very smooth turning motion and not something grabbing. My hand brushes my jaw, rubs against light stubble, and a frown makes its way across my face.

The Follow Me car stops at the holding point just in front of the runway, and we halt behind it. My head turns to look both left and right, but there's nothing to see except yellow sand and an oppressively hot sky.

The preflight checks get completed, mags tested, flaps down, brakes holding, and my voice calls out, 'Golf India Zulu ready for departure.' The response from the tower confirms the wind speed, direction, and that there will be another 10 minute wait.

Really? Why? Military activity in the area? Or am I being fucked with? And I'd just blindly followed the car, but the winds mean Samson will be taking off with a tailwind.

A fully loaded India Zulu is not good with the wind behind her. She wobbles into the air and I don't need that stress.

My gaze takes in the temperature sensor on the Dynon screen and then looks down at my right hand. It's idly resting on the throttle lever and I can see individual bubbles of sweat starting to form. If that's happening to my skin, what's happening under the cowling? How hot is the fuel?

'October Tower. This is Golf India Zulu. I need to take off now or return to the hanger.'

An irritated voice tells me I'm cleared to take off, and I offer my thanks in as pleasant a voice as I can muster. Sometimes being very polite, really, really, pisses people off and that thought puts a lazy smile on my face.

The Follow Me car turns around and drives away. Do I really want to fly or should I go back to the hotel, make love to my girlfriend, and ask her to marry me?

A second later I release the brakes and slowly, smoothly, push the throttle forward. Samson enters the runway and pulls to a stop amongst the long white threshold markings. My eyes pick out

# Phoenix

dozens of black dots where aircraft wheels have hit hard, and I start asking myself questions.

What should I do if vapour lock happens? How much would a crash landing on sand hurt? Will a very gentle climb be the key? Are the met reports compiled in the same way as the UK? My head aches and the sooner we start moving at speed, the sooner cooler air can be vented into the cabin.

My right hand pushes the throttle forward, and we're accelerating. The Rotax is fully awake and it's loud in the cabin. I feed in a little right rudder to correct the pull to the left and the nose wheel lifts off the tarmac. She's sluggish with an 8 knot tailwind but she needs to fly of her own accord. Another couple of seconds, and the main wheels leave the ground.

She feels heavy, and I gently pull the stick back and we climb away from Eddie and Cindy. The radio wakes up and the Tower asks that we climb to 6,000ft above the airfield before departing east.

Glancing down at the Dynon our climb rate is only 200ft a minute. The engine seems fine with that, but there's no time for a leisurely climb to 6k in order to get in and out of Sharm El Sheikh and make Amman by closing time. I need to push her harder.

My left hand pulls the stick back and we pitch up. My eyes narrow on the Dynon as the engine temps start increasing. The readings leave green, pass amber, and approach red.

A facepalm moment happens and I tell myself I'm not going to land at October again. I need to make this work. My head leans against the plexiglass window and my jaded eyes look down past the wheel spats to the airfield below.

It's still hammeringly hot inside the cabin. Scorching air is being vented through both the small window vents and it's circulating around my head and torso.

## Jon Hilton

A call to the Tower follows, 'Golf India Zulu, I'm at 4,500ft and am departing enroute.' There's no reply.

I level out the climb, reduce the strain on the engine, and my eyes are glued to the temperature sensors as they slowly start dropping back down towards green. Did the Tower want 6,000 for a reason?

I know the Egyptian military are carrying out military activity against ISIL. How high does a bullet reach if it's fired straight up? Is Samson at risk from small arms fire?

Is there a height at which I'm considered identifiable and not a terrorist risk?

The Garmin points towards both the Airway and Cairo's Air Traffic zone. The Flightplan says Flight Level 080 and given time we can make 8,000ft, but what the mother of all cocks am I doing above a bloody desert? What's Ava doing today? Is it raining in Bolton? Has Cindy eaten?

Time moves forward and I write down what I want to say to Cairo on my knee board. The voices of jet pilots intrude through my headset as they talk to the ground station. American voices, English voices, Italian, and heavy Egyptian voices.

The Americans are struggling with their reporting points and seem lost. Is that a US accent onboard a commercial jet or military aircraft? The voice doesn't sound like it has a face mask on, so not a fast jet.

Not for the first time, I'm so thankful for being British.

There's a break in the radio chatter and I project my neutral English accent and introduce myself to the Air Traffic guy at Cairo. He acknowledges everything I've said, and asks India Zulu to climb to 14,000ft.

What? I can't do that. It's not on my Flightplan and the engine can't manage more than 11 or 12,000ft. Anything above 10k and

# Phoenix

Hypoxia becomes a risk. What does Hypoxia mean? Even worse decision making and blacking out?

'*Negative, Golf India Zulu unable to climb above Flight Level 1,0*'. He asks again for 14k, and I say the same thing but add that she has a maximum ceiling of 10,000ft.

The voice asks that I climb to Flight Level 1,1. My headspace starts to wonder why they want me above my Flightplan? Do these things just happen, or is there something else going on?

My voice acknowledges the climb to 11,000ft. If we climb slowly, will I be able to acclimatise myself and avoid Hypoxia? And an inner voice tells me I'm pushing too hard, again.

A glance around the cabin and everything is tied down and secured. The yellow life raft is in the other footwell. The Turtlepac is on the passenger seat underneath its towel, and the green file is open with the Sharm plate on show.

The engine shudders.

A quick glance down at the Dynon and the fuel flow readings are dropping. The engine's about to die, and time moves slower.

I gently push forward on the stick. The Turtlepac hose is already attached and ready to be used. My right index finger moves forward to switch off the main tanks and bring the Turtlepac online.

Looking outside the cabin, there's nothing. No habitation, no buildings, no roads. There's sand and a collection of canyons. Water flowed down there once, but not for a thousand years.

Reaching over to the Turtlepac I start slowly pumping the bag, up and down, up, and down. Small bubbles appear in the hose as my eyes watch fuel disappear towards the engine. My head swivels left and right, taking in the nothingness outside the cabin.

The engine readings pick up as the Avgas reaches the Rotax. Right, so all I have to do is keep a bellows action going with my right arm, and fly the aircraft at the same time. And remember to breathe.

Time inches along for 20 minutes and my arm starts aching and wants respite. Sweat has made my T-shirt stick to my chest and arm.

A message flashes up on the Dynon. 'Temperature out of Spec'. Ohh, for fucks sake, really? Does that mean the damn thing is about to fail and kill all my instruments? Is the temperature behind the binnacle north of 50 or so Celsius?

It's like a bloody sauna in front of the damn thing, so god knows what's cooking behind it. What to do?

Keep pumping the fuel into the engine and try to climb faster? Is it time to make a Mayday call and declare an emergency? Should I just get height onside and give myself time to think?

I feel drained, insecure, and my tongue rubs its way over my dry lips and my focus takes in the yellow horizon.

Should I concede defeat and fly down to the deck. Then manage the best landing I can on the alien landscape whilst the prop's still spinning and the Dynon's alive? But would anyone get to me? And who's down there?

Twenty minutes later and we've inched up to 11,000ft. My right arm hurts from continuous bloody pumping but, as a plus, the Dynon's warning message has disappeared. The Outside Air Sensor show's a comfortable 16c and all the readings are back in the green now.

I swap back to the wing tanks and the Rotax doesn't miss a beat. I relax my grip on the stick for a second and she starts to pull left, and the wing drops away.

# Phoenix

I shake the numbness out of my arm, keep a firm hold of the stick, and roll the wings level. An inner voice curses the Germans for botching the repairs. Decision made, I'm bloody voting Brexit.

Height equals stronger headwinds.

I start pressing the buttons on the Dynon, to scroll through the different screens, and figure out how many nautical miles she can manage when pushing a 25 knot headwind. Different numbers stare back at me, and I try to work through best and worst-case scenarios.

Taking a sideways glance at the Turtlepac, realisation dawns that the extra fuel she carries is a necessary evil. That spare bag of Avgas is my lifeline and safety net.

Moments later it occurs to me that the Turtlepac could also be deadly in the event of a crash. And another thought asks how painful being burnt alive would be. My gaze absently trips around the cabin and settles on the repaired section of carbon fibre between my legs.

My train of thought gets interrupted as Cairo call to say bye, and a disinterested voice gives out the next frequency to call. I dutifully switch frequencies and radio to say hi, but there's no reply. That vulnerable feeling starts to bite again, and I find myself taking another slow look around the cabin.

Then lean my head against the window and feel the beat of the Rotax run through my body. This is my bubble. I take a long lingering look at the left wing tip and realise that right now I really want to be a passenger, and not the pilot.

There's jet jocks on frequency somewhere up at 40,000 feet, and listening in it seems they can't make contact with the ground either. A couple of disembodied voices ask that other jets make relay calls on their behalf to different ground stations.

Figuring it's the done thing, I key the microphone and pass my position to an Egyptair jet five or six miles above my head.

We move closer to Sharm and switch to their approach frequency. More jet jocks are talking and the showy buggers seem to confirm their speed in Mach numbers. One voice confirms they're bouncing along at Mach Point Seven Nine. My eyes wander from the horizon down to the Garmin, and coincidentally Samson's managing 79 knots across the sand.

There's another moment of, '*what the fook am I doing here*' as my left thumb hovers over the red button on the stick, ready to call up Sharm El Sheikh International Airport.

If the guy on the ground thinks I'm a dick it'll make life more complicated. My right hand pulls a piece of paper from my green file. My gaze looks away from the horizon and focuses on writing down exactly what I want to say. Another glance takes in the Approach Plate so I can hopefully second guess his reply.

Looking up from my notes, Samson's started rolling left and we're in a 30 degree banked turn. There's a lingering feeling of depression as I roll the wings level again.

Sharm asks that we report overhead, '*Bravo Mike,*' and the chap quotes all the ILS and Localiser details. I repeat back everything verbatim, then my mind races and asks where the hell Bravo Mike is hiding.

The opportunist in me thinks, '*fuck this for a lark*' and I hear my voice politely ask for vectors to the airport. I need them to make it easy for me.

The pleasant-sounding voice gives me a heading to fly and asks that we expedite our landing. There's no time to balance out the tanks, so my headspace is twitchy and on edge.

# Phoenix

Samson passes over the coastline and there's isolated blocks of habitation below the wheels. From above they look like urbanised rectangles surrounded by desert.

We pass over more urban properties and slowly approach the runway. A light-headed me reaches forward to find the flap switch, then wandering eyes look round the cabin to check everything is secured.

My gaze focuses directly on the runway and a hand blindly takes my phone from the centre console and wedges it under my right thigh, like normal. A glance upwards takes in both fuel gauges, at the wing roots, and we've much more fuel in one tank than the other.

All I need to do is touch down, get my paperwork sorted, and then head to Amman. But I'm knackered, drained, and my head hurts. Do I want to do all this again?

We're a mile from the airport, then a quarter of a mile, and then the airport seems huge, massive. There's two enormous runways and a giant terminal building edging a domineering Tower structure.

Seconds seem to take minutes as we approach the runway threshold. It's hot in the cabin, my ears ache, and my body's numb from inaction.

There's a steady descent. And touchdown.

Landing on such a wide runway seems strange. Like a fly landing on a road. The radio sparks up, and a voice orders a left turn and says, '*expedite*.' Samson wheels off the runway and thirty seconds later there's a roar from behind. My head pivots round as a brightly coloured passenger jet touches down and thunders along the runway.

The voice says to switch to the Ground Frequency and I'm politely told where to park. A foot full of rudder keeps India Zulu tracking along the yellow line on the taxiway, and my focus moves from not crashing, to not looking overly stupid.

We roll onto our parking slot, and I close the throttle, pull on the brakes, and shut down the engine. The headset stays half on and half off in case further instructions come through. My shoulders slump forward whilst my hands rub around my face and forehead.

What's the protocol on shutting down? My left hand opens the door and I wriggle my arse so I can get both feet dangling outside the cabin. The newbie passenger jet has parked up a couple of hundred feet away. My mind wonders what the cabin crew, and passengers, must be thinking as they look over.

My inner cheapskate starts to ponder how much I'll be charged for parking next to a Boeing 737. And will the Tower make sure we're not blown away by a set of Rolls Royce engines when she starts up again?

A white Mazda appears and a good looking young guy gets out the passenger door. I'm taken to customs and my attire goes down like a lead balloon with the military. The handling agent doesn't care what I look like, but the soldiers manning the security scanners do not look impressed with my Bermuda shorts and T-shirt.

It's been a tough day, but I'm alive, and whilst any number of things could have happened, I'm fine.

Emptying my bags for inspection eats away at my schedule. Glancing at Eddie's watch I know it's going to be tight flying onwards. I say the same to the Agent as my onward Flightplan ticks down, and he just smiles.

I'm cleared by security and we race back to the aircraft. I jump out of the car, quickly walk round Samson, and carry out a quick inspection. There's light dust everywhere but no more leaking brake fluid, escaped antifreeze, or oil. With my rucksacks safely stowed on board again I push in the Master Fuses, turn on the radio, and ask for permission to start the engine.

# Phoenix

*'Negative India Zulu, your Flightplan has expired and you need to resubmit a new one'*. Really? My head hurts, I'm drained, I need a break, and just don't have the energy to fight on. The handling agent is still in his car, with the air-con going, and his dark aviator glasses stare back at me. I beckon him over.

Sat in my fake leather seat I explain that time has run out and I'm looking to stay overnight. Then point to a large 'open hangar.' It's a big space open to the elements, but away from the jets and offering some protection from the wind.

A smile forms on his face as he explains that the Presidents jet would usually go there. By reply I ask if I can park there overnight. I add a tired smile, and he tells me he'll try to get permission to park there for free.

He makes a phone call, smiles into the handset, and makes various hand gestures whilst walking around in circles. Then looks over at me and gives the thumbs up.

Twenty minutes later Eddie's been heroic again and organised a hotel. I send a message to Cindy and she replies and says Eddie's looking to extend my flight clearance into Jordan until tomorrow.

Samson gets secured in the Presidents spot. I drape my belongings over each shoulder, and make my way through the security perimeter again. Then it's a short taxi ride to the modern four-star hotel.

I'm drained, and not at my best, but there's a need to get into either a pool or the sea to rinse my body of sweat. Am I suffering from dehydration or just general tiredness?

Thirty minutes later I'm surrounded by tourists at the hotel's private beach. There's a pontoon stretching out into an empty lagoon, and I'm drawn to it. I claw off my T-shirt and drop both it and my room key on the yellow sand. Then walk zombie-like along the plastic pontoon, and plunge into the sea as the evening sun starts to set.

The water's crystal clear and I can feel a dozen hours of perspiration dissipate in the cool saltwater of the Red Sea. A hotel steward appears on the beach and waves. He points to a sign and awkwardly says the beach is now closed. I've no fight left in me, and reluctantly paddle ashore and briefly pat myself down.

Slowly walking away from the sea, my tired gaze takes in all the tourists ambling around. None of them look Western. There's been terrorism in Sharm and it looks like all the hotel inhabitants are locals. My business brain wonders if the local hotels have offered special rates to Egyptian nationals simply to keep the resort ticking along.

I manage something to eat in the crowded restaurant, sink four bottles of Sprite and, on Eddie's suggestion, begin the process of trying to extend my Indian Visa. It's a tedious process not helped by both the website not being iPad friendly, and dozens of Egyptian kids running around screaming at each other.

Thirty minutes later I've given up, made it back to the room, and crawled into bed. It's pitch black outside, the room lights are off, and tired fingers send a message to Cindy simply saying, '*Love you.* X.'

And fall asleep.

# Chapter 16. 15th May. Day 10

My eyelids slowly crank open and a reluctant hand reaches over for the phone. The screen says it's a smidge before 5am. I try to figure that into Bolton time, but can't make the maths work. I move my head off the pillow and sit up. My eyes won't quite focus, and my headspace groggily reviews the night's sleep, or lack of it.

The wind had grown into a howling frenzy during the small hours. Through a sleepy haze I thought I'd heard distant gunfire. And each time sleep had let me go I'd scratched at the insect bites on my legs, and they look red raw.

The mental fog starts to clear. I make it to the bathroom and force myself in and out of the shower. And make a conscious decision not to put on the pilot's shirt. I'm nobody's Captain and I won't bloody pretend to be just to impress the locals. Today's plan is smart casual, if un-ironed, instead.

I slowly pack everything away, hoist my two bags onto one shoulder, and lumber towards the hotel reception.

It's a large space with a curved reception desk facing a general assembly area. Comfy chairs and settees are peppered about. No one's there. The receptionist appears and I tell him I want to check out. In response he says I'll have to wait until it's been confirmed that nothing's been signed to the room.

And I hear my voice say, politely, that there's no additional items to pay for, but he ever so slightly sneers.

At 5.30am my patience hasn't properly rebooted, and my headspace shouts out, *'you cheeky bloody sod'*. Those words don't make it to my lips, but I raise my finger and wag it at him, '*I have not charged anything to the room, and you'd better check me out now!*'

His face goes red, and my guess is that he's silently calculating the likelihood of trouble if he causes additional offence. He signs me out and my consciousness feels bad about losing my cool.

A taxi appears outside, and I lug my baggage past the airport-style security scanners and climb onboard. The driver smiles at me, but there's no warmth to it.

It's a two or three mile drive to the airport and halfway there an anxiety attack strikes. My wallet? Where is the bloody thing? A memory surfaces of sleeping with it underneath my pillow for safe keeping, and I've left the damn thing in situ.

I tell the driver to turn around and he looks at me like I'm a useless dick. We do a U-turn and head back to the hotel and pull up alongside the small military checkpoint. He winds down his window and talks to the young Army guard with the rifle. We're allowed back onto the grounds, and I feel both abashed and irritated with myself.

The early morning hangs from me like a dead weight. I awkwardly get out of the minivan, make my way to the reception area, and a quick glance picks out the receptionist. I walk over to him, apologise for my earlier behaviour, and ask for the key to my old room. Then trudge the 400 yards across the hotel grounds and retrieve my wallet.

I slowly walk back the way I came, drop off the key, and put a $20 tip on the counter. Which is my sad sorry way of apologising. The receptionist looks straight at me and won't accept my money, and that makes me feel worse. I leave it there and walk away.

Back in the cream coloured taxi we drive off and make our way to the empty airport. Inside the vast terminal area I ask a lonely looking official where to find the handling agent. Ten minutes later I've found the slim, awkward looking, young man and we both make our way through two sets of security checkpoints and X-ray machines.

# Phoenix

A dozen army guards all point questioning looks in my direction, and I regret not wearing the pilot's shirt and epaulettes. But damn it, I'm not a bloody commercial pilot and will not pretend to be one.

Five minutes later I'm stood in the middle of the airside section of the terminal. It's a huge space void of anyone apart from myself and the handling agent. There's a myriad of shops but they all have their metallic shutters down.

The handling agent doesn't seem to care what I'm wearing and says, '*Right, Captain, I need $400 as handling and parking charge, please*'. I'd been told the previous day that payment could be made in the crinkly Egyptian pounds stashed in my wallet, so needing dollars is news to me.

I stand there feeling drained and uncertain. And tell him I only have a couple of hundred bucks on me. He awkwardly looks down at the polished cream floor tiles and suggests a card payment will suffice.

Unbidden my hand fishes about in my smaller rucksack for my wallet and credit cards. He goes and finds a handheld card reader and his eyes focus on the portable device, but can't get a signal. A pained expression crosses his young face.

I raise my hands and hear my exasperated voice say, '*if you won't take your own currency, if your card reader won't work, and if I only have $300, what can I do?*'

And that's a lie. One thousand dollars is hiding in my wallet, but I'm not in the mood to hand them over when I'd been told I could pay in Egyptian notes. The dollars are my safety net and I'm not parting with 'em. What if an engine failure above the desert means a handful of readies are needed for any number of unknown reasons?

What's the bloody point in having a currency if no bugger wants to use the damn thing?

We start to haggle and agree on $300 and £168 Egyptian pounds. I ask him why he won't accept Egyptian cash, and he just shrugs. With payment in hand his approach changes and he wants me gone, '*Come on Captain, hurry please.*'

A look at Eddie's watch confirms that the countdown to my exit slot is fast approaching, but despite his request to move faster I can't. My energy levels are falling by the wayside as I slowly make my way outdoors into the morning heat.

India Zulu stands at ease in the centre of a large open-sided hangar. There are a dozen green vertical steel columns supporting a roof of sorts, but no walls. The space is big enough for plush corporate jets, and President Mubarak used to keep his toys there.

Samson's attracted a crowd of half a dozen officials. They all seem to want pictures taking of me standing next to her. I feel obliged to stand there and smile, then stand to one side and let them take their own selfies.

The temperature is starting to rise, and it's getting uncomfortable as I begin piling my kit onboard.

A tired looking military jeep is motionless twenty feet from India Zulu. Six lean young men are sat in the back wearing camouflage gear and cradling machine guns. I look over and give them a half-smile whilst a handful of blank faces stare back at me.

One of the officials walks towards me and put's his hand on my shoulder. Then leans forward and whispers not to go near the soldiers or make eye contact. '*They're Special Forces. You can't take pictures of them or talk to them*', he says.

Despite the warning I can't help but wonder what would happen if I stepped out of line. Thirteen stone of Englishmen versus six lots of nine stones. My mind starts to wander away from me. I 'used' to be a Blackbelt in Ju-Jitzu… and maybe…

# Phoenix

….A swift snap kick to the shins of the first chap. Flick at the eyes of the second. Spin around and kick out at the chest of the next unfortunate young fella. Attack the following guy's throat…

And then it occurs to me that I'm getting competitive. Against soldiers. With guns. In a foreign country. A quiet inner voice advises me to, '*Stop being a total fucking dickhead, concentrate on what you're doing, and put a smile on your bloody boat race.*'

I focus on Samson and stow everything onboard. Then check my secondary fuel tank is still in good condition underneath its towel on the passenger seat. And slowly walk around the aircraft and begin my preflight.

Everything is where it should be, and she looks good. Climbing aboard I strap myself in, pull on my green headset, and give a thumbs up to the officials and military types.

My gaze focuses on the Garmin 795, and I scroll through the screen to check last night's Flightplan is still logged in. HESH to NWB to METSA to QTR to QAA to OJAM, Jordan.

Then tell myself to take a moment. I lean my head back against the black faux leather headrest, close my eyes, and try to relax.

The thought comes to me to check the radiator grill to make sure it's not blocked with sand particles. I unstrap myself, climb out of the cabin, and that triggers a look of nervous concern on the faces of the dozen onlookers.

It's forty degrees on the ground now. No clouds. No wind. Just unbroken blue skies.

Satisfied, I climb back inside, strap myself to the aircraft, and turn the Master on. The beacon lights start flashing and the crowd takes a simultaneous step backwards. I call the Tower and ask for permission to start the engine.

Samson is cleared to start up. We're ordered to follow the small yellow 'Follow Me' car that's just swung into view. Releasing the brakes India Zulu rolls forward and I pull on the brake lever to check she'll come to a complete stop. Brake test over I relax and carry-on taxiing. The Rotax is loud in my ears and it's getting swelteringly hot.

The radio crackles at me and the Tower announces that they're expecting two commercial jets, and an expedited departure is required. Meaning bloody well hurry up before our patience runs out.

The prop's blurring away in front of my face as we move forwards. There's a handful of commercial jets on the left. To the right a bright ball of fire sits in the sky and it's watching over a sand-coloured infinity.

My right foot is constantly pushing against the rudder to keep her tracking along the yellow line on the tarmac. I tell myself to concentrate on the taxi markings, or she'll end up heading left and someone might twig that the old girl has a problem. Then there's the risk of being called back and India Zulu being impounded.

It's uncomfortably hot inside the cockpit and the pressure of being at an International Airport weighs heavy. My shirt is sticking to my body as it rejects, again, the idea of being so far from Bolton.

We line up on runway 04L. I keep a heavy foot pressed to the rudder to keep her tracking true, and we take off. Sharm El Sheikh is getting left behind as we climb into the skies.

My left thumb keys the red mic' button, and my tired voice asks for vectors to leave the Control Zone. We head Northeast towards Jordan and Samson climbs over the stunning beauty of the Red Sea. The cabin starts to feel cooler as we continue reaching for the heavens.

My headspace is on edge. Not obsessing about anything, but unsure about what the next handful of hours will bring.

# Phoenix

No matter what kind of job you do, how people feel about you, or whether you've earned the respect of your peers... If you put a person in a brand-new environment and find yourself living off your wits, and subject to the pull of strangers, it's tough.

It plays on your mind exactly how insignificant you are. Add in a lack of sleep, mad heat, a tricky aircraft, and it's hard going. Every little thing feels like a punch to the guts.

And the to'ing and fro'ing over the landing and parking fees pulls me back to the consequences of an emergency landing in the desert. If the engine folds would seven hundred USD be enough to smuggle me out of the desert before the wrong folk took notice?

Isis blew up a Russian Airbus last year as it departed Sharm. My head looks down, past the wheels, wondering how much of a divot a Microlight would leave in the desert floor.

My mind wanders away again and asks whether a Rotax 912 has enough metallic content to allow a surface to air missile to lock on.

My left thumb keys the mic' again and asks the disembodied controller to allow a frequency switch. In return a harshly accented voice replies, in English, that India Zulu should climb to 19,000ft. My mindset sinks, and I explain that it's impossible and that my Flightplan was for 8,500ft.

The fellah ignores me and keeps asking for 19,000ft. But India Zulu can only do, maybe, 12,000ft tops. Should we turn around and head back because he's asking the impossible?

And above 10,000ft hypoxia is waiting. Between 10k and 12k I'd possibly feel light-headed and potentially pass out. Being unconscious means death. Should Samson head back to Sharm?

Or should we head towards the absolute limit of the aircraft and try to climb to 12,000'ish feet? What would keep this controller happy? Are their Military aircraft about? Are jets patrolling the international borders? Is there a risk from ground fire or missiles?

With my hand gently resting against the stick, and my eyes on the horizon, straight and level flight is easy. Every time I look away or scroll through the engine management screens on the Dynon, or check the airway points on the Garmin, we're heading off in a different bloody direction.

There was no time to eat earlier, and my right hand reaches for the bottle of water behind my seat. I look back to the horizon and we've dropped a wing and wandered off course. I take a swig of warm, stale, water and slowly roll the wings level.

The rhythm of the Rotax throbs through my headset. There's an irregular beat to the engine that takes my attention for a handful of seconds.

I key the microphone and report to the Controller, '*Golf India Zulu is climbing, sir*'. He calls three times and each time asks for a position report and our altitude. I keep replying with our position and say, '*we're climbing, sir*'.

In the Egyptian heat she won't climb faster than 200ft a minute. Will the prop' stop again if I push too hard? I take a moment and slip the headset off and listen to the loud throb of the engine.

For a second I thought there'd been a different tone, but maybe I'd imagined it.

The sun streaming into the cabin physically hurts. I absently look outside and stare down at the featureless desert beneath the wheels.

We pass beyond the range of two-way communication and there's no response when I press on the microphone button. I take a swig of water and put the bottle in the centre console.

And the Master Fuse pops out.

From being tired and a touch dehydrated, I'm awake. Jaded, but alert. Without juice from the external power-jack both the Garmin 795 and my phone will eventually die when their batteries run out.

# Phoenix

Will the avionics or radio go next? My sphincter contracts, and my right-hand cups my balls for some reason.

Samson ghosts above a military airfield, just below the left wing, and from 11,500ft up it looks abandoned. Would I be able to land? Should I land? Is it in Israel? A thought floats through my conscious mind that touching down in Israel without permission would be the kind of newsworthy thing that gets noticed.

I press the red button on the stick and try their frequency, but no one replies. A feeling of loneliness sweeps over me again and I just want someone to know our location.

What's the priority in the event of a crash landing in the desert? The need is to find water, isn't it?

My iPhone buzzes and it interrupts my train of thought. It's picked up a phone signal and, even though my Garmin suggests I'm firmly on the Egyptian Airway, the text message welcomes me to Israel's telecom system.

I pull myself away from questioning our location and wedge the stick between my knees. Then take a deep breath and have a stab at figuring out the problem with the power feeds. Why the hell have the fuses tripped? By unplugging the Garmin 795 my smaller Garmin 496 still works.

I begin scrolling through the screens on the Dynon looking for anything unusual. Don't panic, just be calm and logical. Accept the idea of a crash landing and keep functioning, Johnny Boy.

Eddie's baseball cap is protecting my head, but my body is awash with sweat and the sun physically hurts.

My phone blinks at me again and another message welcomes me to Saudi Arabia. The smile of the damned makes its way across my face as my eyes cast from the horizon to the Garmin, to check we haven't accidentally wandered away from the route.

The next twenty minutes are spent trying to fly the aircraft and program the route from the Garmin 795 into the much smaller Garmin 496.

I reach inside my rucksack for Eddie's iPhone battery cell and need two hands. Samson immediately rolls to the left and starts to dive. My stomach lurches. Stay calm, Jon boy. I grab the stick and get her wings level and back on heading, as a feeling of nausea starts to take hold.

Looking outside the cabin there's no roads or civilisation in sight, just sand. The engine tone seems to vary occasionally, and a quick glance at the battery icon on the Garmin 795 shows the power slowly draining away.

I take advantage of the freshly acquired Saudi phone signal and text Simon in deepest, darkest, beautiful Lancashire. *'Fuse keeps popping. Ideas? Very hot here.'* A follow-up text goes to Eddie.

A couple of minutes later Si replies with, '*Have you a lot of things on that are all being drawn through the same fuse?*' My first thought is, '*I'm not alone, I have a friend who knows what I'm facing and wants to help.*' What a bloody hero.

I begin tapping out a message, '*Just to the right of Israel now. Garmin 795 won't charge. Keeps popping the fuse. Up at 11,000ft. Outside Air Temperature 22c. Garmin 496 still being charged. Ideas?*'

I can't wait for a reply and send a follow-up message, '*Reads 13.7volts, Just in the green, bordering yellow. Seems constant but won't take the Garmin 795. Tried switching the beacon lights off, but the fuse keeps popping when I try to power the Garmin… Ideas?*'

My forehead creases into a deeper frown. Deep breath, exhale, deep breath. Then I experiment with shutting off everything electrical in the hope of getting the bloody 795 back online. Nav lights off, transponder off, radio off, Dynon off.

# Phoenix

Simon replies and I feel so bloody relieved that he understands I need his help. His response is, '*Sounds like a dead short of some variety. The cable hasn't been damaged has it and the cable's touching inside the sheath?*'

If it's a short inside the console, there's no chance of it being fixable in flight. And would I even want to try? India Zulu isn't stable enough without an autopilot to make any attempt at repairs whilst airborne.

The engine's running and I have fuel. There's two-way communication with the ground, and the Transponder still works. The sun might hurt, but I'm alive and this isn't disastrous, yet.

Or will all the electrics just fold?

The screen flashes on my phone and a message from Cindy appears, '*Eddie said you had problems with the electrics? Please don't fly if it's not safe… you've achieved so much already. Just getting to Egypt then into Amman is a massive achievement. Love, love, love you. x*'

How do I reply to that? She means well, and I love her. I scratch the side of my face and awkwardly message back, '*love you*'. Now isn't the time to share my anxieties.

We pass further along the Airway and I make another blind call, '*King Hussein Airport, this is Golf Charlie Golf India Zulu, HESH to OJAM, require basic service, please*'.

I get a reply and feel better at being in contact with another human being. Someone knows where I am and that offers hope of a rescue if things go tits up.

My Garmin 795 dies, and the large screen goes blank.

I've got my notes and can plot each remaining leg into the tiny 496. It's not ideal, but it's not disastrous. I clock my wrist to see what my heart rate monitor is saying, and the device suggests my ticker is bouncing along at 40 beats per minute faster than normal.

Tilting my head upwards, the sun seems to be attacking me. My mindset says my arse has been sat in the same spot for too long. Simultaneously an edgy feeling is trying to corrupt my train of thought and wants me to panic.

We fly past a military zone and the radio squeals at me. A disembodied voice asks if I'm a military or civilian aircraft, and before waiting for a reply asks that Samson climbs to Flight Level 14. What to say? How do I respond to that? What triggers a military jet being dispatched to have a look?

The best I can think to say is *'Golf India Zulu, climbing'*. Fourteen thousand feet is not possible. Am I at risk of attack? Are Military aircraft patrolling this area? I have a valid flight plan and that should have been passed on, shouldn't it? Is this a test of nerve? Mine against theirs? Should I turn back?

I'm hot, tired, and stressed. Will I make it through the day? Should I make an unauthorised detour into Israel? They'll help, won't they? Does Bolton have a synagogue?

The Rotax sounds loud through my headset and the 100 horsepower engine is pushing its constant grumblings through my body.

Was there a different tone to the engine just then? I slip the headset off and listen for any irregular beat from the engine. Moving my focus between the Dynon and the phone, my right hand taps out another message to Si saying that the Exhaust Gas figures seem low.

He replies with, *'...you run the risk of detonation which is bad... Detonation is when the fuel pre-ignites before it is supposed... with the piston halfway through the stroke as opposed to its correct timing position, so it is fighting itself and that would wreck the engine. It would sound like a knocking type noise.'*

Did I hear a knocking noise, or was it just a momentary lack of fuel pressure causing the engine to stutter?

# Phoenix

My headspace looks round the cabin and then extends to the yellow horizon. I turn my head to one side, rest it against the plexiglass window, and feel the throb of the engine. Then stare down past the wheels at the vacant sandscape below.

What's Ava doing today?

After a lonely minute, I pull myself together and change to the Jordan approach frequency. The first voice I hear is a jet pilot telling the ground Controller he's running low on fuel and needs to land.

I speak to the chap on the radio and start descending. A glance at the Dynon shows that the outside air temperature at 6,500ft, is 34c. The thought rolls around my mind that the Rotax battery starts to cook itself at anything above 30c.

A little more time trickles through the hourglass and my mindset slowly starts to switch from ditching in the desert, to landing India Zulu. I let go of the stick and she immediately begins rolling to the left and starts diving of her own accord.

I roll the wings level again and slowly shake my head.

When I set up a landing, I want the aircraft trimmed so she descends naturally, I don't want her rolling in any direction. I want to make gentle control inputs and basically let her slowly lose height. In an ideal world one power setting should be sufficient all the way from 1,000ft to 3ft and the flair.

And it completely fucks up my sense of what's right and wrong with the world when she's trying to make a left turn and roll into a dive all the bloody time.

Looking up at the fuel '*sight gauges*' the left tank shows 20 litres. The right tank is nearly empty with, maybe, 5 litres sloshing around. What's that? Maybe 60 minutes flight time left?

I'm tired, I'm stressed, I want respite, and everything is exhausting. I move the stick to the right and start a 30 degree banked turn. We go round in circles for 5 minutes as my crumpled body is pushed against the seat and the compass heading rolls round and around, round, and around.

We level out and she seems 'nearly' balanced.

The radio wakes up and I hear our call sign. The Amman Approach Controller advises that he has other aircraft landing and wants India Zulu to fly a holding pattern. Mentally I'm not up for figuring out headings and reciprocals or anything complicated.

The arrival plate is sat on my left thigh, and it's just a blur. Focusing on anything inside the cabin causes Samson to fly off heading. An inner voice tells me to get my shit together, but then my mind moves away from flying and asks what Ava's up to.

Is she running around today playing with young Amelia? Are they both working on their reading?

A facepalm moment heads my way and I take a time out from flying and start scribbling on my kneeboard. The left wing inevitably starts falling away, and I let it.

Ten seconds later my speech is prepared, the wings are rolled level, and my left hand presses the red microphone button on the stick. I read my lines and in response another heavy Egyptian accent makes an acknowledgement and gives headings to fly.

From his tone he seems to have me down as a competent pilot, but my inner cynic says he's just fallen for the timbre of my voice, and assumed I know what I'm doing. When the reality is that my chinagraph pencil has done all my thinking for me.

Our destination is a decent-sized airport accommodating military kit and lots of small jets. We join left base and turn on final. And I tell myself not to fuck up the landing whilst simultaneously figuring

# Phoenix

that a runway with 10,745ft of tarmac should be enough for a tired boy from Bolton.

A flick of the fingers feeds in the flaps, and I set her up for 60 knots. India Zulu descends towards Amman and the city is everywhere and looks bleached by the sun. Thousands of buildings create a tsunami of urban sprawl that covers the sandscape.

A boot full of rudder cancels out the 10 knot crosswind and we float above the long white threshold markings. My lungs take in a deep breath, and I close the throttle in anticipation of a gentle touchdown.

She glides but won't land. I'm still holding my breath whilst she floats a couple of feet above the tarmac. Samson starts drifting offline. Then one main wheel touches down, followed by the other.

The runway seems huge as my gaze quickly casts around. I've missed the intended taxi point and we keep rolling to the next exit. We take a tight right turn off the active runway and the radio asks that I call the Ground Controller on 100.00.

Squinting up at the sun it feels oppressively hot. Supercharged air is moving through both vents in the cabin windows.

A shadow moves over-head and I tilt my head upwards. An Apache attack helicopter ghosts by a couple of hundred feet above the taxiway. My world-weary eyes focus on the deadly apparition as it transits the skies. It serves to remind me that this is very nearly a war zone in the fight against Isis.

With renewed attention to detail my right hand moves from the throttle and picks up the airport plate. My headspace tries to interpret where the Ground Controller wants India Zulu.

Looking around there's various twin-engined military aircraft, plus a huge Russian military cargo jet, and dozens of Citation types peppered about. We weave around a collection of jets and find our slot. I stop the aircraft and shut down both the engine and electrics.

My left hand moves the door mechanism to open, and the gull-wing door slowly opens itself to the outside world. Intense heat enters the cabin, and my body won't move.

A chap walks over to India Zulu and identifies himself, in English, as the Handling Agent. I sit there, feeling dazed, and let one foot dangle outside the cabin wondering what happens next.

He looks cheerful and by return I smile a tired smile. He says something, which I don't catch, and starts walking around Samson. My headspace wants to talk to him, to speak to another human, but I reluctantly get out a few tools and focus on unscrewing the centre console.

A spider's web of multi-coloured cables stare back at me. They're both intimidating and make me feel scared to touch anything. If I cock up something by mistake, I'll be stranded. Maybe Simon could come out to fix her or, worst case, maybe she'd be written off by the insurance company if something major is kaput.

I force myself to take a happy snap of the nest of cables so there'll be a model of what the bloody horrible mess looks like. And start looking for damaged wires or obvious problems.

The mountings for the external electric points are both very loose. Have they been creating a short? I carefully tighten them up and then break open the insulation around the external cable, leading from the console to the Garmin, and have a gander. And that looks like it could be the problem.

I climb out into the blisteringly hot sun and stretch away the 4 hour flight, then pass the cable to the Handling Agent. '*Do you know anyone who could solder this please?*' He looks thoughtful, then nods.

My iPad is sat on the seat, and I lean into the cabin and type a message to Eddie. He instantly replies saying he's safely got Cin to

# Phoenix

the Airport and she's heading home. A follow-up message says he's organised a hotel for me tonight.

Looking up at the sun it's like a furnace, and the heat feels unhealthy. India Zulu will struggle in these conditions, and I casually ask the handling agent about private hangarage, and he says, '*A thousand US dollars a day*'... and that won't work.

I lean in towards Samson and spread a towel over both the black binnacle, and the Turtlepac, and lock her up for the night. Then hoist my red bags awkwardly onto one shoulder and we make our way through various offices in the terminal building.

One by one I'm introduced to a number of stern-looking men. They all seem preoccupied with paperwork, and I can tell they're not sure what to think of my crumpled appearance.

The unknown seems to worry them, and I sympathise. I tentatively ask about getting a stamp in my passport but get told that as aircrew it won't happen.

One fellah seems like he could cause serious trouble. Small, rounded, hard-headed and someone not to fuck with. He looks me up and down and makes prolonged eye contact. After a handful of awkward moments, I seem to pass muster and he begrudgingly welcomes me to Jordan.

His face seems vaguely familiar, but I can't pull up the name.

With both bags cutting into my shoulder the Handling Agent and I walk through the passenger section of the deserted terminal building. He offers to drive me to my hotel, and we find his car in the small car park and head out.

He feels the need to apologise that his air-con isn't working, and I just shrug and offer my thanks for the lift. It feels stickily hot, even painful inside the car, and the seats are red hot to touch. We start chatting as we mingle with the chaotic traffic, and he seems like an incredibly nice chap. I'm wasted and anxious, but meeting a chatty fellah is welcome. Very welcome.

The car engine overheats and dies. He puts his hazards on, we get honked at by the competing drivers, and we slowly roll to a stop by the side of the dusty road. He curses and apologises again, and I just smile. Every second outside the aircraft feels like a bonus.

Twenty minutes later the car has cooled a little, restarted, and we make it to the hotel. My new friend apologises for the third time, says it's the hottest day of the year, and I just shrug my shoulders.

The hotel is sat on a corner. It's not a great neighbourhood, but it'll do. I check-in and regret asking Eddie for budget accommodation. The guy behind the counter is mid-thirties, lean, well dressed, and looks 'handy'.

My guess is that he's a borne fighter who's used to getting his way. A Palestinian flag is draped across the far wall of the small reception area, and that makes me wonder about his past.

From the way he's appraising me it looks like he's carrying out his own personal risk assessment. He puts on a thin smile that suggests Jonathan Hilton won't be any trouble at all.

I push forward my Brit abroad persona and offer a tired smile. I'm given the key to my room and slowly climb the stairs.

It's a twin room with a rackety sounding air-con unit. An ancient telly sits on a metal stand three feet from the foot of the bed. I heft my stuff onto the right-hand bed, have a shower, and reluctantly hand wash a bunch of clothes in the windowless bathroom.

Then text Eddie to ask about tomorrow's flight. The word is that the Saudi's are withholding the flight clearances at this point, but they could come through at any minute.

There's nothing to be done but climb into bed, try to forget about the day, and fall asleep. It's 8pm.

# Chapter 17. 16th May. Day 11

I wake up early again as some old bloke is wailing out a call to prayer. My conscious mind asks what time it is in Bolton, but I can't figure it out. Looking around the room, there's shirts and undies piled atop the tired-looking radiator from yesterday's cleaning detail.

The window wouldn't properly close last night, and road noise is making its way into the room. The curtains are thin, and sunlight is spraying across every surface of the budget hotel room.

I check my iPad, and there's no news on the revised Indian Visa or flight clearance through Saudi. An inner voice tells me I was weak to let Cindy come over when I should have carried on flying.

Lying underneath the thin sheets I reach for the remote and switch on the TV. A quick flick through all the channels, and there's nothing in English. I reluctantly climb out of bed and peer between the curtains. A dusty road stares back at me with blocks of cream-coloured buildings lazily sat about.

There's a new-looking, metallic, 4x4 pick-up truck sat outside the entrance steps. It belongs to the Hotel Manager and my head tells me he's definitely a player, of some sort.

I make my way back to the windowless bathroom and stare at myself in the mirror. A tired middle-aged face looks back. A slow shower follows and I make my way from the room to the roof terrace. I find a plastic chair and cast a glance around. And can't quite convince myself that putting old plastic chairs on a flat roof equates to a 'roof terrace'.

What to do today? If the Saudi clearance doesn't make it through in the next few hours, it means India won't be possible. Eddie thinks it might be doable if I can set off before dawn tomorrow.

The thought swirls around my mind that I might be able to set off, but will I be able to deal with the bureaucracy enroute and then do three stops in a day? Doable, but unlikely.

Using the sluggish hotel Wi-Fi I find myself Googling temperatures in India and the Middle East. It's pushing 50c in parts of India and tropical storms are brewing in the Gulf of Oman. There are reports of people dying of heatstroke in the online newsfeeds.

If I get caught on the fringes of a weather system that will inevitably screw up Samson's range. Would Pakistan be a possible diversion? The insurance company have specifically excluded Pakistan in their policy. How strong will the winds be at altitude?

The thought crosses my consciousness that Eddie thinks I'm not pushing hard enough. Maybe I'm not the strong character I thought I was, and maybe I should have said no to Cin coming over. A weary feeling pulls at me.

It's 10am, local time, and the sun is blisteringly hot. A sense of unease is tugging away at me. It wants to check Samson over and find out where the soldering is up to. I call my amiable friend, and he answers on the first ring.

The conversation drifts from pleasantries to asking if he could help me gain access to India Zulu. I look up at the skies and the red sun is like a furnace. I mumble that she'll be suffering in the heat, and I plan to jump in a taxi to go check her over. By reply he says that a taxi isn't necessary, and he'll pick me up.

Forty-five minutes later he's outside. With a liberal dose of sun cream applied everywhere I walk out into the ferocious heat. Adnan leans across and opens the passenger door and we set off.

The mental component of the trip is a continuous feeling of loneliness. That sense of isolation seems to apply whether I'm cocooned inside the aircraft, or talking to people I'll never meet again.

# Phoenix

We chat about flying, the mad temperatures, and the rules of Jordan's busy roads. He tells me that if a driver hit's a pedestrian, and the locals seem to have a death wish, that the driver is responsible for the fellah's medical bills.

I express my amazement as a series of brave hearts play Frogger to dodge between bumper-to-bumper traffic. The conversation moves to all the military traffic at the airport and Adnan rolls his eyes.

Isis is an ongoing threat and there's action and reaction. The fighting has led to Jordan going through the pain of absorbing a million fleeing refugees from Syria. Adnan suggests terrorist cells have embedded themselves within that throng of humanity.

I mumble the eternal question of, '*why do people become terrorists?*' His reply comes back as '*Virgins and Whiskey in the afterlife.*' He follows up with an observation that life's losers become terrorists because they can't hold down a job.

I'm staring absently at our dusty surroundings without giving particular thought to anything. Myriad older buildings sit about all with an off-yellow tint painting every surface. Tired sedan cars speed past us with scant regard for safety.

My filter fails to engage and I respond with, '*I've never understood the attraction of a dozen virgins, I think I'd prefer 12 experienced women in their thirties*'. And then realise I'm talking out loud.

He raises an eyebrow in my direction and then agrees with me. For good measure I casually mention that I don't like Whiskey.

It's oppressively hot inside the car, even with the windows down, and my mind wanders towards Cindy and what she's doing. If I die on the flight to India, how will she react? What will my absence do to Ava?

My friend loses concentration for a second, in the midst of the frenetic traffic, and we sideswipe another car. The two separate skins of metal rub against each other and there's a pained squeal from both vehicles. Adnan curses but doesn't stop.

We make it to the airport, park up, get out into the soul-sapping sunlight and quickly head to the terminal building. The aggressive character from yesterday is there, and he eyeballs me. His demeanour says, '*do not under any circumstances fuck with me.*'

A name pops into my mind, 'Omid Djalili,' British comedian and actor. Mentally overlaying both faces they look very similar; except one's guarding his country against foreign threats.

I meekly smile and am led through a maze of offices, airside. It's painfully hot in the sun, blisteringly so. There's military cargo aircraft dotted around, plus private jets, and India Zulu is where I left her, looking tiny.

Walking over I can feel the heat pressing down on my head and shoulders. With Samson's key in hand, I unlock the gull-wing doors and watch as the small piston mechanism pushes the left door upwards.

It's like an oven in the cabin. The window vents are open, and everything is covered, but it's unbearably hot. I walk round to the right-hand wing, open the door, and try to create an airflow of sorts across the seats.

The harsh midday sun drains everything of its colour. I move around Samson and start looking at her carbon fibre skin. Small cracks are flowering on the wheel spats, and the cowling has linear cracks pulling the paint apart.

Likewise, the black stickers marking out G-CGIZ across Samson's flank are starting to shrink in the direct sunlight. Going back to the cabin I rest my right hand on the seat, and it's painfully hot. Looking down more fluid has escaped and is colouring the nose wheel spat.

# Phoenix

I have Eddie's red baseball cap on backwards, and start inspecting the inside of the cabin. The binnacle is too hot to touch. I reach for my small plastic bag of tools in the footwell, and the transparent plastic starts to deform and melt in my hands.

One thousand dollars a day to get her inside. No guarantee on the Saudi permissions. The Indian Visa is running down. What damage is being done to Samson as she sits here in the heat? Can she cope?

The air sits still and there's no breeze at all. Would I be better taking the cowling off to circulate some form of breeze across the components? If I tied linen sheeting over the Rotax would that help?

Will there be more vapour lock issues the longer she sits here? Is the fuel condensing into a vapour right now and escaping through the breather pipes on the wings? Or should the Avgas negate that problem?

My head hurts.

I lock Samson up and remove everything I can carry, then scurry across the taxiway and make my way back to Adnan. He has his customary smile on show and hands me the soldered cables he's had repaired.

I thank him and ask if he can get me back to the hotel. My mind wanders off in abstract directions as he leads us back to the terminal area. The Omid Djalili character is facing towards us, and he turns away as we approach.

And I can just hear him singing, '*Money, money, must be funny, in a rich man's world.*' He keeps singing, makes a vague effort at Dad dancing, and turns round. His eyes meet mine and there's a twinkle there.

Adnan whispers to me that his job is to suspect everyone of being a threat to Jordan, but he's decided I'm not. Maybe singing one of ABBA's finest is his way of letting me know we could be mates.

Leaving the terminal building we make it to Adnan's car. He makes a show of looking at the damaged front wing, and shrugs. It's just too hot to get upset, and he suggests he can pull out a section of the damaged metal later in the evening.

Driving back towards the hotel he stops the car outside a row of affluent shops. I frown and look confused; he smiles and points to what looks like a state-of-the-art ice cream parlour. Multicoloured delicacies sit in the window and he offers to buy me something.

My head's elsewhere, and I politely decline. He smiles and walks off. All I'd want would be a vanilla cornet, flake, and dash of strawberry sauce. Anything else would get you locked up in Bolton.

I follow him inside and he turns to me with a 'tadaar' type flourish. Then hands over an exotic vanilla and strawberry masterpiece complete with an array of sprinkles and an impressive range of E numbers. I thank him, shake his hand, and try to look excited.

Back in the car, we make it to the hotel. He waves and drives off. I walk inside and shuffle past the tired looking furnishings and slowly make my way upstairs to the small room.

Sitting on the bed, I get my iPad out and look for messages from Eddie on Facebook. There's no news on the Permits, but they could come through in hours or it might be days, he says.

Without warning a 'Facebook Memory' flashes up. It's a picture of Ava from two years ago and it takes my breath away. That beautiful, innocent, face looks lovingly back at me. Looking down at my phone, Cindy's face looks up at me from the screensaver.

I lie back on the bed and my tired eyes stare straight up at the yellowing ceiling. In the background the air-con unit is making a grumbling noise.

Five minutes later I sit up, pick up my iPad, and start typing a message to the couple of hundred people following the flight on Facebook.

# Phoenix

'Bad news... I'm very sorry about this... Just checked India Zulu and she's struggling with the heat... She's airworthy at the moment, but suffering... a few bits of plastic inside the aircraft are starting to become malleable and a couple of sections of bodywork are cracking slightly...

There's a couple of other main issues I'm worried about (more later), but I think I've pushed my luck too far already & need to get back to more temperate climes...

There's a mini heatwave going on here (it's been 104f today, and my destination in India is expecting 120f this week). Hence I've had to make a judgement call, and as we're struggling with the revised Saudi permits (which should come through, but may take days) and my Indian Visa runs out shortly, I've decided to turn around and head home.

I'll personally refund any charity donations people have made... I'm very, very sorry. Jon Hilton'

Lying back on the bed again I wonder what the Fox would say right now. He'd probably look at me, head slightly to one side, wry smile on his face, and ask, '*why are you miles away from home flying a sick, written off, aircraft?*'

My glib answer would have been, '*I have no bloody idea.*'

Except to say that the Canada trip was my running away from Dad dying. And maybe this experience is my running away from a feeling that I'm losing my daughter to the new father figure in her life.

When what I should do is try to be a better father and let her know how much she's loved. And maybe it's time to accept the unconditional love Cindy offers, and simply ask her to marry me. And both situations mean getting back to Bolton, centre of the known universe, as quickly as possible.

End of Part 1.

# PART 2. THE TRIP HOME

You'll be pleased to know I've simply summarised the updates I posted on Facebook. There's a couple of additional notes, too.

It would be fair to say that I suffered a little on the trip back. Consequently, I wasn't able to make the detailed notes I did on the outbound leg. Plus, we're up to 70,000 or so words and you deserve a break. Please let your imagination fill in the gaps.

# Chapter 18. 17th May.
# Egypt. Day 12

From Facebook.

*'Jordan to Egypt.*

*If you've ever seen the film, 'Ice Cold in Alex', you may understand I'm on a mission to get home. I seriously need to get back to Barton's Airfield Lodge and throw down a pint... I've changed the status of this page to 'closed' so no one can see what's happening on the trip, unless they're either a friend or hopefully have the potential to be a friend...*

*I'll add more later, but at the moment I'm having a 'mare of a time. Which I can summarise by saying, 'oh not again, please don't, squeeze the bag, anxiety, pressure, sauna-like conditions, arguing, bureaucracy gone wild, suggested threats, manic headwinds & crosswinds'... More insight to come when I've left this very interesting continent. Regards Jon'*

Notes:

What did this mean?

Firstly, I'd been reasonably frank about the dilemmas I'd faced and listed them on Facebook. Subsequently, Eddie was picking up a vibe that the authorities were monitoring the flight and were considering grounding India Zulu. Hence the need was to get out of the Middle East, asap, or potentially lose the Aircraft.

Secondly, I was kept at the Jordan Airport for 90 minutes before being allowed to leave the country. A middle-ranking Intelligence Officer took me away from Adnan's protection and sat me in a separate office. All the while he was toying with my Emergency Beacon, alternately staring at it, looking at the ceiling, and then reviewing my crumpled appearance.

# Jon Hilton

If you're a film buff you might have watched the classic, Where Eagles Dare. There's a scene in there where a dastardly German SS type is chatting to Richard Burton's girly.

They're seemingly just chewing the cud until the nasty pasty German (played in the film by an Englishman) rounds on the woman and says something like, '*but I thought the town hall was on the other side of the street?*'

And then it all turns out to have been an elaborate trap aimed at rooting out deception.

From a cynical, official, perspective I guess it seemed a wee bit odd that someone would make a 5,000 mile round trip, by Microlight, for one night in Jordan.*

My pseudo interrogator talked randomly about various things and mentioned that he'd spent 6 months in York at one point. I feigned polite interest and he asked if I knew anything about the place. By return I said no, but that I'd been to the Railway Museum as a teenager.

He seemed deep in thought whilst absently manipulating the Emergency Beacon as if playing with a Rubik's cube. The top came off and the thin metal antenna uncoiled itself and started flopping about on his desk. He seemed to come to a decision, passed it back to me, and said I could leave.

Adnan subsequently appeared and I asked what the hell had prompted all that. He casually commented that the authorities thought my Emergency Beacon was some form of Scaramanga type concealed gun, and that I might be a spy after all.

I just shook my head and shrugged; he did the same.

When I latterly got to fly there were more headaches and warning messages on the Dynon about a lack of fuel flowing into the Rotax. The engine nearly folded whilst we were up at 11,445ft, and there were more manic moments switching from the main tanks to the Turtlepac, again.

I found myself pumping the bloody bag for an hour to get a constant flow of fuel through to the 99 horsepower engine.

Separate to this, and courtesy of our repeated instructions to climb, we pushed a juicy headwind for a while. According to the Garmin we had a ground speed of 46.4 knots at one point.

In general, it all got a little tedious, but on a positive note I probably burnt a lot of calories that day.

One has to laugh.

*males of a certain age may well have taken a detour at this point.

### 18th May. Day 13.

From Facebook

*'Egypt.*

*Difficult to sleep. The front door to the hotel room wouldn't shut properly. The 'balcony' door wouldn't close & kept rattling. The wind was intense and I knew India Zulu would be struggling all night (wings moving up & down, tail twitching). Every gust rattling the door woke me up.*

*The alarm went off at 4.15am. I needed to get her safe and the plan was to get her to a private airstrip across the Red Sea. Got to Sharm El Sheikh airport for 5am. No one wanted to acknowledge me to start with… but I'd given in (after sneers and too many questions) and put my Captains white shirt on.*

*I hate myself for doing it but in this part of the world it absolutely helps. I woke a chap up at 5.30am to get me through the Sharm security. After paying $470 for the landing fees I sat in the aircraft waiting to go, but the Tower wouldn't acknowledge my flight plan. And in this part of the world, there's no GA flying, and without a Flight Plan, you're goosed.*

*From 6.10am'ish to 8'ish I was sat in India Zulu waiting for the Tower to give permission to taxi. The outside air temp was 30c, and I was sweating like a pig. My Rocket Route flight plan allegedly hadn't come through and Eddie / Ahmed were trying to help.*

*I was fearing the worst and getting worried about a few things. All sorts. We won't let you fly. We'll impound the aircraft, etc. Ahmed tried to submit a flight plan and I hand wrote a flight plan in the aircraft and gave it to the Handling agent. The Tower called and asked if I wanted to fly the 100nm mile trip at 8,000 or 9,000 feet. I said 8,000.*

*He gave me clearance to taxi and gave instructions to climb to 9,000ft. I acknowledged his instructions. No point arguing. We taxied behind the 'follow me' car. Wind gusting. And took off.*

*I flew the vectors I was given and finally found the airfield (it's not on the maps). El Gouna. A private airstrip owned by a rich businessman with five jets. And the hangar was free. The wind was 20 knots gusting 30 or so. I fought the winds and finally landed, taxied to the hangar (wings rocking madly), and met everyone. Security, admin staff, ATC.*

*Then set about getting more US dollars, fuel, and carried out a damn good inspection of India Zulu (more later). By 5pm, I was happy.*

*El Gouna is the kind of place that restores a chap's faith in the Middle East. There's a tiny bit of Blackpool about it, but it's quite lovely. And best of all Samson's indoors, and hopefully I can sleep tonight...'*

Notes:

Oil was splattered all over the nose wheel when we landed at El Gouna. Hence, I took the time with a local mechanic to change the oil and generally look her over.

One of the plastic hoses attached to the engine had melted completely through. We also found that most of the hydraulic brake fluid had managed to escape. And there were heaps of sand embedded in the radiator grill.

# Phoenix

The above aside, the only other things I can recall about El Gouna was a motor cruiser type thing in the marina. It bore the name, 'No Money No Love.' For some reason that seemed worth considering as a general essay on male-female relationships.

Finally, to this day, I still feel bad about wearing the pilot's shirt, and epaulettes, but I wasn't feeling particularly well and couldn't fight folks' preconceptions anymore. I guessed I'd caved into the idea that ground personnel expect certain things of aviators.

**<u>19th May. Day 14.</u>**

From Facebook

*'Egypt.*

*Made a stab at writing down the stuff that happened today, 'real time', so this is a bit of an epic. Sorry…*

*Yet again I couldn't sleep. Found a modern little hotel for £40 a night that included the evening meal. It had a mock Egyptian style look to it that worked pretty well. What I didn't realise was the nightclub across the way would be blasting out 'house music' till 3am.*

*My alarm went off at 4.30am, and I got to the airport at 5.30am. There was another headache with the Flightplan, and bird crap & sand were plastered all over India Zulu. Ahmed was good enough to sort the first issue whilst I got out my sponge. Sunny morning. 30c already. 20 to 30 knot winds, but I needed to go.*

*Got a message from Eddie telling me to be polite to the Air Traffic chaps in Cairo. A commercial jet was 'missing,' and the worry was I might get caught up in matters and get diverted anywhere if I wasn't careful. I chewed a Proplus and took off.*

*The Air Traffic guy asked me to climb to 16,500ft. I said, 'no can do' & we compromised on 12,000ft. Climbing over the sea the engine temps rocketed, and I realised I hadn't put my life jacket on. I hadn't the energy to wriggle into it and started biting my fingernails instead.*

*I heard a lot of Arabic on the radio (they generally speak a lot in English) but Arabic was the language today. It seems like a language that would induce throat ache, or at least sell a lot of lozenges.*

*The engine started to struggle at 11,500ft and I could tell she was going to stop. I quickly attached the Turtlepac fuel cell and she stopped shuddering and came back to life. But that meant manually squeezing the damn Turtlepac (it's like a bag of petrol) to keep forcing fuel into the engine.*

*10 minutes later I switched to the main tanks, and everything ran smoothly again. My Garmin 495 lost its satellite signal, and I began to sweat that the 796 would suffer the same fate. Five minutes later both were in sync again.*

*My iPhone packed up. It wasn't in direct sunlight, but it'd had enough…*

*We went through a number of fuel warnings (i.e. Lack of the damn stuff) and I started manually squeezing the fuel from the Turtlepac into the engine, again.*

*We suffered with headwinds and up at 12,000ft I started experimenting with different throttle settings to eke out the available fuel. Slower means better range, but time drags.*

*The engine got cold, and the gauges went from Green to Yellow. It became a juggling trick to keep her happy. I finally managed to negotiate permission to descend to 8,500, and she seemed better.*

*Time passed, I yawned, and tried to even up my chewed fingernails by nibbling them all. After 7 hours of flying I approached my destination and was vectored in by Air Traffic. The wind was only 10 knots but at 1,000ft I got flipped by a thermal.*

*One second the wings were horizontal, the next they were heading towards the vertical. A few things bounced around the cabin. Completely unexpected. Landed 3 minutes later and struggled out into the sun and a few of the ground crew chaps wanted pictures…*

*Hopefully I'll be in Europe tomorrow, and the temperatures will revert to those India Zulu prefers. Fingers crossed.'*

# Phoenix

Notes:

The issue Eddie mentioned related to an Airbus A320 that had disappeared, north of Alexandria. Correspondingly, everyone was feeling twitchy not knowing if it was another terrorist attack.

The original flight plan was to stay over sand, but we were subsequently diverted over the sea. The radio instructed that we hit various reporting points prior to being allowed to land at Marsa Matruh Airport.

My guess is that the authorities wanted all non-military aircraft out of the way whilst a possible search and rescue operation was underway.

It's a very disconcerting feeling flying over water, and looking down past your wheels, trying to spot wreckage or bodies on the ocean surface.

Separately it's worth noting, I latterly found out, that iPhones seem to struggle and pack up when the ambient temperature is north of 113f (45c). Hence, it would be fair to say, that it was hot in the cabin at the point my phone went on strike.

All in all, it was a long day, and I felt somewhat abused by the end of it.

Incidentally, as a general comment, Marsa Matruh was a key part of the battle for El Alamein during the Second World War.

# Chapter 19. 20th May. Day 15

From Facebook

*'Egypt / Crete*

*Been rough for a few days and not been on form. Early mornings, a couple of long flights, trying to concentrate in that sauna of an aircraft, and generally being dehydrated. i.e. I've got some form of infection.*

*Anyway, not sure I can remember much about today. These are the bits I can recall.*

*Yesterday evening O2 decided my phone had been stolen & text me asking me to call them, which I did. Everything got sorted, and then an hour later they cut my phone off... No phone, no Eddie or Ahmed, no emergency support, no Cindy. Frustrating.*

*Spent 3 hours trying to get the bloody useless hotel broadband to work and get things fixed. And then gave up. Fortunately O2 came back on stream, and I messaged Eddie asking for help with the Flightplan because Rocket Route were being crap again & I couldn't concentrate.*

*He wasn't feeling well and our exchange of messages could have been better. Mostly my fault for being abrupt...*

*Fell asleep at 10.30pm fully clothed and woke at 4am when the geezer started calling the faithful for prayers. If they're going to wake everyone up, why can't they sing something cheery?*

*I put on the Epaulette outfit (it helps with policemen and officials), met my taxi ride at 7am, and asked him to wait whilst I stood in the hotel reception, trying to hook up the wifi.*

# Phoenix

Received a message saying the Flightplan had been sent & I was good to go. Got to the airport & one of the soldiers checked under the car for explosives (that's the third time that's happened).

Went through security and got told my Flightplan had been rejected. It took maybe 2 hours to sort & finally I was asked to sign something saying, basically, that if I crashed it was my own fault. I felt OK at that point and needed to leave.

After the previous day I had worries about running out of fuel (I'd faced big headwinds & without the extra juice in the Turtlepac I'd have left a divot in the desert).

So, I fished out my last $50 and asked for a top-up, at $4 a litre. Took off and flew away from Egypt. Kept scanning the sea for wreckage of the Egyptair jet. It's lonely over the sea. Solo flying is mind-numbing.

Tried to get the Turtlepac fuel into the engine by manually pumping it in but didn't have the energy. The headwinds (always damn headwinds, no matter which way I go) weren't too bad.

Heard an Emirates 'lady pilot' bitch at the Cairo Air Traffic chap for not picking up her five earlier transmissions… Ultimately she was out of range, shit happens, don't be a cow.

Flew to Crete, confused one damn big commercial airfield for another and made myself sound like a burke on the radio. Then swallowed a few ProPluses and got my act together.

It rained in Crete, which was slightly exciting, and the outside air temperature dropped. The engine began to run cold and that needed a little managing. Because I'd left the fuel in the Turtlepac it meant landing with it sat next to me… i.e. Cock up the landing and get doused in Avgas. No pressure.

Courtesy of Eddie, and his friend Kosmos Kimionis, I was allowed entry to a big jet (Ryanair, Easy Jet & BA) airfield. And then admitted to a friend of Kosmos that I was in pain. Like a hero he went and got some antibiotics, and I'm feeling a bit better.

*I'm taking tomorrow off to chill. Hopefully no one starts wailing at four in the morning...'*

Notes:

It's horrible flying over a body of water like the Med' looking down at the waters scanning for wreckage of a crashed jet. It puts a chap on edge.

At Chania International Airport I was asked to park next to a light aircraft that had been flipped onto its roof courtesy of high winds. That could be best described as, 'off-putting.'

And I should have said Kosmos organised a phone consultation with a doctor, and his friend went to get the drugs the medico prescribed.

The symptoms were, sorry about this, difficulty peeing, coloured wee, pain and diarrhea.

It's becoming a recurring comment, but one has to laugh.

21st May. Day 16

From Facebook

*'Crete.*

*Very windy today. 30 knots going on 40 knots. Same tomorrow. Went to the airport to check how well I tied her down. Worst case she'd get wrecked. All's well, though...*

*On the taxi trip back, I spoke to the driver about football & then comparisons between the UK and Crete. Small talk.*

*His wisdom is that the UK is a very productive country because the weather is crap (pardon my language). And in Crete, he said, 'it's difficult to work & concentrate because all we want to do is sleep with women'...*

# Phoenix

*So, there you go.'*

Note:

Aren't taxi drivers interesting fellows?

22nd May. Day 17

From Facebook.

*'Crete.*

*Awake when the sun came up. The Church bells were active at 7am. Got up, showered & went for a walk. Supposed to be too windy to fly but looking at the sky it seemed doable.*

*Walked past an old man, and 50 yards later, an old woman, both begging. I gave each some money. The next left was a grand looking church... I still don't understand why the church doesn't help the poor, but there must be a reason.*

*Poked my head inside & then scarpered before the big fellah upstairs realised a heathen was around.*

*My dehydration / infection thing is clearing up. The dozens of tick or mosquito bites are getting better. I'm afflicted with diarrhea issues at the moment so chewing pills and hoping for the best (more info than you needed?).*

*Just wandered around the town. Texted Kosmos to ask how I get access to the airport. He generously offered to help & off we went. After fueling India Zulu the question was floated as to whether I wanted to fly... Rude to say no...and I was told to jump in the left seat of a Cessna Cardinal.*

*Two chaps got in the back seats. Kosmos tweaked the door mechanism and removed the right window. He haggled on the radio to fit us in between the jets (I'm told Chania is Greece's third busiest airport now) and off we went.*

*Gusting crosswinds pushing the aircraft on takeoff, steep turns, and lots of sightseeing... it all scared the crap out of me (very nearly).*

*I felt wide awake & awash with adrenalin. Hell of an experience. Got dropped off in the town and wandered around. Had something to eat. Missed a call from a Greek number, and then the phone died.*

*Panicked that it was the airport reporting a problem with India Zulu so I raced back to my accommodation (courtesy of www.lifedive.gr) to charge the phone. Only to find out it was one of the owners of the Dive school asking how I was… I said, 'fine thanks.'*

*It seems that between Kosmos and themselves they've decided not to charge for the accommodation (because I'm 'interesting and nice', apparently, said Tasos the retired Navy Captain).*

*So I buggered off to one of the shops and bought a few bottles of alcohol as a thanks…*

*Early night tonight. Tomorrow I may be making a radio call to an Emirates Captain, in his Airbus…*

*And at the airfield I'm aiming for in Italy it seems like a chap has to fly no higher than 500ft above the ground in order to avoid complicated airspace. That could be fun.'*

Notes:

Boy oh boy, did I feel rough.

The Emirates Captain is my friend Tahir Brohi. We were in the Air Cadets together as kids and he flies an A380 now, bless 'im.

Nearly twenty years previously I'd hoped to fly with 'T' and build flying hours in piston engined cargo aircraft, whilst tripping around Zaire and Africa in general.

A corneal ulcer, a girlfriend problem, and a civil war in Zaire put paid to those plans. My life had subsequently taken a different path to his. He'd been following the flight on Facebook and knew that India Zulu was stricken with problems, and he wanted to help.

# Phoenix

In the end we missed each other but his offer to be my guardian angel, above the lonely waters of the Mediterranean, was greatly appreciated.

Did you know that the Airbus A380 has a shower onboard that the pilots can use? Lucky, so and so's.

23rd May. Day 18

From Facebook

*'Crete to Italy*

*A few options to fly to in Italy, and Eddie and I had batted a couple of names about as to where to land. A friend had suggested a different airfield, but I went with Eddie's suggestion of Conte...*

*Up & showered at 6.30am. Filed the Flight Plan and headed to the airport dressed in my red shirt. Sun shining. Tummy still rumbling a bit. I passed by the tourists in the main terminal and got to the Operations Office.*

*Filled in another declaration form and asked what I needed to pay. Fished out my MasterCard and the three guys smiled at me.*

*And then I was asked for the equivalent of five quid. For one of Greece's busiest airports a fiver seems pretty good value. I packed everything into the aircraft and checked and double-checked things.*

*Called the Tower to get permission to start the engine and heard a major 'roarrrrr', then another and another. Three US fighter jets screamed into the sky. I taxied out and saw more fighters rolling in my direction on the opposite taxiway (the military part of the airfield).*

*Figuring they'd be a while I shut the engine down. Without the sound of my Rotax I tuned into a throbbing noise behind me and realised a Boeing 757 was queueing up to get airborne.*

*The noise of its jets was disconcerting. Off-putting. Bugger this, I thought, and called the Tower to ask if I could cut in front of the Top Gun types. Take off* was approved, and off I flew. I took a right turn and then had to start dinking around all sorts of military zones as I cut inland towards mainland Greece. Lots of reporting points, lots of 'give me your ETA for here and there', lots of radio work.

Had to climb as we got nearer the mountains. The engine started to cool and the green readings became yellow. India Zulu wasn't in the mood for 10,000 feet and struggled with 8k. Spoke to Air Traffic and told them I was descending.

Decided I'd keep the engine warm by following the sea at just below 1,000ft. It's out of everyone's airspace, but 1,000ft carries risks, too.

Got a call from a military air traffic controller and we agreed I could climb into their airspace.

More reporting points. More ETA's. More radio work. Found my way to the Greek / Italy border and heard Italian voices. Was told to fly 'not higher than 1,500ft above the sea on QNH 1016'…

Approached the Italian cliffs and, as I coasted in, was told not to fly above 500ft from the ground… Life looks more interesting from 400ft. I found the airfield, a grey stripe in the parched countryside, and changed from the Military controller to the airfield frequency.

Lots of thermals bouncing me about and it felt like being hit by a punch bag.

We landed and I climbed out of India Zulu after 5 hours of flying. Ears numb, back sore, needed the loo. The chap from the radio seemed friendly but said he was hungry and wanted a bite to eat. Did I want to come?

At a restaurant in town he ordered a small beer and asked if I wanted one. He followed it up by saying, 'I wouldn't fly on if I were you.' So I had a beer, too. 30 minutes later we were at the airfield and he was telling me of his recent flu issues and that he'd been arrested in Egypt for a flying related matter. I sympathised…

He's one of the instructors at the airfield. Nice fellow. We spent an hour or two in the sun mucking about with their fuel bowser trying to fill the wing tanks

# Phoenix

*from atop a ladder and generally playing about with the jiggle pump. You haven't lived until you've tasted a mouthful of Avgas whilst trying to get gravity to move fuel from A to B.*

*We both spent another hour removing the Turtlepac fuel cell from the passenger seat. I can put up with a lot in an aircraft as long as I'm not worried about running out of fuel. That's a big issue over the sea and in the Middle East but not so much in Europe. We also tried to protect India Zulu against the gusting winds.*

*Made it to a hotel. Bit knackered.'*

Notes

It was bloody windy, bloody gusty, and I was flying bloody low at points.

# Chapter 20. 24th May. Day 19

From Facebook

*'Southern Italy to Elba.*

*Fell asleep fully dressed last night and woke up too early this morning. My eyes are looking decidedly pink. The clothes I'd hand-washed were still damp and it took a while to get my brain going.*

*Breakfast at 7.30am. I then waited for Antonio to collect me so we could go open the airfield. He had other things to do and appeared at 9.45am. Running it tight for takeoff.*

*I was relying on his generosity so the only thing to do was smile and be polite. He insisted we get something to eat from his friend's cafe and we rolled up outside. With a glint in his eyes, he presented me with a pastry & minuscule coffee with the expectation that I'd fall in love with the Italian way of things.*

*I'm more a sausage and egg toastie type, topped off with a mug of tea, but I went with the flow. The South of Italy is so hugely different from Manchester. If you bought Antonio's chef friend to the Northwest of England, he'd spend the whole time in tears. Quite touchingly Antonio's friend bought me two posters as souvenirs and a 'dinner box' to eat later. Very, very, sweet of both of them. We drove to the airfield, and Antonio wanted to show me a dead snake…*

*He's a genuinely, genuinely, lovely chap but I was in a hurry and gently tried to move matters along. In town the wind had seemed passive; at the airfield it was a distinct 20 or so knots. And blustery. India Zulu was twitching and the tie-down ropes were flexing as the wind tried to blow her away.*

*Antonio & I looked at my route and he made a few suggestions. Everywhere on his screen showed sun across the whole of Italy. If I could manage a 20knot direct crosswind takeoff, I'd be fine. As part of my overall musings, I considered covering up part of the engine radiator, but with temperatures of 25c I figured she might overheat.*

# Phoenix

*I grabbed the food parcel, which turned out to be pastry type things, said goodbye, untied India Zulu, and jumped aboard. Started the engine, waited for the temps to come up, started rolling, and didn't stop until the wheels left the ground.*

*I immediately switched to the military frequency and was told to stay below 500ft.*

*India Zulu took a hit from something, thermal or gust. My left hand had been clamped to the stick, but my right was free, and it launched itself against the top of the cabin, bucking bronco style.*

*My watch, or should I say Eddie's, hit the bulkhead, the strap broke, and it flew off my wrist, and then it started raining pastries.*

*20 minutes later we were clear of the military zone and climbed away from all the buffeting. It started to rain. I feel claustrophobic when rain hits the aircraft. The clouds accumulated and closed in. Serious levels of concentration were required.*

*I tried to climb above the rain, but the engine wasn't having it, the temperatures were dropping, and I had no choice but to put up with the rain, the buffeting, and clag.*

*We ran along a few valleys and found the sea. The sun came out to play. The engine started to cool as I found more mountains in my way and had to nurse her around each one... unable to climb above them.*

*I felt overwhelmingly stressed. Spoke to everyone on the radio and got permission to fly along the coast. The only niggle is that they wanted India Zulu below 1,000ft and there isn't a lot of time to remedy 'problems' at that height if there's a headache to address...*

*The Italians fly at that level, so I figured I would too. The engine seemed comfortable at that height so that was a decided plus. I flew along the coast and was handed from Air Traffic unit to Air Traffic unit. Passing Rome I was directed to a VFR corridor 15 miles out to sea and told to stay below 1,000ft, and then lost all radio contact.*

*That feels very lonely and you try to put yourself in neutral so you don't think too much about the implications of the prop' stopping.*

*30 minutes later I escaped from the height restrictions and climbed. Spoke to Air Traffic and reported in. Then spotted a beautiful little island and the tourist in me took over and I circled to have a gander. The Italian islands are stunning.*

*Made my way to Elba and approached the runway by descending over the other side of a hill. Needed a series of S turns to avoid terra-firma and it probably looked quite interesting from the ground.*

*Landed and have found this place absolutely stunning. Not spoilt by huge amounts of tourism, there's sandy beaches, clear waters, and it's a hidden joy…*

*Incidentally, Napoleon Bonaparte was exiled here after he was taken down a peg or two by the Duke of Wellington…*

*5 hours 40 minutes flying today… hoping for boredom tomorrow…'*

*PS. This isn't me, but this is how you're supposed to land…*
*http://youtu.be/O02PBXVu5UQ.*

Notes:

None to add, really.

The Italians are a friendly bunch, the sun shone; I'd be crap on a bucking bronco. I nearly crashed into the mountains (because the engine was running cold, and I couldn't climb above them) but it was just another day in Johnny's World.

And in terms of accuracy, it's been pointed out to me… that Napoleon did not meet Wellington until after he had escaped from Elba.

Napoleon was exiled to Elba in 1814 after being defeated in the Napoleonic/Iberian wars. In 1815 he escaped from Elba and went to France and formed an army to continue his ambitions.

# Phoenix

A coalition was formed and, under the command of the Duke of Wellington, the battle of Waterloo took place in June 1815. Napoleon was defeated again and then exiled to St Helena in the remote South Atlantic, where he died 6 years later.

<u>25th May. Day 20</u>

<u>From Facebook</u>

*'Elba to France.*

*Penultimate day. These notes are for me rather than anyone else. So the fact that I came within a whisker of falling asleep in flight is a message to me to be careful. And maybe a warning to others not to take flying long distances for granted.*

*Flying a microlight takes a lot of effort and throw in the radio work, second-guessing everything, checking routes, worrying about the weather over 500, 600 or 700 miles, tuning into the sound of the engine, battling a low level of anxiety, etc., etc., it can be tough.*

*That's what I've found. And at the end of all that stress you need to coax a very light aircraft to land… For long-distance flights a heavier aircraft c/w autopilot is pretty much essential… I'll keep this short…*

*Slept ok last night. Got to the airport and my Flightplan hadn't made it. Re-did another, then did my preflight. Decided to cover a certain section of the engine radiator with tape in the hope that would make her run warmer. Took off and realised I hadn't put my life jacket on. Wriggled into it and flew west over the Med.*

*Spotted three firefighting aircraft jinking about above mountainous islands (that looks like so much fun). Sky Demon failed a dozen times over the water. Spoke to various Air Traffic agencies and made my way towards mainland France. Approaching Nice I spotted an Aircraft Carrier.*

*Landed at Lyon, refuelled, and took off for Le Touquet.*

# Jon Hilton

*Got into a cruise configuration, sorted the radio work out, and leant my head against the window... and nodded off... Sorted out my concentration levels and flew on. Experimented with what would happen if I let go of the stick (video later). Found a few clouds and had a play by jinking around them.*

*Landed at Le Touquet after maybe 8 hours flying. Checked into a cheap hotel and going to sleep now. P.S. Think I've hit the sweet spot with the tape covering the radiator. The engine worked well.*

*From Eddie...*

*Yesterday saw Jon Hilton fly from the Italian island of Elba all the way to Le Touquet on the French coast of the English Channel. With a stop at Lyon for fuel Jon made a day of it nursing his aircraft, G-CGIZ, in weather that was not conducive at times for microlight flying to within a stone's throw of the UK and home.*

*Today, weather permitting, he will fly his CTSW over the Channel to England and hopefully reach his home airfield of Barton, near Manchester, to conclude this epic adventure.*

*You can read more about his adventures and misadventures on his Facebook page at https://www.facebook.com/groups/137586931201/*

*We all know this flight started off as a circumnavigation, but the aviation gods decided to throw everything at Jon to stretch his flying skills, and mental abilities, to the limits. He made the hard but correct decision to turn around when it would have been easier to just carry on.\**

*Anyone close to the flight will know just how much Jon had to face each day, and therefore, we salute him on his achievement of flying this small aircraft to Jordan and back... against all odds... and we promise to buy you a beer (make that 10) at the LAA Rally this year.*

*Now take it easy and enjoy the last leg back to your loved ones.'*

# Phoenix

<u>Notes:</u>

I was physically shattered. I full-on fell asleep and she'd rolled into a dive before I woke up. I was 'out' for about 3 or 4 seconds. I woke up completely startled, pulled her from the dive, cranked open both window vents, and started to feel sleepy again...

Not sure what to say, I was overwhelmingly tired.

\* With reference to Eddie's comment about it being easier to carry on...I tried my best. Not sure what else to say.

<u>Last day</u>

From Facebook

'*Le Touquet to Barton.*

*Apart from waking at 2.13am from a nightmare, I'm not expecting anything too exciting today. The engine's working well now and the battery seems to be charging my nav kit. i.e... Both anxieties seem to be resolving themselves. So, this'll be my last update...*

*I failed in what I set out to do, but the more of us that try something difficult or seemingly unachievable the more of us will succeed.*

*Be inspired. Extend your reach.*

*Regards*

*Jon*'

<u>Notes:</u>

Long distance flying is a wonderful weight-loss tool. I misplaced 14lbs over the three weeks.

# **Epilogue**

Golf India Zulu

A week after my return to Barton I took a chap flying from a local radio station. On the climb out from the runway the fuel flow readings started to fluctuate, and it seemed the prop' was destined to stop, again. The decision process was whether to take a tight turn back to the airfield or see if a gentler pitch attitude would help.

I chose the latter and kept the young fellah chatting whilst I casually pointed out ground features. The plan being to keep his eyes away from the fuel starvation messages, in red text, spreadeagled across the Dynon screen in front of his face. With excellent timing the transponder failed as well.

We slowly climbed to a safe height and gently bimbled back to the airfield with this chap none the wiser he'd nearly ended up in a field.

But if you were to play Top Trumps with landing sites... An English field is so much nicer than ploughing headfirst into Italian mountains, ditching in the Mediterranean, or crash landing in the deserts of the Middle East.

My mate Simon subsequently pulled the engine apart. He found a certain amount of 'blue sludge' in the fuel pump mechanism, and that may have been starving the engine of fuel.

The general suspicion is that when the Germans refitted the fuel tanks some of the sealant, or other contaminant, may have found its way into the fuel line and been pottering around the engine.

There's a couple of other points to note.

# Phoenix

After Simon removed the gunk from the fuel pump, 'something' started trying to escape from the wing roots. Gary Masters was subsequently good enough to take the wings off and check over and reseal the tanks.

Since then, the whole 'dropping a wing' thing has gone away and she flies straight and level without any headaches. I've kept various video clips on my phone of her antics in flight so I can recall the hell she put me through. All very stressful, but as a glass half full type of chap, well, she's fixed now, so no problem.

Incidentally, the Germans seem to have been a little mischievous in that one wingtip has a couple of dribble marks in the paint. i.e. the sprayer wasn't concentrating and overdid things a tad when he resprayed the wingtips.

I very carefully checked each wing tip prior to initially retrieving her from Germany. My thought, rightly or wrongly, is that they polished over the dribbled section of paint to avoid any hard questions. And the polish subsequently came off in the rain.

This is all incidental to the terrible job they did cutting out the carbon fibre on the nose wheel spat. Or putting the hole for the fuel drainer in the wrong place. Or not securing the binnacle and generally making the lower cowling look lopsided, etc.

One of the last items on my list of gripes is the 'turning left' issue whilst taxiing.

The Fox finally figured this out after I'd returned to Barton. Whilst both brakes were initially sticking, that wasn't the problem. The CT has two rods that attach to the nose wheel, and one is slightly shorter than the other. Our European brethren had put them on back to front, and she was always destined to pull left.

Hence on short taxiways, especially grass surfaces, the problem wasn't obvious. At commercial airports with miles of smooth runways and taxiways it was a nightmare.

Again, you have to laugh.

The moral of this part of the story? Well, if you ever discover the secret identity of the Fox, my suggestion is to constantly seek his wisdom, do everything he says, and not argue.

You might want to implode and blow a gasket, but experience suggests he's right 90% of the time.

I've written that last sentence in the sure and certain knowledge that if he ever reads this… that a frown will be making its way across his forehead as he starts to dispute the missing 10%.

Gotcha!

# Written Three Years Later

I've cherished a few females in my life but not been able to make the relationships last. Right time, wrong person. And vice versa.

Miscarriages have played a role, too. And whilst you might think this type of personal tragedy brings people closer, in my experience it does the opposite.

Like Samina and Ava's Mum, my relationship with Cindy failed.

There were health issues on my return from the Middle East, not least severe fatigue. A phone call to the health centre led to an emergency assessment.

An apologetic Practice Manager handed over a yellow letter bearing the words, '*you have the symptoms of Cancer.*' It went on to say that it would be a wise move to attend all subsequent appointments whilst they continued their investigations.

I have a specific memory of taking the letter from her hand in a state of numb incomprehension. Twenty minutes later I found myself sat in a B&Q car park watching families walk past the car carrying tins of paint, plants, and all manner of DIY kit.

It hit me like a hammer that my life might stop, but for everyone else it would continue. It was a cold moment of palpable desolation. A fear of the unknown and a sense of loss that I'd miss out on the milestones in Ava's life.

For ten days you could say I wasn't mentally or physically at my best. And with poetic timing Cindy was presented with an exciting self-employed opportunity that she wanted to pursue. The role needed her complete focus and she decided to depart our relationship.

When the results finally filtered through it turned out the health centre had jumped the gun a little. The diagnosis wasn't, in fact, the big C.

The suggestion being that the symptoms matched the version of Hepatitis that comes from, let's politely say, poorly prepared food. My guess is that it started in Egypt and might explain why I was feeling so damned tired and miserable all the time.

And that seemed to have been layered on top of the dehydration and kidney infection that started to trip me up somewhere around Jordan. Maybe that additional veneer of misery contributed to my coming home.

Then again, if I hadn't felt ill maybe I'd have continued onward with that stupid, gung-ho, approach I seem to adopt. Maybe Samson would have coped with the thunderstorms and additional heat in India, or maybe she wouldn't.

Maybe I'd have coped when the Hepatitis properly kicked in. Or maybe I'd have lost focus somewhere and piled headfirst into the deck.

*** 

A handful of months after the Cancer scare Cindy and I organised to meet up again.

We met at a rather nice local restaurant and chatted through a few things. From matters being lighthearted she suddenly asked if I'd been seeing anyone whilst we were apart, and I said no.

I asked the same question whilst buttering the toast that accompanied the pâté. She went coy and said she had been seeing someone, but it hadn't worked out. She then proceeded to tell me, in explicit detail, about their sexual relationship.

And I must admit I found that a little off-putting. Nevertheless, she said she loved me and wanted to become an item again. And I sat

# Phoenix

there with uneaten toast in one hand, whilst my jaw was on the floor, and didn't know quite what to think.

Despite a handful of misgivings, we subsequently did get back together. At the same time you could say the pâté moment knocked me about a little, and I never quite looked at her in the same way. Maybe some things should be left unsaid.

Weeks rolled by and Ava, myself, and Cindy were out and about somewhere. We were most likely joking and being silly, as was our way, when my darling daughter looked up at Cin and solemnly asked, *'can I call you, my mummy?'*

And my best guess is that Ava returned home and innocently mentioned that conversation to her Mum. Maybe she'd said it in the same way she'd sleepily told me she had a new Daddy... and three days later all hell broke loose.

You could say I was put through one of the worst days of my life. Ava's mum baited me to the point of losing my temper, which I did unfortunately.

It seemed, reading between the lines, I was being given a choice between seeing Ava or having a relationship with Cindy.

A day later I tried to chat to Cin about events. She seemed distracted and wasn't properly paying attention. Yet on some level she must have been hearing what I was saying.

She tilted her beautiful face to one side, looked up at the ceiling, and absently said, *'I just need someone to put me at the centre of everything they do.'* And in that moment, I knew that Ava would always come first and that I wouldn't be able to meet Cindy's needs. My relationship with her subsequently died.

Despite letting Ava's Mum know of the break-up, I've been stopped from seeing my daughter for the last six months. And her mother seems hell-bent on rewriting Ava's past and future in a way that doesn't include me.

Hopefully, this book will show Ava, at some point, how much she's been a key part of my life.

After the original crash in 2015 I chose not to go to the pub, get drunk, and generally stare into space. I went straight round to see Ava, hugged her, and simply spent time by her side.

And as the summer evening wore on, and the curtains were drawn, I read her a bedtime story until she fell asleep. Maybe a parent's love for their child is what life is all about. Maybe that surpasses everything else.

To bring matters to a conclusion, I'd suggest the preceding 85,000 or so words could best be described as a love story, rather than a book about flying. With that love encompassing the aircraft's namesake, Samina, and Cindy, and most of all, Ava.

Ultimately, this is my message through time to my beautiful daughter.

*'As I write this, baby, you're 7 years old and life will undoubtedly bounce you around as you get older. Please try to be the best person you can be, work hard, and help those that need your support. Whatever happens in the future, I will always love you.'*

And finally, to anyone else who has struggled to this point… it's my wish that you wrap your arms around those you love and give the blighters a bloody big hug.

Have a happy life, please.

JH

Note:

You may have noticed an absence of pictures within the narrative. That was to avoid giving away what happened. If you wanted to add a little extra flavour to the story, you could head to Facebook

## Phoenix

and search for 'Microlight in the Middle East.' Assuming FB still exists when you read this, there's pictures galore in store.

# Time Capsule

I did warn you in the prelude that I'd written a summary of my existence to this point. I should also say that the timeline gets horribly mashed as different elements tangle and untangle themselves, but here goes;

My journey towards aviation started with Mum, Dad, and myself attending a long distant careers evening at Turton High School.

There were all sorts of professional folk in numerous classrooms promoting different vocations, and we aimlessly wandered into one such room. Pictures of aircraft were pinned on felt-covered exhibition boards, and a chap in a blue uniform was standing by the door idly chatting to my English teacher, Mr Elliot.

Mr Elliot was the kind of stuffy type that I've never understood and, from day dot, he'd marked me down as a cocky trucker. He spotted me, said hello, and simultaneously sniffed at the idea of my becoming a pilot.

My teenage psyche didn't quite know how to respond when he quietly said, '*Forget it, Hilton, you're too tall to fly in the RAF, and you're not clever enough.*' He didn't say that in front of my parents of course, it was a little sideways dig whilst they were off looking at pictures of 1980s jet fighters stuck here and there.

But even at the tender age of fifteen, Mr Elliot's demeanour and comments got under my skin and irked a little. Having said that, maybe I should have thanked my former nemesis because in that classroom, at that moment, he gave my life direction.

Unfortunately, fate intervened shortly afterwards and emergency surgery was needed on my stomach. A twisted Omentum, and complications after the operation, took me away from school

# Phoenix

during my last year and I left with a paltry three GCE's, all at grade 'C'.

Mum and Dad weren't exactly inspired, but Dad figured he could fund my way into a grammar school to sit A levels. Consequently, all three of us met the Vice-Chancellor at Queen Elizabeth Grammar School in Blackburn. And this chap informed my parents that there might even be a place for me at Oxford or Cambridge, if I buckled down.

I could see my parent's eyes twinkling at that point, but it seemed like a bit of a stretch to me.

Firstly, I wasn't comfortable with the idea of my parents funding my education and secondly, I wanted to earn money and gain my own independence. Hence, without any great planning, and to the chagrin of my parents, I ended up leaving full-time education.

And found myself living the high life as a trainee Civil Engineering Estimator, on a Youth Training Scheme, earning a whopping £25.00 a week.

That led to my latterly becoming a Tunnel Engineer, which I wasn't great at, and then to becoming an Estate Agent, which I was a little embarrassed about.

How do you go from one occupation to the other?

I guess you could say I was being lazy, cocky, and somewhat stupid all in the same instant. And from the vantage point of time, I have to say those three adjectives seem to have played an interesting role in my life.

For those unfamiliar with tunnelling, a tunnel drive involves digging a big hole in the ground, known in engineering terms as a shaft. When you're deep enough, a laser is embedded high in the shaft wall and the miners then dig a tunnel in whichever direction the red dot sends them.

# Jon Hilton

We'd finished a series of tunnels, in Ashton Under Lyne, and a member of the engineering team was needed to remove the laser from one of them.

The normal plan of action would have been to get a couple of ladders lashed together and go from there. But that involved time and effort, so, with a casual nod towards the miners, yours truly climbed inside a large metal earth-moving bucket. And then politely asked the crane driver to hoist me into the skies.

The plan was to use the crane as a lift and lower a younger me down into the depths of the shaft to retrieve the laser. A simple, quick, solution, I thought.

Basically, I was suspended above a bloody big hole in the ground by a crane. And then felt weightless, looked up to see the chain had snapped, and don't remember a great deal after that.

Fortunately, the bucket only fell thirty feet or so. It subsequently bounced off the concrete floor of the shaft and it went one way, and I went the other. The damn thing had been built to carry 4,000kg's of earth, and it'd been empty when I climbed in, hence the chain snapping was a tad surprising.

An ambulance took me to hospital and the X-rays suggested a compression fracture of the lowest section of my spine. There was a loss of feeling on my right side, but nothing hugely debilitating and I felt better after a couple of hours.

The next day I went back to work, picked up my theodolite and optical level, and started wandering around the site, again.

One of the middle-aged Irish miners took me to one side and in that gentle Southern Irish brogue told me to get the previous day's incident recorded in the accident book. The logic being that that might be insurance against my spine taking a turn for the worst in the future.

# Phoenix

'Elth and safety weren't the big deal they are now, but the site agent was switched on to the idea of future insurance claims. He looked at me, as I was sheepishly peering around his door, and said nothing had happened that warranted entry into the blue accident book sat on his desk.

And that was the point I started to wonder about working for the firm.

At the same time, the Channel Tunnel project was just getting started and they desperately needed Junior Engineers. I gave thought to upping sticks and moving down south but, after working a couple of night shifts in Sheffield, I was beginning to have reservations about Tunnel Engineering in general.

Whilst I was wondering how my life might pan out a couple of other work events occurred.

Firstly, a teenage labourer had an unfortunate coming together with a bench saw. He'd been cutting planks of wood in the site compound and was feeding the timber through the saw with two hands.

Sadly, the spinning vertical circular saw didn't have a guard in place to protect the user. And he was pushing the wood through the circular blade as it revolved at 60 odd times per second.

Maybe the young chap wasn't paying attention, but steel met flesh and seven of his fingers went walkabout. I wasn't there at the time, but I was latterly told his screams could be heard throughout the acre wide compound.

The senior engineer was in one of the cabins nearby, and he tried his best to deal with matters. He consequently picked up the lifeless digits and put them in a small cardboard box. Then gingerly gave them to the ambulance crew and the medicos had a stab at sewing them on some hours later.

We didn't see the young man on site, again.

Although, as a postscript to this incident, a year later I went on a family holiday with the family to Majorca. The four star hotel was near to Magaluf (or Megamuff as I believe it's known these days) and my baby sister wanted to go to a water park somewhere in the main resort.

We queued up for the biggest and scariest water slide, and a bunch of young lads were 10 people in front of us. One of them looked familiar, and I looked down at his hands. It was the young fellah from site.

From a quick glance it seemed that his fingers had been sewn back on, but they were pointing in different directions and seem to have been shortened.

Anyway.

The week after the fingers incident, I turned up at one of the active tunnel drives, to check the laser, and found a crane had fallen down the shaft. Yep, you read that right.

The crane was using the kind of bucket I'd climbed into a month before. The miners were digging out the ground and shovelling earth into it. When it was full, the bucket was hoisted out of the shaft, its contents were emptied into a wagon, and the bucket was lowered down again. The process was repeated over and over throughout the day as the shaft got deeper and deeper.

The crane had a warning bell fitted that rang when the bucket was overweight and too heavy to be safely hoisted up. According to the miners, the bell was regularly kicking off and the crane driver unilaterally decided the noise was becoming a tad tedious. Consequently, he wedged his hanky between the bell and ringer and got on with the job in hand.

And the laws of physics kicked in, and the crane slowly started to lean forwards. Time speeded up and a 20 ton Ruston Bucyrus RB22 crane dived headfirst into the shaft and wedged itself in-situ. Fortunately no one was hurt, the driver managing to leap out in

# Phoenix

time, and the miners ran into the tunnel, but it was a damn close affair.

Twenty minutes after all the excitement had occurred, I found myself stood by the side of the circular shaft, at ground level, looking down at the underside of the crane. And all I could think was, *'maybe I need a new career.'*

And courtesy of a random job advert in the Bolton Evening News, I ended up working as a valuer for an estate agency chain.

From what I recall, the management wanted tall, slim, vaguely handsome young men who could string a sentence together. It didn't say that on the job advert, but all the valuers I met seemed to fit that profile. And I guess I did, too.

Roll forward two years, and I can't say I was particularly thrilled at being an Estate Agent either, so I revisited the flying idea.

Although, as another postscript, if you want to get propositioned by mature women, Estate Agency is definitely the way to go. I'm digressing here because certain things just stick in a chap's mind, but...

On two separate occasions, randy females deliberately poured tea onto my nicely creased suit pants in order to get me to take them off. And one newly single lady kept me at her house 'till midnight and wouldn't let me leave until I'd accepted her proposal to play gentleman's leapfrog.

Possibly the strangest memory I recall, was of two women in their forties who trapped me, all on my lonesome, in their property. It was a café at the front, had a private eating area in the middle complete with wooden benches, and a residential section to the rear.

They disappeared into a side room, stripped down to their underwear, draped white bedsheets over their heads, and chased me around whilst simultaneously grabbing after my manhood and cackling.

An innocent younger me was completely bloody non-plussed and I leapt onto a couple of the benches as a way to leg it away from the ghostly apparitions. I subsequently made it into the toilet, locked the door, and managed to escape to freedom through the small window.

In my defence, I'd just turned twenty-one, had only just got a girlfriend, and wasn't quite mentally prepared to be jumped on by two horny middle-aged ghosts… It's funny the things that wedge themselves into a person's memory.

And yes, I was a late starter where females were concerned. I grew up watching classic films on Sunday afternoons in which the hero was generally a gentleman. I guess my early years were framed by the likes of David Niven, Cary Grant, and Gregory Peck.

I did pick up the pace a little as I slowly matured and, from a naive innocent, it would be fair to say I became a little mischievous in my later years. I was always faithful in relationships but, when single, there was definitely a twinkle in my eyes.

And all that completely changed when my daughter came on the scene many years later. From footloose and fancy-free, I became an adult almost overnight. I was in my early forties at the time, and becoming a grown-up was somewhat overdue, I guess.

\*\*\*

Anyway, back to my narrative.

With Mr. Elliot in mind, who I later learnt had failed the RAF selection process as a younger man, a 22 year old me decided to get a PPL. Hence I withdrew all my savings, packed my bags, and headed to a flying school in Missouri.

# Phoenix

The day I arrived at the Flight school I found myself sat in the Chief Flying Instructors office nervously waiting for my induction. And with wonderfully poetic timing, the burly local sheriff walked in, complete with gun in holster, and arrested her.

The suggestion being that the school was a cover to run drugs up and down the great United States of America. Hence I was gruffly informed that the flying schools' assets had been frozen, and the dollars I'd just parted with were forfeit whilst a court case was set in play.

And eight weeks later, after living in an abandoned US Airforce base for the interim, the local community took pity on me and decided to fund my flight training. It has to be said the Americans can be a wonderful bunch.

During that spell in the US, I came into contact with a chap who offered me a job as a crop spraying pilot. By return, I said I wanted to finish my flying licenses and do things properly, but he wanted me there and then.

I'd seen a couple of bent and broken Boeing Stearman's on the back of flatbed trucks by that point and I was acutely aware of the implications of bouncing off hedgerows and telegraph poles. The fella made the offer of a Green card to secure my services, but I decided to pass on that opportunity in favour of returning to sunny Bolton.

My life has been full of *'what if'* moments. And who knows how matters might have played out if I'd been braver and accepted his offer.

There were memories that I cherish from that time in the US, like having a good natured argument with a flying instructor at the end of a night flight. We'd just landed at a decommissioned Airforce base, and the runway was huge. No one was around, and the runway lights seemed to head towards infinity.

Likewise everywhere else was shrouded in complete darkness, and there was a pitch-black abyss below the wheels. And the instructor was questioning whether we'd actually touched down. I said we had, but he was adamant we hadn't.

We had landed, of course, it just happened to be the absolute lightest of a kiss against the tarmac. He finally humphed and said, *'well done on the landing.'*

The only other significant memory I carry from that time was another night flight above either Missouri or Mississippi. My instructor, the same chap, had just welcomed his firstborn into the world and was somewhat tired. Consequently, he kept nodding off.

The plan had been to just potter around the skies for an hour or so, but I got bored. I woke him up, and we agreed to head to a small town on the horizon.

A grid pattern of lights suggested the place was home to 10,000 or so folk. Everywhere was pitch black, and there was no definition between sky and ground.

We pottered overhead, and my instructor suggested pulling the power so we could, I guess, be at one with the world. I stopped the engine, and we just glided in circles above the centre of the town.

It was a beautiful experience, but then it got interrupted. One second we were quietly appreciating the moment. And then everywhere went white. The kind of white you see in the bible.

Every part of the cabin was awash with the purest of pure heavenly light. For a fraction of a second, I thought I'd died.

Another second passed, and both of us realised the aircraft had been pinged by a searchlight. We jumped into action, I fired up the engine, and we headed back to the airfield vowing to keep the incident to ourselves.

# Phoenix

If you ever see a Xenon Searchlight being switched on, you'll get a vibe as to what I'm talking about.

The two of us latterly decided we'd floated over the centre of the township. Maybe over the police station. Possibly they'd heard us, heard the engine go quiet, and taken aim.

I can't say what death will be like, but if it involves a white light blinding all the senses, then I've got a head start on everyone else.

\*\*\*

On my later return to Blighty I tried to save as much money as possible with the aim of funding a commercial ticket. Life inevitably got in the way and, eight-or-so years later, I separated from my girlfriend, abandoned life as an insurance broker, and trundled off to Florida with a wodge of cash.

The plan was to self-fund my FAA training with the intent to meet a mate of mine in Africa, and get a flying job. I'd known this chap from Bolton's Air Cadet squadron and Tahir, mostly known as T, was working as a newbie commercial pilot in Zaire.

Incidentally, T was mentioned part way through the previous chapters. His life took a different direction to mine and he latterly went on to Captain an A380.

During those happy months in Florida, I guess I got a little cocky. I ended up having regular landing competitions with the instructors as a way to pass the time. That was great fun and, dare I say it, I was a little bit unbeatable.

Possibly as a way to bring yours truly down a peg or two, the flying school started sending me to Orlando International to collect paperwork and other bits and pieces.

Those were intense adrenalin-filled experiences. I have to say that regardless of whether you're a man or a woman, flying solo into such a huge jet airport will put hairs on your chest.

# Jon Hilton

On one occasion I was on the huge taxiway, strapped to a single engined put-put, sandwiched between an Airbus and a Boeing 737. And I was wondering whether the passenger aircraft in front would blow me into the clutches of the bigger jet behind.

At precisely the same time, I looked up and saw Jesus staring back at me.

It turns out it wasn't God's eldest; it was the image of an Eskimo painted on the tail of a 737-400. But when you're living on your wits and experiencing things for the first time, it's easy to get confused. You may have read that and thought, so what? But at that moment I swear I nearly peed my pants.

Later on in my commercial training, as part of the cross-country nav' test, my Cessna and I (N5363Q) floated directly over the Daytona Speedway heading into Daytona Airport. We subsequently flew onward through the Bermuda Triangle to Freeport in the Bahamas.

Alas, the flying school didn't provide an inflatable life raft, and I can tell you the first time you're out of sight of land, with the sea stretching from horizon to horizon, it's an interesting experience.

On the return trip, some point past midnight and in the pitch black, I was allowed to fly along the runway at Cape Canaveral. This may be long forgotten history by the time you read this, but Cape Canaveral was where the Space Shuttle launched from and landed at. So gaining permission to fly at 200ft above the runway, in the dark, was damned exciting.

If you're bored, you might want to Google '*night-time Space Shuttle launches.*' They were majestic to watch, and I saw two of 'em whilst studying in Florida.

Separately, and this might not paint me in the best of lights, I have a vivid memory of herding cows around a copse of trees on a cross country flight somewhere in the Florida Keys. I was in a Cessna

# Phoenix

Aerobat at the time, and swooping around the blue skies was enormous fun, incredibly stupid, but fantastic fun.

Incidentally, cows don't seem to move very fast even when an Englishmen is whooping and a hollering at them from a hundred feet above the deck. They just ambled around the isolated group of trees and seemed to take it all in their stride.

Likewise if you've ever heard of the Vomit Comet, that's a brilliant experience in a Cessna. If you get matters right, you can have '*things*' just float in midair as you fly up and down in a parabolic motion. As I say, I was a lot younger at the time and maybe a little less safety conscious, but that was great fun, too.

And then I got homesick and phoned my girlfriend, Joanna, from a roadside payphone and pledged my undying love to her. A day later I'd binned my US commercial flying course in favour of pursuing the much more expensive CAA licenses. The intention being to return to the UK and get a commercial job here.

Hence, I waved goodbye to sunny Florida with an IMC rating, Multi-Engine rating, Night rating, and a couple of hundred hours in my logbook.

Sadly, Joanna and I didn't last. She'd offered to move around the country with me as a precursor to my getting an airline job, but changed her mind and didn't want to leave Salford. I guess that soured our relationship a tad, and we parted ways.

At the same time, and it does seem to happen a lot, fate kicked me in the goolies again, and a Corneal Ulcer got in the way of my flying. This was the early 90s by that point, and a bout of laser eye surgery would have buggered up my medical certificate. So I reluctantly shelved the idea of flying for a living and slowly got on with trying to establish a normal life.

\*\*\*

# Jon Hilton

I'd gone back to living with my parents at that point, and they weren't best pleased at having an unemployed oik living with them again. Hence I needed employing. I wanted the salary that went with my former occupation, Insurance Broker, but figured I'd role the dice and see what was available.

So I took matters into my own hands and started writing letters to firms all over the Northwest asking for a job, any job, as a matter of urgency.

One of the few replies I received was from a Searchlight company. It turns out there are only half a dozen or so such firms in the world. They were good enough to offer me a position and I took the equivalent of a pay cut, which is an academic perspective when you're unemployed, to relaunch myself in a new direction.

I started life there as an export clerk, but it would be fair to say I had ambitions to take on the Sales Managers job. Hence, filled with a certain amount of misplaced confidence, I stayed late one night and figured out how clever the fax machine was. Then sent three hundred fax letters to firms all over the world saying my employers could manufacture anything.

There were a handful of replies but one, most notably, came from a chap in Paris. He was involved in a project that required powerful, weatherproof, fittings for a client he was working with.

To that point, the scheme was about to die because none of the commercially available lighting kit was hardy enough for the environment he had in mind.

He didn't realise it, but he needed marine searchlights and I was the chap to help. So I borrowed my boss's Audi, managed to get a 500kg marine-grade searchlight onto a trailer, and drove through the Channel Tunnel to Paris.

I rocked up at their industrial unit, at the end of Charles de Gaulle airport, and was asked to shine the searchlight around the night skies. I politely mentioned that the searchlight could be seen from

# Phoenix

twenty miles away and that it might not be the wisest of ideas with jets tootling about. But Jean-Marie was adamant that was what he wanted, and he didn't think it'd be a problème.

So I duly pointed the 7kw Xenon, the equivalent of one hundred million candles, into the night sky and took a bow. The project they had in mind was the Eiffel Tower, and the searchlights were just the job.

I promptly skedaddled back to Bolton with a big grin on my face and worked up the costs of supplying four rotating searchlights. Only to be told the firm didn't want the order.

The logic being that the kit needed a certain amount of programming to create a revolving beam effect, and the searchlight firm didn't want the headaches associated with the £50k order.

I jumped up and down, threatened to resign, and ultimately found a compromise where the firm would supply the searchlights, but the Frenchie's could do the automation. And twenty odd years later the kit is still there, and I'm quite proud of that.

That said, the firm initially rejecting the order had caused an element of friction between myself and the older guard. And that was confounded shortly afterwards by the Disney Corporation.

My employers had had a fallout with a major architectural lighting distributor in London, and I'd been tasked with getting them back on board.

I travelled down to the smoke and begged and pleaded with them to start working with us again. They did, and we picked up an order to manufacture light fittings for the tennis courts on the Disney Cruise ships.

The catch was that the kit had to be designed from scratch around the specific lamp the lighting designers wanted to use.

Everything became a rush to make the kit on time, and tempers got a little frayed. Not least because there wasn't sufficient time to prove the design. Consequently, 50 or so lights were packed in wooden containers ready to be shipped whilst one fitting was put on test over night.

I'd decided to work late that evening and was mid-paperwork when I decided to take a break. I ambled into the testing area and for some inexplicable reason picked up an atomizer, the kind folk use on plants, and sprayed water onto the test fitting. The front lens shattered, the glass fell out, and all the electrics in the test bay tripped.

I came into work the next morning to a proper, major, telling off. Words to the effect of, *'How dare you, what were you thinking, we can't send the fittings out now, and it's all your fault!'*

A thirty-one year old me was somewhat mesmerised as half a dozen individuals rounded on yours truly. I pulled myself together and pointed out that the fittings were for outdoor use, and glass raining from the heavens might hurt the little kiddies as they served and volleyed their way around the tennis courts.

That argument held some sway. But I definitely got their attention when I said that an electrical fire on board a cruise ship could lead to corporate manslaughter charges.

A handful of high-ups started to look a little sheepish at that point, and I was subsequently re-adopted into the good lads club. That said, a week later, I got dragged down to a posh area of London to explain why the lighting order hadn't been dispatched on time.

In return, and with epic opportunism, my employers were asking that the price of each unit, at a couple of hundred pounds a go, would need to be renegotiated upwards.

Consequently myself, the design manager, and the general manager were sat around a large table, in the lighting firm's multimillion pound HQ. And we were being interrogated by half a dozen of the world's leading lighting designers.

My boss told the assembled group that we hadn't realised the searchlights would be used outdoors, and they'd need to be redesigned. And you could hear a pin drop as the room went silent.

The scariest man in the room looked at me and said, *'you knew they were for outdoor use, didn't you!'*

I looked down at the opulent meeting room table, as it became the centre of my world, closed my eyes, and then looked up and said, *'yes.'*

We were kicked out of their building fifteen minutes later with instructions to get the fittings ready asap, at our expense. My boss glanced at me as we were getting into his silver Audi and looked a little awkward. *'Don't worry,'* he said, *'everyone knew the fittings were for outdoor use. I was just trying to find an angle.'*

I figured that was the end of my lighting career, though. Generally being shamed in front of the top table of UK lighting designers didn't seem like a good thing.

A week later, I got a call from a London number. It was the guy who'd put me on the spot, and he asked if I wanted a job. I said yes, and asked why he was interested in me. *'You've got integrity,'* he said, *'and I'm going to give you a chance.'*

A month later I'd jumped ship and began commuting to the big smoke to start my career with them as a salesman. They were turning over circa' £20 million a year and seemed able to offer an interesting career.

In an attempt to repay the faith they'd placed in me I followed up various lighting orders that seemed to be on the cusp of dying. One deal I successfully resurrected was for the supply and installation of the lighting kit on the Millennium Bridge across the Thames.

I was credited with being the Project Manager, but I have to say I had no idea what the hell was going on. Fortunately, there was a brilliant foreman on-site, and he took on the majority of the day to day technical duties.

Incidentally, I told the engineering team, before the Queen opened the bridge, that the damn thing was somewhat flimsy and was acting like an aerofoil. By return, I was told to shut up, or I'd be removed from the project. In later years it became known as the "wobbly bridge" and subsequently cost circa' £5 million to fix.

If you're old enough to recall the bridge saga, you may have heard stories about folk "walking in-step" causing it to wobble. I stood on the bridge before it opened, and it seemed very lightweight. My perspective was that it would have always needed a redesign.

During that time, I also briefly met Lord Foster whose firm were the Chief Architects on the project. He tore a strip off one of his team whilst I was milling about, with reference to the height of the handrails, and I have to say he scared the hell out of me. That said, I did get offered a lift in his Range Rover, which I declined in a state of sheer terror.

Unfortunately, the lighting firm had a few financial issues round about the millennium. Specifically Foot & Mouth Disease was blighting the UK at the time and sadly, and somewhat bizarrely, that was affecting the sale of lighting kit to theatres.

And with equally bad timing we'd completed a chunk of work on the Millennium Dome, and they were disputing our invoices.

Hence, a handful of months after I rose to the lofty position of Group Marketing Manager, I loved that title, they went bust.

Not long afterwards I set up my own firm, Legal Brokers Ltd. And if you asked me how that happened, I'd have to say there've been times when I've simply been a butterfly on the breeze.

\*\*\*

# Phoenix

From an "adventure" perspective, and over the decades, I trundled off and did... a safari in Kenya, got caught up in a rip-tide off Australia's Gold Coast, completed a charity bike ride around Beijing, and tried Freefall parachuting (none of that tandem malarkey).

I also picked up my basic Hang-Gliding licence, took part in the Colour Festival in Jaipur, and got sunstroke in Rio. I ran the Bulls at Pamplona and finished the Berlin, Paris, New York, Moscow, Reykjavik, Los Angeles, and Sahara marathons.

The Sahara trip involved leaving in a refugee camp for a week. As a nod to administrators the world over, if someone tells you to buy camouflage gear for your fledgling armed forces, try to avoid buying kit suited to the jungle. ie. your chaps will stand out. That said the Sahrawi people were very friendly.

Separately, I did the Glastonbury and British Grand Prix, things. Both were good fun.

I got invited to row the Atlantic with a couple of guys, but Dad had just passed away and I wasn't in the right place to sit in a boat for 2 months with near strangers. With hindsight it might have been a good distraction.

***

With the Berlin, Paris, and Pamplona runs I was somewhat poor during those times in my life and was living a little hand to mouth. Consequently, I spent a handful of nights sleeping rough on each of those mini-adventures.

With Pamplona, I kept trying to hide from the seedier elements loitering around and slept underneath a park bench for two nights. In the end the bull run was somewhat over subscribed with enthusiastic ediots and I got cut from the event twice.

On each occasion I pegged it back to the main grandstand area, slid in between the scaffolding poles holding up the seating, and got back into contention for the fun run.

Humorusly, my last attempt at taking part meant I was nearest to the half dozen or so bulls that were about to be released. And there I stood, aching, unwashed, filled with adrenalin, and nervous as fook.

And that was when a young South African chap came over to me and said he wanted to do the run with yours truly. He had a rolled up newspaper in his hand and seemed a little too wide eyed for me.

That was when I was informed that your average half a ton bull isn't attracted to colour, the big buggers are attracted to movement.

My South African loonie wanted to run alongside me because he thought the black monsters would make for the rucksack, with all my belongings inside, that was dangling from my left hand. His plan was to thwack the nearest bull with his newspaper in some kind of taunt and see what happened.

At which point I realised I was in the midst of some form of the Darwin Awards event.

The upshot was that 50 or so folk were injured during the run, but non fatally, and I managed to sprint like a champion to safety. I will say I felt thoroughly alive at the end of the event.

That said, if you do the run yourself, and make it into the arena, you may subsequently wish the bulls skewer more loons. ie. it doesn't end well for the poor bovines.

*** 

Anyway, with respect to sleeping rough…. With Paris, I fended off a deadbeat who was trying to sexually assault a young woman at some point during the wee small hours. And with Berlin, I was freezing and scared most of the time.

# Phoenix

I don't advocate rough sleeping, but it'll open your eyes to poverty. The Germans, this was the year after the Berlin Wall fell, looked down at me with looks ranging from indifference to sheer contempt. Those experiences taught me a lot about humanity.

And for good measure, I completed the San Diego Triathlon and the British and South Korean Iron Man events.

\*\*\*

I front crawled my way through a Relay Swim across the English Channel and had one of my many near-death experiences whilst training off the South Coast.

A handful of us set off together, in relatively calm seas, to reach a metal buoy a mile or so out to sea. The conditions turned decidedly worse, and my comrades turned back, but I'd lost sight of them and pushed on.

The waves were angrily rolling along with something like 2 meters between the bottom of each wave and its top. One second you're in a water-filled trench, and the next, you're thrown up towards the skies, and that goes on and on as the waves go about their business. And there I was bobbing up and down at the whimsy of the weather gods whilst front crawling my way to the buoy.

Feeling colder and colder I made it to the big hunk of metal, as it lurched from side to side, and tread water for 5 minutes staring at it. All the while trying to figure out how to safely climb onboard the bloody big thing without getting hurt.

A yacht blithely sailed past and I yelled at it, but didn't get a response. So I took a deep breath, thought warm thoughts, pointed myself towards the shore, and launched myself into front crawl again.

My goggles were ripped from my head as wave after wave pummeled against me. I spent an hour battling the elements and used every ounce of strength I had left as I swam onwards.

# Jon Hilton

Unbeknown to me, my friends had made it back to shore and, fearing I'd drowned, called out the Air Sea Rescue helicopter. With a twist of irony they'd given the authorities the wrong location, and the helicopter went searching 5 miles north of my position.

With my energy levels flat-lining, I front crawled my way towards the distant shore. The tide was constantly pushing me off course and the rocks at the very tip of the headland seemed my only bet to make landfall. My inner coward new that if I didn't put in a mammoth effort I'd have been lost to the Atlantic.

As I neared the headland, and inbetween deep breaths, I recall lifting my head out of the cold water to focus on one specific point of the storm defences. And saw my compatriots, four grown men, anxiously walking up and down the secluded access path in front of the boulders.

They spotted my yellow cap from a hundred yards away and started sprinting. Two of them fell over as the waves crashed against the shore and bathed them in the cold waters of the Channel.

They helped pull me ashore… and we all went and got a cuppa.

As an incidental comment, during our earlier training sessions, the chaps will tell folk how I squealed like a pig each and every time I jumped into a cold Bolton Reservoir. I loathe the cold and am not what you'd call fearless in that regard.

If you ever try outdoor swimming, without a wetsuit, in February, in the Northwest of England, you too may make emasculated noises as your manhood retreats into your midriff.

By comparison, the other chaps just got on with their swimming and made no noises. They were a tough bunch.

***

Another experience came to mind whilst jotting this stuff down. And that was my tumbling out of control during my Freefall

# Phoenix

parachute training in San Diego. I plummeted from 10,000ft to 2,000ft until an instructor, who was the spitting image of the actor Gary Busey, dived earthwards at breakneck speed and pulled my parachute cord.

At the time, a group of us were dropping from the heavens somewhere between Southern California and Mexico. Looking down I could see a dividing line of sorts forming the border. A shanty town of makeshift Mexican properties was leaning against it, and the US side seemed completely empty.

The Santa Rosa mountains were on my left and the sea was on the right. The sky was pure blue with a misty tint to the horizon, and the ground looked parched. From altitude, a handful of black dots, US Immigration jeeps, were roaming across the landscape trying to scoop up those making illegal entry into SoCal.

And every time I reached behind me to pull the cord, my world went haywire as I tumbled out of control.

The funny thing about that experience was how slow terminal velocity felt. And it's interesting how my consciousness seemed to take a detailed look at my surroundings in a kind of, *'this is interesting'* type manner.

As if my brain was taking one last glimpse at the world and wanted to annotate everything before it was too late. I also recall feeling incredibly calm about the prospect of becoming a pancake.

And then Mr Busey's look-a-like saved the day.

*\*\*\**

Separately, and I appreciate I'm jumping around here again, I got introduced to the notion of self-defence at an early age.

I'd seen an old guy being threatened and embarrassed in a pub when I was 14. Mum and Dad always took the family to the same pub, the Black Swan, for Sunday lunch. I'd have chicken in a basket and play as many games of Galaxians on the sit-down video game as my pocket money could stretch too.

The pub had two sections; one for families and one for young men to play pool and be as loud as they wanted. It was a bit of a tribal affair; our side kept apart from their side.

And one of the young "Mods" wandered into the family section and took exception to an old guy who was holding up the bar.

The younger male, clothed in a denim jacket, jeans, and Doc Martins, started to tear a strip out of him. By contrast, he was stood there wearing his shirt, tie, nice pants, polished shoes and was visibly wilting under the humiliation he was being subjected too.

The young guy was swearing, getting animated, and maybe 20 families watched the verbal beating. No one from the family side told the young man to go away, or said anything, they just watched. And I didn't have the balls to stand up for the old fella, either.

That was my first introduction to bullying.

Roll forward twenty years, and the father of my then-girlfriend was being threatened by a bodybuilder type. So I figured I should learn how to defend him, and that morphed into a five year journey to becoming a Black Belt in Ju-Jitzu.

Consequently the training regime led to broken fingers, broken toes, and broken ribs. On one particular day, I was driven completely bonkers courtesy of what you might call *'disagreements'* with both British Telecom and British Gas. It was a perfect storm type incident and, very foolishly, I lost my temper. In an attempt at resetting my state of mind I tried to put my fist through a wall.

If the younger me, I was late thirties at that point, had considered where the load-bearing walls were in the house, then I'd most likely have put a hole in the plasterboard. As it happened, I didn't have

# Phoenix

that degree of foresight, and bone met brick. Consequently, my right hand needed surgery and pinning. All very silly, on my part.

Looking back through the years, the wall incident was the most annoyed I've ever been. That said, Bolton can be a tough old place and knowing you can protect your friends and family is quite reassuring.

I haven't fought anyone since my school days, and the martial arts thing is more about personal confidence. Plus, Ju-Jitzu puts a greater emphasis on self-defence, and that suits my personality.

As a general comment, though, if anyone says they do Ju-Jitzu, my advice would be to avoid throwing punches at them or kicking them. By all means, shout at them or call them names, but it wouldn't be wise to attack them.

Despite the previous paragraphs, it's worth noting that I'm one hell of a coward. I'm scared of everything and always look over my shoulder expecting trouble.

*\*\**

One other item to mention, I guess. Mr Elliot, my nemesis, wasn't particularly impressed with yours truly, and you may recall he commented that I wasn't clever enough to join the RAF.

My dad was always the smartest chap in the room and, for whatever reason, my younger brother decided to get his own IQ tested. He subsequently passed the Mensa tests and got issued with a card for his teenage wallet. I was probably early twenties at the time.

Feeling a little inadequate, I took the official home tests and got a letter saying I'd passed. The next step, they said, was to pay sixty quid or so (I can't remember exactly how much) and attend Manchester Metropolitan University for a supervised test. I didn't feel the need to pay up and let things lapse.

A year later, my brother got his degree, and, as the older brother, maybe I felt a little miffed at the idea of being the thickie in the room. Hence, I took the unsupervised test again, and the resulting letter suggested I was a borderline candidate for membership but that I should get in. Humorously, they'd spelt my surname wrong on that letter.

Why am I scribbling down this drivel? Whether the letters were correct, or whether I'd have passed the supervised tests or not (or whether it was just a money-making scam), the key element here is confidence.

If a person believes they're a clever cookie, there's a decent chance they'll attempt ambitious things because they have the confidence to at least try. Throughout my life every time someone has said, '*you can't do that.*' I've replied with, '*why not?*'

And that approach stems, rightly or wrongly, from having a degree of self confidence, and taking a somewhat stubborn approach to matters.

If you're a young 'un reading this, my advice would be to focus on the positives in your life and don't let anyone stop you pursuing your dreams.

Sometimes the folk that say, '*you can't do that,*' are the ones who haven't done anything.

***

Bringing matters around to my purchase of India Zulu, I guess the flying dream was still nestling somewhere in my consciousness. So, after a few more years had trickled through the hourglass, and the eye ulcer had resolved itself courtesy of an acidic solution, I bought a Microlight and started flying again.

The first dozen or so flights involved jaunts to various nearby farm strips, and then my ambitions and horizons started to expand.

# Phoenix

Trips to Wales, Scotland, Northern Ireland, Europe, and the Alps followed. On the latter trip I flew around the Chitty Chitty Bang Bang castle, which was fabulous to look at. And I managed to win the GPS category of the Round Britain Microlight Rally, too.

I mentioned, at one point, about flying a couple of hundred feet above the runway at Cape Kennedy. This was the launch centre and touch down runway for NASA's space shuttle programme.

And if you squinted I guess you could say I have another tenuous connection to that iconic piece of technology. The space shuttle programme had numerous 'alternate' landing sites dotted around the globe in case the beastie dropped out of orbit prematurely. One location was up in Scotland.

At the point I bought India Zulu I was still within what's called the 'kill zone'. That's a figurative number for pilots that tends to range from 50 to 350 flying hours. In essence more pilots die in that zone than any other, mostly due to either inexperience or over confidence.

On one day, early in my ownership of India Zulu, I'd filled Samson up with fuel, had a cup of tea and toastie in the airfield cafe, and decided to aviate. The plan was to just explore 'somewhere', and I took off and headed north to look at a place called Ailsa Craig. It's a bloody big rock in the sea.

I floated around it, looked at all the birds nesting, and decided I needed a wee. The nearest airfield was Campbeltown, formerly known as RAF Machrihanish, and the 3km runway was a possible landing point for the Shuttle.

The airfield was abandoned, no one was on frequency, and I desperately needed to pee. The problem was the wind. It was blowing a hoolie and the massive windsock was full and pointing directly across the runway. My guess was that in excess of 15 knots was throwing it's weight around.

I lined up on the runway, but Samson was getting thrown around, so I spun about, mid-final, and landed on the taxiway. Then jumped out, relieved my bladder, whilst simultaneously watching the wings jiggling around as the wind whirled around us. I hurriedly jumped back on board and took off again.

In a way it was great fun, but when you actually "crash an aircraft" you look back on all the instances when one was way overdue and think, *'what a fool'*.

I guess I'm an adult these days and hugely more risk averse than I used to be.

And when you think about it there is a fine line between being, in your own mind, and adventurer versus being a reckless twit. I've been both.

Apart from my crash, if it was wind shear, I experienced similar events prior to landing at Nuuk in Greenland, and during heavy rainfall at Lille. One minute everything is fine, and the next someone is stepping on the aircraft and forcing her to earth. And then you're released, and start swearing.

Hey, ho.

***

Time inevitably marched on, as it does, and my dad's health took a turn for the worst. A virus attacked his brain, which led to seizures, and those led to heart issues.

Dad was always such a physically strong fellah, and watching him struggling to breathe was ripping me apart. I guess I needed something all consuming to fill my mind, so, in a somewhat cowardly fashion, I jumped in India Zulu and flew my ill-equipped Microlight to North America. The flight led to Wick, the Faroe Islands, Iceland, Greenland, and Canada.

The day I left Barton I realised I needed to be with dad, hence it became a race to complete the trip and get home again.

# Phoenix

At different points in the flight across the Atlantic I very nearly had wheels trailing in ice laden clouds up at our ceiling of 11,000 or so feet. If the clouds had inched higher we'd have been encased in the white stuff and I'd have been a gonner. Similarly, to avoid icing issues, there were times when my aircraft and I were barrelling along at 30 ft above the Atlantic, at 2 miles a minute, whilst sleet was assaulting Samson.

I landed at Iqaluit, slept for six or so hours, and raced home. And a couple of days after returning to the UK, nature took its course and the old fella passed away.

There's a 2,000-year-old poem which reads, '*The moving finger writes and having writ moves on.*' The suggestion being that time moves forward, and there's bugger all we can do about it.

There was no intention to court any awards, but the flight to Canada led to being awarded the Britannia Trophy. I asked permission to take my beautiful 3-year-old daughter to the ceremony, and we headed off, with her Mum, to the Royal Aero Club to meet the Duke of York.

T'was an evening amongst the great and the good and a memory I'll cherish. Ava's Mum and I clashed, as was our way, but hopefully the pictures will stay with my daughter forever.

The sadness about the day was that, as the son of a Coal Merchant, Dad would have loved being there. The old sod would've been all blaze' and cocky. And I'd have bet money he'd have repeatedly blurted out, '*where's Randy Andy?*'

When the Prince finally ghosted into the elegant building, complete with bodyguards, he seemed like a genuinely nice chap. I'd heard he could be both rude and abrupt, but my wonderful daughter seemed to charm him.

I held Ava in my arms, standing beside the Queen's middle son, and felt incredibly proud to be British.

And strangely, I felt a little sorry for Prince Andrew. Having a succession of people fuss and fawn around a person, by virtue of birth, must be so damned tiresome.

***

And, as away to square the circle, it might be worth contemplating death. I have three scenarios for consideration, my grandads demise, my father's demise, or taking matters into a persons own hands.

As a youngster I heard that my Grandad passed away peacefully in my Nana's arms. That struck me as a gentle ending and was quite soothing to hear as a young pup. As I got older the real story emerged that my randy, elderly, grandparents were having a romantic get-together and grandad checked out courtesy of an ill timed heart attack.

The mind boggles at this point. I just hope the moment was at the end of the process with a beautific, cross-eyed, smile creeping across his face.

The second scenario, would be Dad's passing. He picked up a brain eating virus which led to complications. And within six months he'd checked out. If I were to get sickly I'd want the whole deterioration process over a lot swifter than that, though.

As a side note, Dad's ashes sat in the crematorium for longer than the norm'. Consequently, it seemed to be an after thought that he was returned to the church for the funeral process. He wasn't expected back on the day his box arrived at the church and there was a summer fete going on.

And somehow, god knows how, his little cardboard box seems to have ended up for sale on the Tombola stand. Fortunately, no one won his ashes, as I imagine that may led to a little disappointment on the part of the winner.

# Phoenix

As it was the mistake was realised and he was discreetly removed from sale. You have to laugh, I guess.

The last option would seem to be a 'Dignitas' type exit. A friend of mine knew an elderly lady who went down this route. She flew to Switzerland and, however these things are agreed, was told to wait 6 months for her departure date. My friend suggested she had a terminal something or other, and didn't want nature to take it's inevitable course.

And a week after she'd returned home, she got a phone call saying they'd had a cancellation. And off she went again, business class, to meet her maker.

Death is a funny old thing in that it greets us all at some point. Personally, I'd like to aim for the cross-eyed orgasmic look at some future undetermined point.

*** 

The rest of my future, to this point, is unwritten. A part of me wants to fly around the world in India Zulu. And a part wants a quiet life without any great excitement.

At present, I simply carry out charity flights as a way to both give something back to society and make reparations for the life I've been lucky enough to lead.

I pay all the flying costs and take folk flying who might appreciate a different perspective on the world. Any money subsequently donated goes directly to a Cancer Charity in Liverpool via www.justgiving.com/jon-hilton.

***

All this brings me up to date, I guess... Farewell, and don't forget the chocolate.

Jon

Printed in Great Britain
by Amazon